The Dow Jones-Irwin Guide to
COLLEGE FINANCIAL PLANNING

The Dow Jones-Irwin Guide to COLLEGE FINANCIAL PLANNING

Paul M. Lane

Dow Jones-Irwin
Homewood, Illinois 60430

© DOW JONES-IRWIN, 1981

All rights reserved. No part of this publication may be reproduced, stored in a retrieval system, or transmitted, in any form or by any means, electronic, mechanical, photocopying, recording, or otherwise, without the prior written permission of the publisher.

This publication is designed to provide accurate and authoritative information in regard to the subject matter covered. It is sold with the understanding that the publisher is not engaged in rendering legal, accounting, or other professional service. If legal advice or other expert assistance is required, the services of a competent professional person should be sought.

From a Declaration of Principles jointly adopted by a Committee of the American Bar Association and a Committee of Publishers.

ISBN 0-87094-267-0
Library of Congress Catalog Card No. 81-67120
Printed in the United States of America

1 2 3 4 5 6 7 8 9 0 K 8 7 6 5 4 3 2 1

For Dad

Preface

The completion of this book is due in large part to the help of over 3,000 families and students that forced me to learn some of the intricacies of the financial aid system. They were always patient and helpful as we explored the system and tried to learn how it might function for them. I could not write this without acknowledging my wife, Bonnie, for her patience and support. Special thanks go to Doris Statler and my parents and the many colleagues who helped in a variety of ways. The actual work on the manuscript would not have been completed without the assistance of Mrs. Inez Brown, whose constant checking, double checking, prodding, proofing, and organization has helped to bring this book to completion.

Paul M. Lane

Contents

SECTION I THE INTRODUCTION

1. **To the Reader** 3
2. **Should You Consider Aid?** 5

    The Worry Is Not Merely Parental. College Costs Will Increase. Why Should You Apply for Financial Aid? If You Think There Is No Aid for You. Your Home Does Not Disqualify You. Financial Aid Is a Process and a Strategy: *Tax Returns. Confidentiality. Family Case Studies.* More Than a Process—A Strategy.

SECTION II THE PROCESS

3. **The Application Process** 15

    Calendars: *Local Scholarships. Untapped Money. Handicapped Students.* The Processing Year. Tax Years Are Important: *Importance of Line 31. Record Keeping. Student's Earnings.* Application: *How It Works.*

4. **The Application** 25

    How Long until You Hear? Common Form. State Aid Application. Institutional Application. Pell Grants—BEOG. Where to Send Aid Applications. Verification Procedures. Formulas for Calculating Aid: *Uniform Methodology. Pell Grant.*

SECTION III   THE FAMILY CONTRIBUTION

5. **The Organization of the Family Contribution** — 35

   Parents' Income. Parents' Assets. The Student's Contribution.

6. **Parents' Contribution from Income** — 40

   Taxable Income. Nontaxable Income. Allowances: *Income Tax. Social Security. State and Local Taxes. Employment Allowance. Medical and Dental Expenses. Maintenance Allowance.*

7. **Calculation of Available Income** — 48

8. **Parents' Contribution from Assets** — 52

   Home Equity. Other Real Estate and Investments: *Stocks. Bonds. Land Contracts. Trust Funds. Other Securities. Real Estate. Businesses. Farms. Cash. Net Worth.*

9. **Calculation of Parents' Contribution from Assets** — 70

   Asset Protection Allowance.

10. **Student's Contribution from Income** — 74

    Student Income.

11. **Student's Contribution from Assets** — 78

SECTION IV   GENERAL STRATEGIES

12. **How Many Will Be in School** — 87

    Parents' Contribution. Case Example. Impact on Aid. Apply for Aid for All Students. Apply Every Year. Strategies. Planning. Should Parents Go to School? Check School Policies. "Stopping Out." Strategies When Filing for Aid. Formulas Do Not Distinguish Cost of Schools. $80,000 Income Receives Aid. Professional Schools Count. More Students, More Aid. A Case of Large Assets. Maximize Your Aid. Which Assets Should You Use? Planning.

13. **Using Your Income Taxes in the Aid Application** — 100

    Business Income (or Loss). Thirty Months. Real Estate. Scott Case I. Case I—No Changes. Case II—Investment in Real Estate. Case III—Larger Real Estate Investment. Case IV—Addition of Small Business. Capital Gains and Losses. Split Losses and Gains. Effect of Loss. Farm Income or Loss. Protection of Assets. Other Ventures—Oil! Plan Ahead. Adjustments to Income. IRA and Keogh. Financial Aid and Tax Planning Go Together.

SECTION V AVAILABLE MONEY

14. The Philosophy of Aid Packaging   117

Types of Aid and Packaging. Two Types of Financial Aid.

15. Sources of Aid   125

Pell Grant: *Pell Grant Formula. Pell Grant—Student Eligibility Report.* Guaranteed Student Loan. Parent Loans. Campus-Based Programs. SEOG. NDSL. CWSP. *Six Major Federal Programs.* State. Institutions. Private.

16. Loans   134

NDSL. How Is the GSL Used with Aid? *Difficulty with Family Contribution. GSL Helps When Family Contribution Falls Short. Loan Dollars Are for Educational Purposes. GSL Limits. Graduate Students. Change in Situation. Multiple Loans. Use the GSL if Possible. Changes Possible. Protect Yourself. Strategies for Using GSL. More GSL Ideas. Financial Guardians. Where to Apply. The Application. Processing Delays. What if You Are Refused? The SDSL. Why Banks Participate. Potential Changes. Higher Interest Rates. Use the GSL or SDSL if You Can.* Parents' Loan Program: *Ease of Payment. Nonliquid Assets. A Major Financial Resource. High Interest Rates. Guardians.*

17. Packaging   153

Aid Packaging and How It Works.

SECTION VI SPECIFIC STRATEGIES

18. Divorce   159

Aid Is Based on Child's Home: *Financial Aid and Tax Status. Stepparent's Income. Yours, Mine, and Ours!* Divorce and Separation: *Get Information. Financial Aid Is Not Judgmental. Disappearing Parents. Where Should Students Live?* Educational Support Agreements: *Definitions of Aid. Benefits of Lump-Sum Settlements. Check Divorce Agreement. Nonpayment. Planning a Divorce.*

19. Gifts to Students   173

Gifts from Relatives. Give It to the Parents of Students. Give It after the Students Are through College. Planning. Parents Saving Tax Dollars and Losing Financial Aid. Joint Accounts. Education Accounts. One Man's Solution. The Message.

20. Small Trusts   182

Possible Avoidance. Warning. How Do Trusts Work in Financial Aid? Trusts of $50,000. Trust of $35,000. Small Trusts. Planning Your Estate.

Does Your Children's Guardian Know about Financial Aid? Plan Ahead. Check Your Estate Plans.

21. **Independent Students**   187

Definition. Is Independence Important? Things to Be Considered. Planning for Independence. December of Junior Year in High School. Separate Residence for Students. $1,000 Support. Independence as a Financial Aid Strategy. Total Family Financial Aid Planning. Other Factors. Changing Regulations. Using the GSL to Gain Independent Status. Changes in GSL Could Limit Independence. Independent Student Who Works. School Policies: Investigate School Policy on Independent Students.

22. **Social Security and Veterans' Benefits**   201

Find Out if You Qualify. The Financial Aid Office Needs to Know. Financial Aid Treatment of Social Security Benefits. Cash Flow Problems. Find Out How Much Aid Officers Expect. Computation of Family Contribution with Benefits: *Student Assets Plus Benefits. Assets of Rich Families. Plan Ahead.*

23. **Pell Grant (BEOG)**   208

SECTION VII   MORE EXAMPLES

24. **Case Studies**   215

$20,000 Income. Importance of Assets. Number in Family. $32,000 Income. Cash Flow. School Policies on Bill Payment. Three in College. Effect of $90,000 in Assets. $55,000 Income. Three in College. Investment Strategies. $65,000 Income. Conclusion.

SECTION VIII   THE FUTURE

25. **The Future**   229

Financial Aid Will Change. Reduction in the Federal Aid Programs. Changes in State Programs. Institutional Aid Programs. You Can Help Yourself. Using History as a Guideline.

SECTION IX   APPENDIXES

Appendix A   Glossary   235

Appendix B   Resources   245

Appendix C   Sample Questions   251

Index   257

Section I
THE INTRODUCTION

Chapter 1
To the Reader
Chapter 2
Should You Consider Aid?

Chapter 1

To the Reader

Readers will use this book in different ways, depending on their purpose. Ideally, anyone who is trying to plan ahead and maximize their financial aid situation should consider all the possibilities. In order to help those with limited time, we have prepared a list of some of the areas that you may wish to refer to in detail.

Parents

Introduction
The Family Contribution
General Strategies
Available Money
Appendixes

Attorneys

Divorce
Gifts to Students
Small Trusts

Relatives

Gifts to Students
Small Trusts

College and University Trustees

The Process
The Family Contribution
Available Money
The Future
Glossary*
Resources*

Pastors and Counselors

The Family Contribution
Available Money
Divorce
Independent Students
Future
Appendixes

Author's note: All names used in examples throughout this text are fictitious.

Bank Officers
The Family Contribution
Loans
Gifts to Students
Small Trusts

Guardians
The Family Contribution
Loans
Small Trusts
Independent Students

Accountants
The Family Contribution
Using Your Income Taxes in Financial Aid
Gifts to Students
More Examples

Students
Student's Contribution from Income
Student's Contribution from Assets
Available Money
Appendixes

High School Counselors
The Process
The Family Contribution
General Strategies

Available Money
Specific Strategies
Appendixes

* Readers will find the Glossary and Resources helpful in providing background for important names and symbols used in the text.

This is a book for everyone that is even remotely interested in the workings of the financial aid system. While the system is dynamic and, therefore, constantly changing, understanding it can be most helpful in maximizing your student's aid, in counseling families, in administering institutions, and in making income and estate plans.

During the writing of this book, significant changes have gone on in the financial aid system as a result of political changes within the country. We have tried to address the impact that these may have in the section entitled "The Future." The list of questions in Appendix C is meant to help you obtain the most current information possible at the time you actually need it. Unfortunately, for too many families, financial aid has been a mystery. It is time we made it possible for everyone to understand how it works and how they can take advantage of it.

Chapter 2

Should You Consider Aid?

Have you thought realistically about how much your child's education may cost you? Most parents, even those that have started on the process, are surprised to find out the real cost of educating a young person through the college years. Educational expenses sometimes exceed $10,000 a year. The size of cost increases is often over $1,000 a year at private schools. Parents find themselves making major changes in their life-style or dipping into accumulated capital.

The Worry Is Not Merely Parental

A grandmother once assured me that she had provided for her grandchild's education by setting aside a trust of $50,000 for her two-year-old grandchild. My projection is that the trust may only cover the first two years of educational cost at a private school in the year 2000, and might be entirely used in attending four years at a state university.

College Costs Will Increase

Inflation, no matter what economic progress occurs, will necessarily continue. College and university costs can only be expected to increase. (See Table 2-1.) Even should we, as a people, be able to control our inflationary pressures, educational costs will still spiral upwards. Faculty salaries, building programs, and so forth have not been able to

TABLE 2–1
How Much will School Cost?

12 Percent Increase in Tuition and Fees*		Year	14 Percent Increase in Tuition and Fees*	
$ 7,500	$10,000	High school sophomore	$ 7,500	$10,000
8,400	11,200	High school junior	8,550	11,400
9,408	12,544	High school senior	9,747	12,996
10,537	14,049	College freshman	11,112	14,815
11,801	15,735	College sophomore	12,667	16,890
13,218	17,623	College junior	14,441	19,254
14,804	19,738	College senior	16,462	22,000

* Twelve and 14 percent are typical of the inflationary increases. It is not rare for a school to be charging tuition and room and board fees of $7,500 a year in the private sector; there are a number that have already topped $10,000. If we assume that the student is currently a sophomore in high school, we can then use $7,500 and $10,000 as our base-year costs.

keep pace with inflation; there is a backlog of necessary expenditures as well as continual quality improvements.

WHY SHOULD YOU APPLY FOR FINANCIAL AID?

Each year more and more families are applying for and receiving financial assistance. However, many families that should be applying for assistance have not done so because they thought that they were not eligible. State and federal governments are making billions of dollars available to those families that have properly filed for aid and have indicated a need. If you feel that you would like assistance in covering the cost of postsecondary education, in particular college and university expenses, it is worth your time to apply for aid.

Be aware that more and more people are not only applying for but receiving substantial sums of tax-free dollars through financial aid. You cannot afford not to at least apply, particularly if your child is contemplating one of the more expensive schools which may cost you $7,500 and up. (This cost would include tuition charges, fees, room and board, books, personal spending money, travel to and from school, and miscellaneous other items.)

In order to maximize aid one must plan strategies long before the time to apply. Start planning when your child is a junior in high school.

If your income is less than your congressional representative's ($60,663), you may be surprised to learn that you have a reasonable chance of qualifying for some kinds of assistance. Some of our legislators in Washington believe that their children should also qualify for financial assistance when they apply to college. To make this happen, major changes in the financial aid laws will be required. Many of these changes have already been put in place, and many more are being actively considered.

Chapter 2: Should You Consider Aid?

If You Think There Is No Aid for You

Tax-free dollars help dramatically. Consider how much additional income must be earned to pay for $1,000 of college cost at different income levels. Using the recent federal tax table and assuming a net state tax rate of 4 percent, the results are:

Taxable Income	$25,000	$36,000	$46,000	$60,000
Federal tax rate (married taxpayers filing a joint return in 1979)	32%	43%	49%	54%
State tax rate (assumed 4 percent)	4%	4%	4%	4%
Marginal total tax rate	36%	47%	53%	58%
Amount that would have to be earned to generate $1,000 after taxes	$1,563	$1,887	$2,127	$2,380

The impact of tax-free dollars increases dramatically as the taxable income increases. Thus, the family in the $46,000-income bracket for taxable income that files for and receives $1,000 in assistance has received the same as if the family had received an income increase of $2,127.

The effect of financial aid becomes even more dramatic as we consider increasing amounts of aid. For example, suppose the family with $46,000 taxable income wanted to earn enough money to match $4,000 of financial aid. In order to do this, they must earn an additional $8,500—increasing their income by almost 20 percent.

You are contributing to the financial aid funds when you pay your state and federal income taxes. Therefore, if you have college-age children or are going to college yourself, you might as well get what you are entitled to of these tax-free dollars. Many families have hesitated to apply saying that they are "too proud" to apply for assistance. They are determined to make it on their own. Their independence is admirable, but their sense of financial planning is questionable when so many are getting assistance from the various aid programs that are available.

It does not cost much to apply for aid. However, it may cost you a great deal to overlook this potentially substantial source of assistance. It may be possible that you or your child has many more opportunities open to you than you thought possible. Good financial planning for educational expenses will include making the most of these opportunities.

Apply for financial aid if you would like help, feel that you should be entitled to some, or are just interested in getting all you can from the government in the form of tax-free dollars. In my years in financial aid, I have seen countless families who think they are far too wealthy to receive financial aid. Many of these people are now educating their children with the help of financial aid. They accepted hearsay from friends that they would never qualify. This hearsay however is contradicted by facts and good planning. The system changes significantly each year. Thus, a family that does not qualify under one year's formula might qualify for some assistance the next year.

The whole system of financial aid is political. Politics govern all levels of financial aid—the federal government, the state government, and even institutions. While one might expect laws to be made and administered so that the poorest receive assistance first, this is not always the way financial aid works. In fact, many of the recent changes have made it easier for upper-income families to receive assistance while some less fortunate cannot qualify for sufficient help.

Your Home Does Not Disqualify You

Almost every time a financial aid discussion is held someone in the audience who listened to the hearsay of well-meaning but ill-informed friends will bring up several of the myths about financial aid and why it is not worth applying for. One of the most popular ones is about owning your own home. The question usually goes something like this: "Is it true that if you own your own home, you cannot get assistance?" This is not true at all! In fact, changes in the law for awarding federal funds to students excluded any consideration of the home value for the 1982–83 academic year and beyond. Many people who own their own homes are receiving federal aid, sometimes in large amounts. Sometimes people will refer to neighbors or friends who have situations similar to their own. If the neighbors or friends don't qualify, they think they won't either. The key here is *similarity*—not identity. Each situation requires individual planning. Each family unit is different, and your neighbors may be in different situations than you think they are.

A good example of this was the doctor neighbor of a financial aid director who had been advised by the financial aid director not to apply for assistance. When he came to talk with me, explaining that he could not afford to send his daughter to the school of her choice, we reviewed the situation and found that he could qualify for substantial assistance. After some discussion, we surmised that the financial aid director who advised him had assumed things about the doctor's financial situation without asking any of the necessary questions. Beware of anyone who tells you that you will not qualify for aid who does not ask a number of exploratory questions and do a considerable amount of calculation. Get yourself properly represented on the aid application so that you and your family can qualify for the maximum amount of assistance.

FINANCIAL AID IS A PROCESS AND A STRATEGY

The application process is comparatively simple. At one time, applying for financial aid required filling our numerous financial aid

Chapter 2: Should You Consider Aid?

forms, each of which might be treated differently. In most cases today, the application process has been simplified considerably, and schools are using one of two major forms to determine the ability of your family to contribute. The advantage to this is that no matter what kind of form you file you should end up with about the same amount of assistance.

The federal forms as well as those used by most schools are primarily based on the federal income tax form. Families that have completed their income taxes and have these forms available usually find that it is not too difficult to complete the necessary financial aid forms. Those that have not yet done their taxes, when attempting to fill out the financial aid form, find that they have to do a great deal of estimating. This estimating is not only laborious but also frequently leads to errors in the financial aid form which can dramatically affect the amount of aid they can receive. The earlier you file your financial aid forms (usually by the end of January), the sooner you are going to hear about financial aid. Early filers usually have a better chance to get aid; so plan to have your taxes done early.

Tax Returns

Some schools may ask for a copy of your tax return to verify the information that you put on the financial aid forms. Since this is increasingly the only realistic audit procedure for schools wishing to verify the financial aid information, when you have your taxes prepared, have extra copies made in order to have them available to mail out as needed.

If you have completed your tax returns, you will find most of the financial aid information that will be requested of you rather easy to complete with the possible exception of the asset information. If you have a variety of assets, make a list of your assets, their current market value, and what you owe against them. This list will help you greatly as you complete the necessary forms for a financial aid application.

Plan to (or have a professional) do your taxes early, preferably in January. If you own a small business or farm, do your year-end taxes as soon as possible. Do not delay. Those who have to pay additional funds can still hold the tax return until April 15 or whatever their due date is.

Confidentiality

Many parents are concerned about the confidentiality of their records, particularly their asset and income information. Financial aid officers are a very professional group and treat this information in the appropriate confidence. I cannot think of one occasion where the confidentiality of information has turned out to be a difficulty for anyone in the financial aid process. It is a fear not founded on fact. Most likely, hearsay has again replaced fact.

Family Case Studies

To give you a feel for how financial aid may work for different families, consider these families that have successfully applied for aid.

Annual Income $14,000. The Joneses are a traditional financial aid family, receiving assistance in large quantities. Mr. Jones is a laborer who owns his own home. There are two children. The family income was about $14,000 in 1980, and they have assets totaling about $24,000 including equity in a house and one major investment (see Table 2–2).

TABLE 2–2
Expected Parents' Contribution for Three Families

	Jones Family ($14,000 income)*	Malone Family ($34,000 income)†	Taylor Family ($88,000 income)‡
Taxable income	$14,000	$34,000	$88,000
Nontaxable income	0	0	0
Assets (net)	24,000	28,000	25,000
Expected parents' contribution per child	0	1,500	5,700
Total parents' contribution	0	$ 3,000	$17,100

* Family size, 4; number in college, 1.
† Family size, 4; number in college, 2.
‡ Family size, 9; number in college, 3.

Mrs. Jones does not work outside the home but is an industrious homemaker who has worked hard improving their home and raising the two boys. Under the financial aid formula in use for the 1981–82 school year, this family would not be expected to contribute to their child's education.

Not surprisingly, many families in this and similar situations do not feel that they can afford the cost of education. It is unfortunate they are unaware of how much assistance they actually can receive. The Jones family did not think they could afford college even though they were willing to make extreme sacrifices to be able to do so. When they originally filed for financial aid, they made a mistake in how they listed their investment which caused their expected contribution to increase to $40 a month. That would have been too large a portion of their monthly budget. Proper planning rectified this.

Annual Income $34,000. The Malones are also a family of four. Mr. Malone is a high school teacher, and Mrs. Malone works in a doctor's office. Together they have an income of about $34,000 (see Table 2–2).

Chapter 2: Should You Consider Aid?

They have two children planning to attend private colleges and, thus, were preparing for staggering educational expenses. They believed, before they came to the office, that they would never qualify for any aid because their income was too high. After properly putting their financial information through the system, we found that they would only be expected to contribute $125 a month for each student in college, or a total of $250 a month out of their combined monthly gross of almost $3,000. With this information the Malones felt free to investigate the schools that their children were interested in and which they thought would provide the best education. In fact, they found that it was going to cost them approximately the same, no matter where the boys decided to go to school—a community college, a four-year public state institution, or a more expensive private school. The Malones did not feel that the $250 a month was going to be easy. But they felt they could afford that amount far easier than the over $12,000 per year they would have had to spend without financial aid.

Annual Income $88,000. Dr. Taylor and his wife have a combined income of just over $88,000 with which to support their seven children. To most people that would seem like more than enough to feed and clothe a family as well as to take care of college expenses for the children. However, the Taylor's third child was interested in going to an exclusive private college, and the Taylors were properly advised to apply for financial aid. Dr. Taylor is only in his mid-40s and has just recently attained his current level of income after years of specializing and developing a practice. The Taylors have relatively few assets, primarily the $25,000 equity in their home (see Table 2–2). Mrs. Taylor's work is mostly voluntary in the community. However, she does make about $1,500 in "pin money" as she calls it as a paraprofessional helper with the board of education. These things, plus keeping the house and being the chauffeur for the children, have kept her more than busy in recent years. The Taylors were pleased to find out that they could receive aid for Lisa, the third child, to enter the more expensive college. They were even more pleased that Lisa's two older brothers might also be eligible for aid at their respective institutions now that there were three in college. The Taylors were not only grateful for their aid but grateful for a system that understands that high-income families like theirs also have need for assistance in financing the burden of higher education. But the gratitude here is ill-founded. They were not truly "given" anything. They received what they were due.

MORE THAN A PROCESS—A STRATEGY

If you need assistance with the cost of higher education, apply for aid. Your application should be done as part of an overall plan. You must know as much as possible about different options in order to formulate an effective strategy. This will then yield you tax-free dollars. Detailed discussions follow of the process of financial aid as well as a variety of strategies that you can use in preparing to file for assistance. Remember that you are applying to have your own tax dollars returned to you. You are entitled—minimally—to this money. Now you must properly plan to get it.

When I first started in financial aid I believed that it was for the truly low-income family. At that time my conservative beliefs would not let me accept the idea that our increasingly socialistic system would provide assistance to higher-income families. Recently, as the Congress has sought to provide more and more assistance to families in all income ranges (particularly those of its own members), I have become persuaded that anyone who would like help should try. Further, it has become obvious that there are a number of things that one can do to greatly increase the chances of receiving assistance. This concept of planning for financial aid is the basis for the remaining chapters of this book.

Section II
THE PROCESS

Chapter 3
The Application Process
Chapter 4
The Application

Chapter 3

The Application Process

CALENDARS

There are a number of different calendars operating on and influencing the financial aid award cycle. Obtaining the maximum possible financial aid requires good planning. You must coordinate the student's application to school(s) and applications for available moneys. Thus, the calendar is important for you as you begin the overall planning process.

The elements of this planning process calendar include the following:

1. Admissions Application. Most colleges and universities require the student to complete an admissions application and be accepted before financial aid can be awarded. It is advisable to apply early so that you will have the maximum chance of receiving funds, especially in this time of fund shortages.

2. Institutional Aid Applications. Many schools will have their own aid forms or perhaps require a supplement to the federal forms to determine your student's eligibility for need. Obtain this form from the schools that you are considering, and find out the deadline for filing it with the financial aid office.

3. Federal Form. This form is used for application for the Pell Grant (formerly the Basic Educational Opportunity Grant, BEOG) and other federal programs. All students should file this form.

4. State Aid Forms. Most states have their own financial aid forms which are usually obtained from the high school counselor. You should obtain the form and also learn the date it should be filed. *Remember always to apply to one in-state school if you wish to maximize your aid possibilities.*

5. Special Scholarship Forms. If you are applying for any special scholarships, be sure to check out their complete regulations: what forms must be filed and the appropriate deadlines and supporting documentation.

Most forms have to be filed earlier than you think, so plan ahead to complete the entire application process in plenty of time. Make up a financial aid application calendar like the one shown here.

The Financial Aid Application Calendar

School name	Sample University			
	Date Should Be Filed			
Admissions application	November 25			
Institutional aid application	January 1			
Federal aid application	January 30			
State aid application	January 30			
Special scholarship application	December 15			

The deadline for applying for financial aid is the time students should narrow down their choices of schools to no more than three—this means January of the senior year. Nothing is achieved by putting off the selection of a school unless the school does not announce its admissions or financial aid until April of the senior year. One of the advantages to applying only to the schools that you most want to go to is that these schools, if they want you, will fight harder to make you the best possible aid award. There is competition among schools for students. Take advantage of the schools' eagerness and let their "generosity" help you. Your mutual satisfaction—their enrollment and your finances—will result.

Chapter 3: The Application Process

Local Scholarships

If you plan to apply for local scholarships of any kind, check to see what forms they require. Many of them are now using need as criteria and have early deadlines for filing the necessary forms. Late in the junior year or early in the senior year of high school check with the high school guidance office; also check your church, civic clubs, and your parents' employers.

Untapped Money

Many times at financial aid workshops questions have been raised about the supposedly millions of dollars of scholarship moneys that are just waiting to be claimed. On a number of occasions we have paid for students to subscribe to one of the services in order to see how helpful they can be. To date it seems that instead of chasing these elusive dollars the best thing you can do is to qualify for federal, state, and institutional moneys that are readily available to students with need.

The definitions of need may surprise you; at some of the private schools families with incomes of $50,000, $60,000, and even $70,000 may be receiving assistance. It is common for families with incomes under $50,000 to be receiving aid. This does not mean that everyone qualifies, but enough do.

Handicapped Students

If you have a student that is in any way handicapped, however minor, be sure to check with your rehabilitation department to see what if any benefits may be available to help with educational costs. Benefits vary from area to area; some of the assistance is quite substantial and, even more importantly, is not need-based. If you are not sure where to start, check with your high school counselor. Also contact the department of social services in your area. If you do not have a contact person already, you may have to make several phone calls to locate an individual who can be helpful. The end result will almost always be affirmative.

THE PROCESSING YEAR

Assume that we are applying for financial aid for the freshman school year which runs from September until May or June. This segment of time is called the award period. The processing year, or year in which you file your aid application, is generally the preceding academic year. The base income year is generally the last taxable year completed prior to filing for financial aid.

For example:

1. Award period   September–June, college freshman
2. Processing year   September–June, high school senior
3. Base income year   January of junior year to December of senior year in high school

These different years have evolved over time to meet the needs of the rapidly changing financial aid system. The award period or year makes a great deal of sense. Obviously the award is going to be distributed during the academic year in which the student is attending the college or university. The award period can get far more complicated when we start considering summers and the possibility of schools with 12-month calendars. Fortunately, you do not need to be concerned with that. If you are contemplating such an institution, they should automatically make all the appropriate adjustments for you in the award period.

For any academic or school year, the processing year would be the preceding year. This is of great significance to you as the application for financial aid should be initiated as early as possible in the processing year, usually in January or February. A very few schools have asked people for special applications in the preceding fall. Some private schools and the National Merit Scholarship Corporation are about the only organizations that asked for these special financial aid applications in recent years. Most schools would like you to apply based on the previous year's taxable income as near the beginning of the following year as you can. You should plan not only to get your tax return ready by the end of January so that you can be prepared to file for aid but also to fill out the financial aid forms in January and start the process on its way. From the time you file a financial aid application until the time you receive an actual financial aid award, sometimes as long as 12 weeks will pass. More often it is between six and eight weeks, depending on the school and how early you file.

The third year that was mentioned is the base (taxable) income year. Many parents wonder why we go back a whole year. The reason for this is quite logical. As more and more federal and state dollars have become a part of the aid process, there has been a need to have verifiable information on the financial aid application. It has been decided that the best and easiest source for that information is the U.S. income tax return. Thus, many of the questions refer directly to your income tax form. There are two important messages in this concept.

TAX YEARS ARE IMPORTANT

The first is that financial aid officers will be using the preceding year tax base as the basis for their decisions. This means that spring of the

Chapter 3: The Application Process

junior year in high school is the time to start some financial aid planning. Ideally, you have been planning for years. Realistically, you are extemporizing. Many people have found ways of shifting income around in order to keep their taxable income low during the years that financial aid may be available. You may want to do the same. As an example, if you had a choice, it would be to your advantage as a parent to take the higher income in the tax year ending in the junior year of high school and the lower income in the tax year ending in December of the senior year of high school. There will be more details on this in later chapters.

Importance of Line 31

The second important message is that for federal aid everything is focused on line 31 of the U.S. Individual Income Tax Return (Form 1040). (See Figure 3–1.) If you wish to apply for financial aid with some sophistication, watch for things that you can do to affect line 31. Things that come after line 31 have very little positive effect on financial aid with the exception of large medical bills.

Record Keeping

Record keeping is an important part of applying for financial aid. At workshops it is always suggested that you keep a financial aid application calendar of what needs to be done when. An example of a calendar was shown earlier in this chapter. You will find that there are different schedules for the federal, state, and institutional processes, and you will want to have these all distinct in your mind so that you always have a maximum chance of obtaining aid. Many people find it helpful to keep the admissions information on the same calendar so that they can keep everything up to date by constantly checking the calendar and adding necessary items from time to time.

Another suggestion that people have found helpful is to keep a copy of everything to do with financial aid or admissions so that when you need to refer to them they are organized and readily available. You are in a much better position to deal with a question from the financial aid office at the institution if you know where all the material is and what was mailed when. When you have your income taxes completed, make several extra copies so that you have them readily accessible. One of the problems is that many people do not keep good records, and then they find it difficult to deal with a financial aid office or a state agency that is trying to get consistent information. One of the most important things to keep available is your acknowledgement forms that you have filed the proper financial aid forms. These forms generally contain the code

FIGURE 3-1

Form **1040**	Department of the Treasury—Internal Revenue Service **U.S. Individual Income Tax Return** **1980**	
For Privacy Act Notice, see Instructions	For the year January 1–December 31, 1980, or other tax year beginning .... 1980, ending .... , 19 ...	

Use IRS label. Otherwise, please print or type.
- Your first name and initial (if joint return, also give spouse's name and initial) | Last name | Your social security number
- Present home address (Number and street, including apartment number, or rural route) | Spouse's social security no.
- City, town or post office, State and ZIP code | Your occupation ▶ | Spouse's occupation ▶

Presidential Election Campaign Fund
▶ Do you want $1 to go to this fund? .... Yes ☐ No ☐
If joint return, does your spouse want $1 to go to this fund? ... Yes ☐ No ☐
Note: Checking "Yes" will not increase your tax or reduce your refund.

Requested by Census Bureau for Revenue Sharing ▶
- **A** Where do you live (actual location of residence)? (See page 2 of Instructions.) State ___ City, village, borough, etc. ___
- **B** Do you live within the legal limits of a city, village, etc.? ☐ Yes ☐ No
- **C** In what county do you live?
- **D** In what township do you live?

Filing Status
Check only one box.
1 ☐ Single
2 ☐ Married filing joint return (even if only one had income)
3 ☐ Married filing separate return. Enter spouse's social security no. above and full name here ▶
4 ☐ Head of household. (See page 6 of Instructions.) If qualifying person is your unmarried child, enter child's name ▶
5 ☐ Qualifying widow(er) with dependent child (Year spouse died ▶ 19 ___). (See page 6 of Instructions.)

For IRS use only ☐

Exemptions
Always check the box labeled Yourself. Check other boxes if they apply.
- 6a ☐ Yourself ☐ 65 or over ☐ Blind
- b ☐ Spouse ☐ 65 or over ☐ Blind
- c First names of your dependent children who lived with you ▶ ....
- d Other dependents:
  | (1) Name | (2) Relationship | (3) Number of months lived in your home | (4) Did dependent have income of $1,000 or more? | (5) Did you provide more than one-half of dependent's support? |
- 7 Total number of exemptions claimed ....

} Enter number of boxes checked on 6a and b ▶
} Enter number of children listed on 6c ▶
Enter number of other dependents
Add numbers entered in boxes above ▶

Income
Please attach Copy B of your Forms W-2 here.
If you do not have a W-2, see page 5 of Instructions.

8 Wages, salaries, tips, etc. .... | 8
9 Interest income (attach Schedule B if over $400) .... | 9
10a Dividends (attach Schedule B if over $400) ...., 10b Exclusion ....
c Subtract line 10b from line 10a .... | 10c
11 Refunds of State and local income taxes (do not enter an amount unless you deducted those taxes in an earlier year—see page 9 of Instructions) .... | 11
12 Alimony received .... | 12
13 Business income or (loss) (attach Schedule C) .... | 13
14 Capital gain or (loss) (attach Schedule D) .... | 14
15 40% of capital gain distributions not reported on line 14 (See page 9 of Instructions) . | 15
16 Supplemental gains or (losses) (attach Form 4797) .... | 16
17 Fully taxable pensions and annuities not reported on line 18 .. | 17
18 Pensions, annuities, rents, royalties, partnerships, etc. (attach Schedule E) .... | 18

Please attach check or money order here.

19 Farm income or (loss) (attach Schedule F) .... | 19
20a Unemployment compensation (insurance). Total received ......
b Taxable amount, if any, from worksheet on page 10 of Instructions .... | 20b
21 Other income (state nature and source—see page 10 of Instructions) ▶ .... | 21
22 Total income. Add amounts in column for lines 8 through 21 .... ▶ | 22

Adjustments to Income
(See Instructions on page 10)

23 Moving expense (attach Form 3903 or 3903F) .... | 23
24 Employee business expenses (attach Form 2106) .. | 24
25 Payments to an IRA (enter code from page 10 ___) . | 25
26 Payments to a Keogh (H.R. 10) retirement plan ... | 26
27 Interest penalty on early withdrawal of savings ... | 27
28 Alimony paid .... | 28
29 Disability income exclusion (attach Form 2440) ... | 29
30 Total adjustments. Add lines 23 through 29 .... ▶ | 30

Adjusted Gross Income
31 Adjusted gross income. Subtract line 30 from line 22. If this line is less than $10,000, see "Earned Income Credit" (line 57) on pages 13 and 14 of Instructions. If you want IRS to figure your tax, see page 3 of Instructions .... ▶ | 31

E.I-36-2425717   U.S. GOVERNMENT PRINTING OFFICE 1980-313-251   Form **1040** (1980)

Chapter 3: The Application Process

number of your application and other data that is particularly helpful in finding your file at the processing centers. Keeping these acknowledgement forms can speed up the process should you decide to apply to an additional school for financial aid. They are also helpful if you have neglected to send your information to your state agency or other scholarship opportunity. These acknowledgement forms will usually be sent to you about three weeks after your application is received by the processing center.

Student's Earnings

Another item to keep track of is the student's earnings. If the student has substantial earnings, even though it may not be necessary to file a tax form, be sure to keep the records handy with other financial aid information. You will then be able to provide proof of the income or expenses when you are asked.

APPLICATION

If you have kept good records, the actual application will not be difficult. Be sure that you know exactly what information the state and the institutions to which you are applying want and when they want it. Be sure that you have duplicates of everything that you have sent to the various organizations so that you can replace them if necessary. In correspondence, always provide, in addition to your return address, a phone number where you can be reached and the best time to reach you. This information will greatly decrease the turnaround time for your application. This is particularly true for the phone number and the best days or times to reach you. If you can be called at work, please list that number so the aid officer can get in touch with you. Without this information the financial aid officer simply puts your file aside until time is found to write. A letter may have to be complicated whereas a phone conversation could get right to the heart of the problem. Many institutions do not have sufficient financial aid budgets to permit calling you. Therefore, if you are concerned about a problem or delay in the application, call the financial aid office. For the best results, request that the financial aid officer have the file on the desk.

The forms are printed in the summer and early fall for distribution to high schools and colleges usually in November. During this whole period, the continual process of changing and modifying financial aid formulas, regulations, laws, and other procedures continues. One of the difficulties with financial aid is that you have to stay on top of all the changes if you wish to be successful when you apply for aid. Clearly, one of the changes is less and less reliance on information about assets and more and more decisions based on tax returns. There have even been discussions in the financial aid community that perhaps the form will evolve into an attachment to a copy of your tax return.

The importance of aid filing in January has been stressed. In a number of states and institutions it is first come, first serve for financial aid funds. It has happened on several occasions that the school or state has run out of funds and the late applicants have not gotten their full awards. Many families tend to stall, thinking it not that important. If tax-free dollars are important to you, you should consider the impact of those tax-free aid dollars before you decide not to file or to put off filing until later in the winter or early spring.

How It Works

The determination of financial aid is based primarily on two major components: the family contribution and the cost of the school being considered. With these two factors, a whole assistance package can be built for the student with tax-free dollars.

The *family contribution* is a financial aid term for the amount of money that under financial aid theory the family should be able to provide toward the cost of the student's education. Because this is theoretical, some families will contribute more and are able and willing to do so, and some families, of course, do not feel that they are able to contribute the amount indicated as the family contribution. Each year the family contribution for the student is recalculated, based on the family's updated information. The expected family contribution may be recalculated during any award period should the family experience a radical change of events such as loss of primary source of income, accident, or major uninsured loss.

The family contribution is determined by the use of formulas that have been developed over a period of time between the financial aid community and the federal and state governments. Colleges and universities are showing interest in the particular components that make up these formulas. Slight modifications can substantially increase or decrease the need for dollars in the financial aid system by large amounts. Some members of the financial aid community believe that ultimately the formulas may be adjusted purely to act as rationing devices for aid. If you can understand some of these components of the formulas, you may be able to take steps necessary to maximize your aid eligibility through the aid system.

The family contribution is made up of essentially four major parts, as shown in Figure 3–2. All of the information to determine each of these parts is collected on the original form that is filed with the processor. The first section is the parents' contribution which is divided into two

FIGURE 3-2

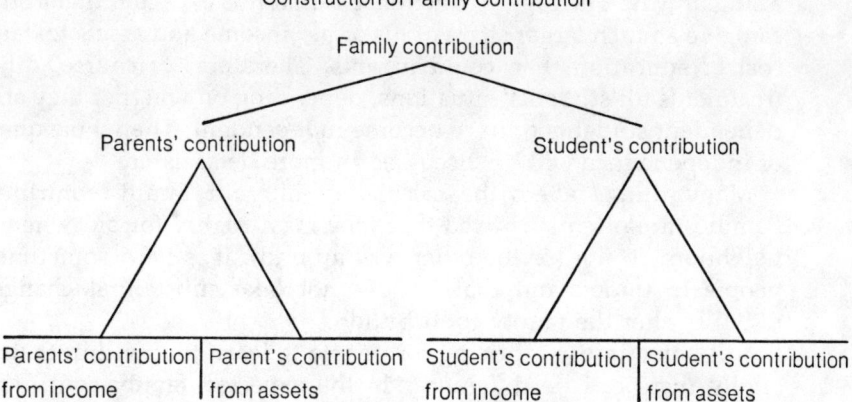

Construction of Family Contribution

major parts—the parents' contribution from income and the parents' contribution from assets. The second section is the student's contribution which is composed of the student's contribution from income and the student's contribution from assets. The parents' contribution from income is calculated by taking their total income and then subtracting a number of different items. These items are allowances made for clothing, food, shelter, cost of getting to work, medical expenses, and state and federal income taxes. Theoretically, when all of these things are subtracted, there should be some money left over which is considered to be available income. Some parts of the system are quite flexible. For example, if there are two parents working, there is a provision for the cost of the second parent being employed. On the other hand, many of the allowances are standard across the country. They do not take into account the extreme differences in cost of living from one area of the country to another.

The parents' contribution from assets is calculated by determining a net worth for the parents. This is essentially done by subtracting all the debts against assets from the assets' current market value. If you overestimate the value of your assets and underestimate your debts, you are costing yourself money. Most people make this mistake.

Once a net worth has been determined, a large amount of the assets are set aside as a reserve for retirement or emergencies. A small percentage of the remaining amount of assets or an income supplement is added to the parents' available income to come up with a total figure from which the parents' contribution is determined. The parents' contribution is determined in total first, and then if they have more than one student in college, the parents' contribution for the individual student is calculated.

The student's contribution from income and assets is determined in a similar way. The biggest difference is that it is expected that a student can give a much larger share of his or her income and assets toward the cost of education than could parents. There are, of course, different treatments for students' situations, depending on whether they are still dependent students or have become independent. The whole question of independence will be discussed in more detail later.

Many things affect the calculation of your family contribution. Families are often surprised that they may qualify for aid when their neighbors do not (or the other way around). It is hard sometimes for people to understand that it does not take substantial changes to radically alter the family contribution.

It is sometimes surprising for people to learn that within their own family there can be differences in the expected family contributions between children. There are two major items that are likely to produce this: first, the amount of savings that the students report and, second, the year in school of the students. Thus, in the case of the Wheelers, they found that their son, Jeff, who was a junior and had considerable savings of his own, required a much higher family contribution than Jane who would be a freshman and had spent her junior summer in high school touring Europe with her band group and therefore had no savings. Students are expected to earn and save (and have available for their educational costs) different amounts, depending on their year in college. The more advanced students are in their education, the more they are expected to earn over the summer. Thus, a senior would have much larger expected summer earnings than a freshman and, therefore, would require a larger family contribution.

Chapter 4

The Application

The application itself is an important part of your financial aid planning and strategy. You should find out as early as possible what is involved in a financial aid application for the schools that your student is interested in attending. Schools as well as state programs vary in their application processes. It is essential that you keep all options distinct.

Because of the many changes that the financial aid system has undergone, often counselors may be unsure just what is going to be required in the application process. Nevertheless, you need the information. So get the best estimation possible and a copy of the most recent forms. Some schools with limited resources and high cost have been forced into collecting much more detailed information to ration their own institutional dollars. You will want to find out these policies early in the financial aid planning process as this could affect the amount of institutional aid that your child could receive.

It is important for you to remember that financial aid and admissions officers in colleges and universities often do not see it as their job to help you qualify for more money. It is analogous to asking the IRS for tax tips. As inflation has continued and there have been difficulties in obtaining sufficient state and federal subsidies for education in some areas, the financial aid officer has become more and more of a rationer of limited resources. The officer feels the need to "protect" the school's money. You want to do everything you can to get the largest available ration for your student.

One of the most important things that you can do is to be sure that you have a clear understanding of the financial aid application process at each institution to which your student is applying. If it is unclear to you, call or write to get your specific questions answered. As mentioned earlier, you should create a financial application calendar for yourself with all the dates clearly established. Be sure to verify also that the admissions papers are filed on time because that is usually crucial to getting adequate financial aid.

How Long until You Hear?

If you have filed a complete financial aid application and admissions information, you will usually hear from the schools in a variety of ways, depending on the processing system they use. There are a number of different ways financial aid officers handle financial aid applications. One of these is "rolling." This means that as the financial aid application is received it is processed, and you are likely to hear relatively rapidly—perhaps six weeks or less from the time you file your application. Another method is "batch processing"; the aid forms are processed together in groups. A third way that is frequently used is to mail out financial aid awards with admissions acceptance letters. This means that even if you file for financial aid early you may have to wait until your admission is complete to find out not only if you will get assistance, but also how much you will get.

Common Form

The first element for a financial aid application is the common form found at almost every school. Most institutions accept either the Financial Aid Form or the Family Financial Statement. Many schools, particularly the public institutions, also accept the Pell Grant (Basic Educational Opportunity Grant) form. Application begins, obviously, with completion of the form. This usually means answering *every* question (even if it means entering zeroes in some places to indicate that you have read and responded to the question). An unanswered question will result in a delayed or rejected form. When the form is complete, mail it to the processor (listed in the application instructions). In the past, envelopes for mailing have always been provided along with the forms. Before you mail it, be sure to make a photocopy of what you are sending and place it in your files. On more than one occasion we have been able to help a family whose forms were apparently delayed in the mail because they had a copy of what they sent in. That information was used to do a hand analysis and then estimate their aid. Be sure to respond rapidly to any request for

Chapter 4: The Application   27

additional information, verification, or questions in order to avoid delaying the process. Some of these questions can be eliminated by being sure that your form is neat and clear when you put it in the mail.

State Aid Application

The second element that you should consider is the state application. Most states have some kind of need-based assistance programs. These have become increasingly popular as we as taxpayers have elected to support them through our federal government subsidy to state financial aid programs. If you are not sure whether your student(s) will be going to school in the home state or another state, apply for the state aid. I have always recommended that people interested in financial aid apply to at least one institution in their home state and to their state's aid program. The additional gift assistance that may be available may make your home-state institution look better to you than the other schools that you were considering.

State forms vary substantially. Your high school counselor knows about the procedure in your state. In general, many states use the FAF (Financial Aid Form) or the FFS (Family Financial Statement) so that there are less forms to fill out. State questions have often been found on a supplement to these two forms. If they are not there and you cannot get the information from your high school guidance office, then get the name of the state agency that handles financial aid and write them a letter requesting the complete application information.

Institutional Application

The third element of the financial aid application is the supplemental institutional aid form. Some schools do not have their own application; others have very simple ones; some have complex documents. These institutional aid forms have become increasingly complicated as the Family Financial Statement, the Financial Aid Form, and the Pell Grant or BEOG application have been simplified. If the school where you are applying has an institutional application form, you should get a copy of the form and be sure that it is completed and returned to the school as soon as possible.

Pell Grants—BEOG

Another item that is often asked for is the BEOGSER, or the Basic Educational Opportunity Grant Student Eligibility Report. When you file either the Financial Aid Form, the Family Financial Statement, or the BEOG (Pell) form, you will probably have filed for the BEOG (Pell) SER.

The SER (Student Eligibility Report) usually comes in triplicate. Be sure that you keep all three copies until you have decided which school you will be attending. In the interim period if one of the schools to which you apply requests the SER, photocopy the original and send the photocopy to the school. When the school is finally selected to enroll in, then it will be important to send them the BEOG (Pell) SER in its original form and keep a photocopy for your records. The originals will be used by the school to obtain the money for the student. Do not be discouraged if the BEOGSER form indicates that you are not eligible. Thousands of students are getting assistance even though they are not eligible for BEOG.

Should the SER request additional information or verification of information, you should provide the information requested and return it as soon as possible for further processing. If you are not clear what is being asked, seek the help of a financial aid officer or try calling the BEOG toll-free 800 number listed on the BEOG information.

Where to Send Aid Applications

How many places should you send your financial aid information? When you complete the financial aid application of your choice (Financial Aid Form or Family Financial Statement), you will have the opportunity to release that information to a number of organizations. Where to send the information is almost always one of the questions asked when we get to that section of the aid application at the workshops. Some choices are:

1. BEOG. There is usually a question that reads something like this: "I give permission to send information to BEOG." If you indicate yes, then you will be automatically applying for the BEOG. You will as a result eventually receive a BEOGSER in the mail.

2. Your State. If you have found out that the state scholarship commission in your state requires the financial aid application you are completing, be sure to request a copy for them (see 3 below). As we mentioned earlier, some states have their own applications and others use the Family Financial Statement or the Financial Aid Form.

3. Colleges and Universities that You Are Considering. (There is usually a place where you can list several colleges and universities and/ or the state agency that you wish to have receive copies of the information that you are submitting on the application.) By the time you are filing in January of the senior year your student should be able to narrow college choices down to about three schools. Since it costs money to forward the application to each school or agency you list other than the Pell (BEOG), it may be important for your student to consider limiting schools at this time.

Chapter 4: The Application

4. Local Scholarship Competition(s).

Each year the financial aid forms seem to go through a number of changes. These changes are usually agreed upon during the winter and spring. There are a number of parties working in an informal coalition to create the form. These include the U.S. Department of Education, state governments, and educational interest groups. Compromise is at best difficult to achieve in trying to represent the many different groups that are interested in getting information on the form and trying to create a document that will be simple enough that everyone will be able to understand it. As the document has been simplified, there has been more room for sophisticated applicants to play with the figures if they so desire. This is to your benefit. Your overall strategy will guide you.

Verification Procedures

Once the information is released to the financial aid office or state agency, your data is verified. The most common way of doing this is to request the parents' income tax return. More recently the colleges have also started requesting the student's income tax return. The requesting of tax returns has grown out of two important areas. First, the colleges and universities are concerned for the accuracy of the information being submitted. Second, and more recently, to be sure the records agree, federal government requires validation of BEOG information for a percentage of those people receiving the BEOG. It is possible that you could be asked for considerably more information than that shown on your tax return, but that is a rare case. Some institutions have a policy of verification for every aid applicant and, therefore, will automatically request your income tax return.

Many states also review a portion of the aid forms that they receive. Again, the primary source for the review would be the income tax return. At the present time I know of no institution that is actively verifying asset information except through those items that automatically show up on the income tax forms. So, if you show dividends on the income tax forms, it is very important that you list something under investments when you get to the asset portion of the form, or the state or college aid officer is going to wonder where the dividends are coming from.

FORMULAS FOR CALCULATING AID

Uniform Methodology

One of the formulas that has been used is called the "uniform methodology." This procedure was developed by a coalition of interested parties and has been adjusted each of the last several years in major and minor ways. Some of the adjustments have helped many higher-income families to qualify for assistance.

You would not know that you were having your aid calculated using the uniform methodology. This would all be done automatically for you. Thus, when you mailed your form to the processor, a family contribution would automatically be determined for you unless you file only the federal (Pell Grant) form.

It is important that you know at this point that individual schools have the right to adjust the formula within certain limits. Many do so. Therefore, the title of uniform methodology refers to a process that is becoming less uniform.

Pell Grant

Another major formula is the BEOG (Pell Grant) formula. Many students will have this automatically calculated for them as well as the uniform methodology when they file an aid form. The formula is one that is used to determine the disbursement of federal government grants, in particular the Basic Educational Opportunity Grant, (the Pell Grant). There has been considerable consideration given to making this the only formula used in the aid system for the disbursement of all federal and state dollars. The difficulty with this concept is that this particular formula has served more as a rationing device than a true determination of need. In many ways that could be bad for financial aid applicants. But on the positive side there is less information to check and, therefore, perhaps more ways to apply.

Processing

The information needed for processing these formulas is collected on the previously discussed aid forms, which should be in your high school counselor's office in November and should be filed, if at all possible, sometime during the month of January. Recently the three most common forms have been the FAF (Financial Aid Form), the FFS (Family Financial Statement), and the BEOG (Basic Educational Opportunity Grant). The first two were used by most schools giving substantial aid dollars to students. In the case of both the FAF and the FFS, the processor to whom you mail the form automatically computes the family contribution for you using uniform methodology. Assuming that you have released your information to the Basic Grant (BEOG or Pell), the processor will then automatically estimate your eligibility for that award as well.

When processors determine the family contribution for each student, there is little room for variation. Standards have been set for certain "benchmark cases," and the different systems must provide similar results. Over the years we have had a number of families submit the same information to both major processors (FAF and FFS) and have found that the family contribution usually works out to within a $50 range almost every time. When there is more variance, the reason is usually because the family submitted different information on one of the forms.

When the processor is finished, the information is forwarded to the financial aid offices and state agencies as directed by the family. Families should, then, be particularly careful to see that they have sent their information to all the correct organizations. It is not uncommon for a family, in the rush of completing the form, to forget or to omit a state agency or a college or university. Until that error is found and corrected that portion of the aid process comes to a complete standstill. We have always recommended that students release their information to all schools that they are seriously considering and that they be sure that any other groups (such as state agencies and local scholarship organizations) also are sent a copy of the information.

Section III
THE FAMILY CONTRIBUTION

Chapter 5
The Organization of the Family Contribution

Chapter 6
Parents' Contribution from Income

Chapter 7
Calculation of Available Income

Chapter 8
Parents' Contribution from Assets

Chapter 9
Calculation of Parents' Contribution from Assets

Chapter 10
Student's Contribution from Income

Chapter 11
Student's Contribution from Assets

Chapter 5

The Organization of the Family Contribution

The family contribution is traditionally made up of four parts.

Family Contribution

Parents' Contribution		*Student's Contribution*	
Parents' contribution from income	Parents' contribution from assets	Student's contribution from income	Student's contribution from assets

Each of these has an important role in financial aid planning and strategies. Good use of them will maximize your student's potential for aid.

Parents' Income

The first area to be considered will be that of parents' contribution from income. Recently this has become very dependent on the U.S. Individual Income Tax Return, line 31, the Adjusted Gross Income. This has eliminated much of the subjectivity in income reporting that has been a part of the aid system. You should be aware that aid professionals are beginning to ask themselves what the real influence of things like depreciation and optional retirement plans are on taxable income and whether these should be added back into income to determine a better estimate of cash flow.

For the present though, the major consideration for income is focused on line 31 of the tax form, nontaxable income, and the allowances that are subtracted from these. This is one of the areas in which joint tax and financial aid planning can help to reap significant rewards.

Parents' Assets

The second major portion of the parents' contribution comes from assets. This is the area where most families make mistakes when filing for financial assistance. We overvalue our assets and underestimate our liabilities, and this greatly reduces financial aid. I continually tell people this in the workshops that I have given; nevertheless, many of them still try to impress others with their assets instead of getting my message to be realistic. To give you an example of what overestimating your assets can do, let's consider the Merritt family.

When the Merritts were completing the Financial Aid Form they listed assets (for financial aid purposes) of $100,000 and debts against those assets of only $25,000. The net worth or assets less liabilities was then $75,000.

$$\text{Assets} - \text{Liabilities} = \text{Net worth}$$

When the Merritt's student did not qualify for financial aid and they felt that they could not afford to pay the bills, a review of their situation indicated that the assets were really only about $80,000 and their debts were really about $40,000 for a net worth of $40,000.

$$\text{Assets} - \text{Liabilities} = \text{Net worth}$$
$$\$80,000 - \$40,000 = \$40,000$$

The difference in the assets reduced the family contribution by almost $2,000 a year, or enough to qualify them for some state and federal assistance. What they did the second time around was to look at their assets more realistically. The Merritts were asked to think about what their home was really worth if they had to sell it and not what they would like to get out of it under ideal circumstances. Some families have even learned to recognize the selling costs, including real estate commissions (7 to 9 percent), taxes, and legal fees in determining the real value of their property. (One family even suggested that they felt they should deduct the capital gains that they would have to pay if they were forced to liquidate their home.)

The Merritts were further asked to consider the true value of their stock portfolio, not what the high was for each stock. After reviewing each of these assets required for consideration on the Financial Aid Form, the Merritts then totaled their realistic assets and found that they

Chapter 5: The Organization of the Family Contribution

really only had assets of $80,000 instead of the original $100,000. The same process is followed with debts or mortgages against assets. Many of us like to forget how much we owe, but that is important in figuring out financial aid. If you have a debt that qualifies, by all means list it.

Thus, be realistic in determining the asset portion of the parents' contribution in order to help the student qualify for the maximum federal and state assistance. This is an area of such importance that it bears repetition. A large number of families make mistakes in overestimating assets and underestimating liabilities. They end up depriving their students of potential assistance.

THE STUDENT'S CONTRIBUTION

The student's contribution is a very important part of the financial aid picture. The student's contribution plus the parents' contribution make up the total family contribution. Once again, the family contribution is the number which we subtract from the total cost to determine aid eligibility. Variance in student contribution among family members is one reason why two children from the same family can have such different needs, even when the schools they are attending have the same total cost.

Student's contribution + Parents' contribution = Family contribution

Total cost − Family contribution = Aid eligibility

There are three major segments to the student's contribution which are considered in most financial aid calculations:

1. A contribution from the earnings that the student will have the summer before school starts. This is a predetermined expectation at many institutions and in the national formula.
2. A contribution from the student's assets. Students that have accumulated savings or other assets are expected to contribute from these resources to help with the cost of their education.
3. Recently the federal government has begun to take a closer look at students' past earnings records from the previous tax year. This has just started in the BEOG (Pell Grant) program, but it is likely to become more important in other aid sources as well.

In my experience the student's contribution is often the one that causes the most trouble for students and parents. Many students appear to forget that they, as well as their parents, are supposed to be making a significant contribution to the cost of their education. Numerous times students come into my office and complain that there is not enough aid and that there is no more help available from parents. A careful review of the situation shows that the student is not contributing the share expected of him or her.

If you decide to apply for aid and you receive an award, be sure that you review it carefully. Most awards will tell you how much the parents are expected to contribute and how much the student is supposed to contribute as well as how much aid the student will be receiving. To avoid problems, the parents should review this and make sure they feel that they can come up with their share. Just as important, however, parents must sit down with the student and be sure that he or she has the resources (or will be able to earn enough) to provide what is expected of him or her. If the money will be available, then there should not be any difficulty. However, if the money is not going to be available, you should discuss this with the financial aid office and know what the consequences are going to be.

A brief example of the kind of problem that you can run into is as follows. Joel came into the office complaining that he did not have enough aid to make the necessary fall payments for his freshman year. In reviewing the situation the following information was available:

Charges for the year	$6,300	
Books, supplies, etc.	700	
Total cost		$7,000
Less:		
Parents' contribution	$3,000	
Student's contribution	1,500	
Total family contribution		4,500
Aid eligibility for Joel		$2,500

Joel's aid award showed that he was to receive $2,400 in financial assistance for the year. The initial bill for the first semester from the university was one half the total cost of $6,300 or $3,150.

Total bill		$3,150
Resources for first semester:		
Financial assistance	$1,200	
Parents' contribution	1,500	2,700
Unpaid balance		$ 450

Joel complained that he did not have enough financial aid to pay his bills and that he had not even begun to buy his books and supplies. He also needed money for entertainment and other miscellaneous expenses. He thought that he had been misled by the school into thinking that his parents would not have to contribute more than the $1,500 a semester for a total of $3,000 a year. As is often the case with students, he felt that he would not be able to go to school.

After a short review of Joel's case, it became clear that he had not listened when the discussion had turned to the student's contribution. It had not occurred to him that he should plan on spending his own hard-earned money for his education. Joel spent his summer earnings as fast as he made them and did not give much thought to his responsibilities at the university. As has always been the case, we tried to work out something for Joel so that he could stay in school and live frugally. He used more of his savings then he expected to make the payments that first year. After this incident Joel was careful to check on what he, as a student, was expected to contribute to the cost of his education.

A similar problem that we have with students' contributions is that some students plan to pay all or part of their parents' share in addition to their own. Of course in most cases it is difficult for students to earn enough to pay both shares, and they soon find themselves in financial trouble. The key to success is to be sure that everyone takes responsibility for their contribution seriously. This means both students and parents.

Chapter 6

Parents' Contribution from Income

Traditionally there have been a number of considerations in the calculation of the parents' contribution from income. These are listed and their use explained below.

Taxable income.
Nontaxable income.
Allowances:
    Federal income tax.
    Social security (FICA).
    State and local taxes.
    Employment allowance.
    Medical and dental expense.
    Standard maintenance allowance (taxable and nontaxable).

The income in the home refers to the home in which the child lives in the case of divorce or separation. Thus, if a couple is divorced and the child is living with the mother, then the father's income is not directly included. Some schools may elect to consider this as an option in the disbursement of their own funds, but generally the resources of the home in which the child lives are the only ones considered.

Recently it was decided that stepparent's income would be included if the student lived with the stepparent for more than six weeks and/or received $1,000 or more in support. If you are divorced or involved in the possibility of one, you may wish to read the chapter on divorce and

Chapter 6: Parents' Contribution from Income

separation later on in this book (Chapter 18) to help you figure out the best financial strategies for that situation.

TAXABLE INCOME

The taxable income we mentioned can be found on line 31 of your Form 1040 U.S. Individual Income Tax Return. The most important thing that you can do to help yourself in both tax planning and financial aid planning is to keep that figure as small as possible. A number of specific strategies that you may wish to consider with your tax advisor are discussed in Chapter 13.

NONTAXABLE INCOME

Nontaxable income includes the following (plus those listed on the worksheet to calculate income):

Social security
Child support
Veterans' benefits
Tax-free interest on bonds
Untaxed portions of pensions and capital gains
Living and housing allowances
Ministers' housing allowances
Unemployment compensation[1]

Assuming that you have used the worksheet to determine your total income, it is time to look at what the formula does with this information.

ALLOWANCES

Income Tax

The first allowance is made for the U.S. income tax that you pay. It is important to note here that once you have determined your income for line 31, for financial aid purposes you might as well pay a large tax on that line unless your tax rate is considerably higher than 50 percent. Deductions that come after line 31 are probably not of help to you. Try to determine if you might qualify for financial aid before you start structuring your finances to take advantage of the system. With the

---

[1] Unemployment compensation can be taxable under certain circumstances. You should verify this when you do your taxes.

Worksheet to Calculate Income

Income from line 31, IRS 1040, 1980	_____
Nontaxable income:	
Social security..	_____
Aid to Families with Dependent Children	_____
Welfare benefits	_____
Railroad retirement benefits	_____
Disability income.....................................	_____
Untaxed portions of pensions and capital gains	_____
Child support	_____
Veterans' benefits....................................	_____
Tax-free interest on bonds............................	_____
Living and housing allowances	_____
Ministers' housing allowances*	_____
Unemployment compensation†	_____
Nontaxable Income	_____
Total taxable and nontaxable income	_____

* For ministers' housing allowances, if you do not know the value, use 20 percent of ministers' salaries.

† Check income taxes; sometimes unemployment is taxable.

exception of most of your medical deductions, not many of the itemized deductions help you with financial aid because they come after line 31 and serve only to reduce your federal tax. (This is good, but at the same time, it is likely to reduce your financial aid at an even more rapid rate.) For example, if you gave $1,000 to your favorite charitable institution and were in the 50 percent income tax bracket, it would have the following effect on financial aid.

Parents' Contribution from Last $1,000 Income

	Tax	Spendable	Parents' Contribution*
Before gift	$500	$500	$235
After gift ($1,000)...............	0†	0	470

* Assumes the highest rate at which income after allowances can be used for financial aid for parents' contribution from income.

† Tax reduction of $500 due to charitable gift.

You must be careful in thinking about these things as obviously there are other things to consider such as the impact on state and city income taxes if you have those kinds of taxation. This would be true for any of the things that appear under the itemized deductions including interest expense, contributions, miscellaneous deductions, and casualty or theft losses. Obviously, if you have interest expenses and the other itemized deductions, you should take them. However, if you have a chance to make these deductions optional or defer them, then you may want to consider the financial aid impact. If we refer back to the example—before the gift, the family had $500 in spendable income.

Chapter 6: Parents' Contribution from Income   43

They were expected to give $235 of it to help with the cost of education for their children, leaving a spending power of $265. After the gift the family had nothing because they had given away $1,000 and were expected to contribute $470 ($235 more) to the cost of educating their children.

Another area that should be looked at carefully when filing for financial aid is that of income averaging. The effect of income averaging is to reduce your income taxes and leave your income intact. It is important that you are aware that any reduction in taxes will increase aftertax income and, therefore, decrease financial aid. Thus, the impact of averaging may be negated by the corresponding decrease in financial aid. Some families have indicated that they have prepared their tax forms without averaging completely and filed those with financial aid offices. Then they have gone on to average for filing with the federal government. I would not recommend this. It is illegal. If you are going to average, it is important that you be aware of how it may impact your financial aid. Remember, financial aid is tax-free.

Social Security

There are several allowances that are subtracted from taxable and nontaxable income. The first one discussed was the U.S. income tax. The second item usually is the FICA tax, commonly known as the social security tax. To find out how much you paid into this for last year, check your copy of the W–2 form (or your tax records, if you pay it yourself). For example, the FICA tax rate recently was 6.13 percent on the first $22,900 of income. If both you and your spouse were working, take the 6.13 percent times each income for the first $22,900. Thus, if parent A had an income of $15,000 and parent B an income of $25,000, you would compute your FICA as follows:[2]

Parent A: Since $15,000 is less than $22,900, then FICA = 6.13 × $15,000 or $919.50.

Parent B: Since $25,000 is more than $22,900, then FICA = 6.13 × $22,900 or $1,403.77.

You cannot do much to change this nor should you worry about it for financial aid purposes as it is subtracted out of your available income to determine the parents' contribution.

State and Local Taxes

The next allowance that is made against income is an adjustment for state income taxes and other taxes that may affect your cost of living.

---

[2] Note the percentage rates and maximums change periodically. Also, rates are different for self-employed individuals.

This is generally a fixed percentage of your nontaxable income plus what you report as income on line 31 of Form 1040. A recent table that was used for calculation of uniform methodology has been included (see Table 6–1). If you find that you actually have a state and local tax

TABLE 6–1
State Tax Table

	Percent of Total Income		
State	$0–$5,999	$6,000–$9,999	$10,000 or more
Puerto Rico, Texas, Wyoming............	7%	5%	4%
Florida, Louisiana, Nevada, Tennessee, West Virginia.......................	8	7	5
Alabama, Arkansas, Georgia, Indiana, New Mexico, Ohio, Oklahoma, Washington.........................	8	7	6
Alaska, Arizona, Idaho, Kansas, Kentucky, Mississippi, Missouri, Nebraska, New Hampshire, North Carolina, North Dakota, South Carolina, South Dakota, Virginia.............................	9	8	7
American Samoa, Canal Zone, Colorado, Connecticut, District of Columbia, Guam, Illinois, Iowa, Montana, New Jersey, Oregon, Pennsylvania, Trust Territories, Utah, Virgin Islands..................	10	9	8
Delaware, Hawaii, Maine, Michigan, Rhode Island........................	12	10	9
California, Maryland, Minnesota, Vermont............................	12	11	10
Massachusetts, Wisconsin	12	12	11
New York.............................	13	13	12

* To use state tax table: Take total taxable and nontaxable income and multiply by the allowance rate. For example, $20,000 income in New York State:

$$\$20,000 \times 12 = \$2,400 \text{ allowance}$$

Source: Reprinted with permission from *CSS Need Analysis: Theory and Computation Procedures for the 1981–1982 FAF*. Copyright © 1980 by College Entrance Examination Board, New York.

burden that is considerably higher than is indicated by this table, it would be wise to point this out to financial aid officers at the schools to which you are applying for assistance. Send them some back-up data such as a copy of your state income tax return, sales tax statements, or whatever. If the figure on the table is more than you now pay in state or local taxes according to your records, don't worry about it. That figure is automatically used unless appealed. In reviewing a large number of cases for financial aid purposes we have found this estimate of state and local tax burden to be fair and equitable.

Employment Allowance

Another allowance that is made against your total income is the "employment allowance." In the basic formula it is assumed that one person in the family is working with all the related expenses of getting to work. If there is a second parent in the home that is working, an additional allowance is made for the cost of that person working. This allowance is 50 percent of the first $4,800 of gross income reported. This allowance often helps families to qualify who thought because a second parent was working that they would be ineligible for assistance. This allowance, like many of the others, is supposed to be automatically revised each year to reflect changes in the consumer price index.

Assume a family with one parent working reports an income of $35,200 on line 31 of the Form 1040. The example shows what happens (based on the 1980 tax year and 1981–82 uniform methodology) if a second parent goes to work and earns $9,000.

Income to be reported on Line 31 with only one parent working	$35,200	
Income of second parent	9,000	
New total household income	$44,200	
Second parent income		$9,000
Less deductions:		
Income tax (43 percent married joint)	$ 3,870	
Social security tax (6.13 percent)	552	
State taxes (assume 6 percent)	540	
Total deductions		−4,962
Spendable income		$4,038
Less employment allowance		2,400
Amount considered for financial aid		$1,638

The maximum rate at which a family contributes from income after deductions for the uniform methodology formula is 47 percent. So, to find out how much of the second parent's income could be considered available for part of the family contribution it would be necessary to multiply $1,638 by 47 percent.

Amount available for financial aid × Maximum expected contribution
= Family contribution from second income

$$\$1{,}638 \times 47\% = \$770$$

The second income would not affect financial aid substantially in this case and would provide considerable aftertax spending power for the family.

Income	$9,000
Spendable income after taxes	4,038
Increased family contribution	770

Even after paying the $770, the family would have an increased spendable income of $3,268 for the year.

Some families have learned this early and have split the working income more evenly. This is especially easy to do if you own your own business. The important message remains that in this situation, the second income of $9,000 is not likely to affect aid by more than $770. This could vary with different federal or state tax rates.

Many single-parent families are now receiving aid because the "employment allowance" recognizes their special expenses such as child care. It is important to remember here that the income on which you file for financial aid is the income in the home in which the child lives. Thus, if there is one parent in the home in which the child lives, then that is what is considered for financial aid purposes. Since divorces are somewhat complicated at best there is a chapter devoted to them later in the book.

Medical and Dental Expenses

Medical and dental expenses are another area that may affect financial aid. Many families have given up keeping track of this because of the standard deduction on their income tax forms. If you have substantial expenses in this area, it is advisable to keep *detailed* records as they may help you in financial aid and may be worth showing to your tax preparer. For financial aid purposes, medical expenses beyond 3 percent of income may reduce the expected family contribution even if you do not itemize deductions.

What we are looking for is the total amount of medical expense less expenses covered by insurance. These can include the following:

Medicine
Doctors
Nurses
Hearing aids
Eye glasses
Ambulance
Drugs
Dentists
Hospitals
Dentures
Transportation

The most commonly overlooked expenses in my experience are eye glasses and transportation. For transportation you can take 9 cents a

Chapter 6: Parents' Contribution from Income

mile, plus parking fees and tolls (1980 income taxes). Some people have planned to move optional noninsured medical procedures to a year when they could help both with taxes and financial aid. This, of course, only works if your medical bills not covered by insurance exceed 3 percent of your total income.

Maintenance Allowance

The standard maintenance allowance is the final amount subtracted from your total taxable and nontaxable income to figure out how much of your income is considered available. This is a predetermined amount based on the number in the family and the number that will be attending college in the following year. The larger the reported size of the household, the larger the standard maintenance allowance will be. For example, in a recent period, the amount for a family of four with one child in college was the same throughout the United States—$10,850. (For a family of four with two in college, the amount would be $9,640.)

The way to increase this figure is to increase the number of people you report as being part of the household. Sometimes families do not consider everyone that they should include.

Size of parents' household includes:
Parents.
Students.
Other dependent children.
Possible other members who live with you and receive more than half of their support:
Relatives.
Student's grandparents.

On more than one occasion we have helped a family to receive appropriate federal and state assistance simply by recognizing the true need of the family. This was done by showing how many people were really living in the household.

Chapter 7

Calculation of Available Income

In the preceding chapter a variety of allowances against total income were discussed. Once all these calculations are done on the income, the total of allowances can be subtracted from the total income to arrive at a figure called parents' available income. This amount may be considered available for the total college expenses of the family at amounts ranging from 0 to 47 percent. The 47 percent level is the maximum level and would only occur in the higher-income brackets in most families unless almost all of the income was tax-free and there were few other deductions.

The set up is like this:

Total taxable and nontaxable income for 1980*		$44,200
Less allowances:		
U.S. income tax (four exemptions)	$10,312	
FICA	2,140	
State and other taxes (assume 9 percent)	3,978	
Medical and dental expenses	0	
Employment allowance	2,400	
Standard maintenance allowance (family of four)	10,850	
Total allowances		29,680
Parents' available income		$14,520

*Figures are for a family of four with two parents working and one student in college (second parent earns $9,000).

Chapter 7: Calculation of Available Income

Assuming that this family did not have sufficient assets to be considered in calculation, these parents would only be expected to contribute $4,289 toward the cost of their one child in college, based on the commonly used uniform methodology. The student should then easily get aid at colleges costing more than $5,000. For example, just based on the parents' income:

	A	B	C	D
School cost	$9,000	$7,000	$5,000	$3,000
Parents' contribution from income	4,289	4,289	4,289	4,289
Aid eligibility (considering only parents' contribution from income)	4,711	2,711	711	0

If the family size increased to six with the same income, there would be some substantial differences in the parent's contribution.

This next example shows the change that results from increasing family size.

Total taxable and nontaxable income for 1980*	$44,200
Less allowances:	
U.S. income tax (six exemptions)	$ 9,452
FICA	2,140
State and other taxes (assume 9 percent)	3,978
Medical and dental expenses	0
Employment allowance	2,400
Standard maintenance allowance (family of six)	14,970
Total allowances	32,940
Parents' available income	$11,260

* Figures are for a family of six with two parents working and one student in college.

Again, assuming that this family did not report sufficient assets to be considered in the calculation, these parents would only be expected to contribute $2,858 toward the cost of their one child in college. This student should easily get aid at colleges costing $3,000 or more, including some of the state institutions.

	A	B	C	D
School cost	$9,000	$7,000	$5,000	$3,000
Parents' contribution (from income)	2,858	2,858	2,858	2,858
Aid eligibility (considering only parents' contribution from income)	6,142	4,142	2,142	142

Notice that the child from the six-member family is eligible for approximately $1,400 more aid at schools A, B, and C. The parents' contribution for the family of four was $4,289. In the six-member family with everything else the same, the parents were only expected to contribute $2,858, or a difference of $1,431. Some people who have applied for aid have missed out in the past because they have not counted everyone in the household. This oversight is especially common in families with grandparents or other relatives living in the home, or in families who have quasi-independent children that are really receiving their support from home. Each year the rules for members of the household are spelled out clearly. This is certainly an area to watch as you complete the form.

To show the effects of other changes it is probably worth examining a couple more cases using the same basic format. The first will be a single-parent family. The parent has the same income, files as head of the household, and has four deductions.

Total taxable and nontaxable income*		$44,200
Less allowances:		
U.S. income tax (higher taxes)	$11,891	
FICA (note change as only one person working)	1,588	
State and other taxes (assume 9 percent)	3,978	
Medical and dental expenses	0	
Employment allowance	2,400	
Standard maintenace allowance (family of four)	10,850	
Total allowances		30,707
Parent's available income		$13,493

* Figures are for a family of four with one parent and one student in college.

Assuming that there were not sufficient assets to be considered in the calculation, this parent would be expected to contribute $3,807 toward the cost of the child's education. This student should get aid at colleges costing $4,500 or more.

	A	B	C	D
School cost	$9,000	$7,000	$5,000	$3,000
Parent's contribution (from income)	3,807	3,807	3,807	3,807
Aid eligibility (considering only parent's contribution from income)	5,193	3,193	1,193	0

It is interesting to note that the single-parent family actually has a smaller contribution based on the factors that we are considering at this point than the two-parent family of four. The major reasons for this are

Chapter 7: Calculation of Available Income

probably the increased income taxes that have been estimated and the applicability of the employment allowance.

The final example in this section, using the same information, is the traditional family of four with one parent working, two children, and one parent at home.

Total taxable and nontaxable income*		$44,200
Less allowances:		
U.S. income tax (four exemptions)	$10,312	
FICA (only one person working)	1,588	
State and other taxes (assume 9 percent)	3,978	
Medical and dental expenses	0	
Employment allowance (second parent not earning income)	0	
Standard maintenance allowance	10,850	
Total allowances		26,728
Parents' available income		$17,472

*Figures are for a family of four with two parents, one working, and with one student in college.

Making the same assumption on assets—that there are not enough to be included in the calculations—these parents would be expected to contribute $5,677 to the cost of their child's education. The student should get assistance at schools costing $6,000 or more.

	A	B	C	D
School cost	$9,000	$7,000	$5,000	$3,000
Parents' contribution (from income)	5,677	5,677	5,677	5,677
Aid eligibility (considering only parents' contribution from income)	3,323	1,323	0	0

You can see that based on their income this family has the least aid eligibility of all four situations that we have examined. The family could increase its aid if some of the income could be attributed to the nonworking parent or if there are more members of the family that are not being counted.

It never ceases to amaze me that in these somewhat similar families there is a range of parent's contribution from income of over $2,500. It should be reason enough for you to apply for aid and find out where you would be in terms of parents' contribution.

Chapter 8

Parents' Contribution from Assets

Traditionally, the area of parental assets has been one of great difficulty for financial aid officers. There are a number of assets that are considered:

    Home equity
    Other real estate and investments
        Stocks
        Bonds
        Land contracts
        Trust funds
        Other securities
        Real estate
    Businesses
    Farms
    Cash

HOME EQUITY

One of the major areas of debate in financial aid for years has been the use of home equity. Home equity is the market value of the home less the mortgages and/or debts against the house.

$$\text{Market value} - \text{Mortgages and debts} = \text{Home equity}$$

Chapter 8: Parents' Contribution from Assets

For most families the home is one of the largest investments, and the correct treatment of this major asset has been extremely important to the whole aid picture. Recently Congress has passed legislation which may eliminate home equity from consideration in federal programs. The financial aid professional community is divided on the appropriate use of home equity.

To correctly deal with home equity you must determine the real market value of your house. Most people are not professionals in real estate and wonder how to do this. Be realistic—think about how much your house would be worth if you had to sell it within a couple of weeks. *Remember that it is of no value to you to increase the value of your home.* If your neighbors are asking $100,000 for their house, you may figure that they are selling for $90,000. How long has their house been on the market? How quickly did it sell? Is your home as nice? Honestly? Many people have found it helps to read the real estate section of the newspaper, to visit an open house or two, to ask a realtor friend for a quick appraisal that is realistic. Other people are lucky enough to have a state or local home appraisal system that is accurate. If you have such a system in your area that is keyed to market value, you could use the market value determined by that system.

Be careful—do not use insurance values unless your home is new. The Howard family is a case in point. The Howards' home had the following values:

Insurance	$85,000
Appraised by the Howards	$70,000
Realtors' appraisals (three)	$50–55,000
Actual sale price (after one year)	$47,500
Quick sale price (estimated)	$42,500

The difference in the amount of aid their student could qualify for would be significant, depending on which value the Howard family selected for their house. You can readily see that the estimated quick sale price is one half the insured value of this older home. The Howards could increase their need by as much as $2,400 per year by using the quick sale price as the real value of their home.

During a recent series of workshops many families had to be reminded that their home value might be less than it had been six to nine months before as mortgage rates were climbing and home sales were falling off rapidly. If your home would be difficult to sell because of some factor such as high mortgage rates, be sure to consider that fact when you give the current market value. Again, the key to success at the aid game is for you to be honest with yourself about the real value of your home in today's marketplace.

One of the important things to remember is that currently the financial aid office has no quick method to determine the value of your home. Unlike the income tax form which can be used to check the income you report on the aid form, there is no verifying document for home value. On rare occasions a real estate assessment for property tax purposes may be requested, but this remains a rare event. Your ability to determine the real value of your home is being tested.

The second part of the home equity equation is the liabilities including mortgages, loans, and debts or liens against the house.

Market value − Liabilities = Net worth (determined by you)

When you ask most people what is owed on their home, the immediate response is the estimate of the amount of the first mortgage that is yet to be paid. If we are considering a family that has a home with a realistic market value of $90,000, the first mortgage may be $56,000. Under these circumstances the asset would show for financial aid purposes as follows:

House market value		$90,000
Less:		
First mortgage	$56,000	
Net worth		$34,000

But many times families neglect to list other debts against the house that they should include. Now suppose that we consider the same house and the other debts against that house which, like mortgages, would have to be liquidated if the house were to be sold. These might include a sewer assessment, a land contract or second mortgage, a debt to parents from whom money was borrowed to make the down payment, a home-improvement loan that is a lien against the house. If you are not sure of something but you think it is a debt against the house, count it as part of what is owed. You may not count purchases on credit cards or other forms of consumer credit. Looking at the same house considering some of the other debts, there will be quite a difference in net worth.

House market value		$90,000
Less:		
First mortgage	$56,000	
Land contract or second mortgage	10,000	
Sewer assessment	2,000	
Debt to parents for down payment	5,000	
Total owed	$73,000	
Net worth		$17,000

When all the debts are considered, the net worth of the house is reduced by one half. These few changes could reduce the family contribution by almost $1,000 and perhaps significantly increase the amount of financial aid awarded. Each year there are slight adjustments on what the formula will allow for debts against a house, so read the fine print on the aid forms. Again, if you are not sure but you believe it is a debt against the house, include it in the total.

Worksheet to Calculate Home Net Worth

Quick sale price of house (what is it worth?) .... _____
Less:
    First mortgage (check with mortgage company) .... _____
    Home improvement loans .... _____
    Land contract .... _____
    Second mortgage .... _____
    Debts secured by home (i.e., debts to parents) .... _____
    Other—1. .... _____
            2. .... _____
            3. .... _____
        Total owed .... _____
Net worth of home .... ========

There are very few ways for financial aid officers to check this information except to ask you for a copy of your mortgage statement and an explanation of the other debts. Be sure that you keep a written record of how you figured what was owed on your house so that you can back up your claims if necessary. The worksheet provided in this section should give you such a record. Be sure to check your actual mortgage statements for figures. Most people think that they have paid more on their mortgages than they have.

Members of Congress, as I mentioned earlier, are interested in helping their own families (and others like them) qualify for aid. There has been a great deal of consideration given to eliminating home equity from any consideration in the financial aid formula. In the fall of 1980 legislation was passed in Congress eliminating the consideration of home equity for federal programs. Schools and states are not required to use this formula, and they may not because it will greatly increase the aid eligibility of many families.

But because of this, many families with expensive debt-free homes may now qualify for some federal and perhaps even state or institutional assistance. Eliminating $100,000 of home net worth from consideration could reduce the family contribution by over $5,000 under some circumstances. This would help many families in the higher income brackets qualify for aid—particularly those with incomes between $35,000 and $75,000 a year. The treatment of home net worth continues to be a subject of debate and would be an important area to check on as you begin the financial aid planning process.

The listing of home value has been one of the largest areas of error for families seeking aid. Many families have deprived themselves and their students of the opportunity to receive federal and state assistance by improperly listing their home value and debts against the home.

Others have been deprived by the effects of high inflation on home values. Many West Coast families who own relatively modest homes have found their equity is in excess of $100,000, based on conservative current-market prices. The elimination of home equity will, in some people's minds, help to equalize the tremendous differences in cost of living in this country. The important point is to remember that if you are asked to list your home value, list it realistically. Your aid will be affected by this valuation.

The King family readily comes to mind. When they first applied for financial aid and explained how needy they were, they were informed they would probably qualify for assistance. After the application was processed, the family found that their student would not receive any assistance at an expensive private school even though they had a relatively modest income. We spent some hours counseling this first-generation American family and found that they had apparently over-valued their home by almost $40,000. Correcting this one factor made the student qualify for significant amounts of assistance. In this case to change the value we used the state assessment of real market value which we confirmed with a realtor in the area. The Kings then had to go back and refile their forms with the state and federal governments in order to get the assistance to which they were entitled. Unfortunately, because they filed incorrectly, they were too late for a portion of the state aid. This is why it is so important to start the whole process early and to do it right the first time.

The second year the Kings and I sat down early in January and listed everything correctly, and they were able to get substantial help for their student. Further, it was possible to forecast some of the help that would be available for the other children that were coming along. Let's hope that you can avoid the same mistakes and receive the money that you are entitled to.

OTHER REAL ESTATE AND INVESTMENTS

Once the home has been properly considered in the financial aid application, then it is time to consider other assets. There are essentially three other major components to be considered. They are: (1) other real estate and investments, (2) businesses or farms, and (3) cash in the bank. It will help you if you understand how each of these has been treated in the past and probably will continue to be treated in the future. The listing of these assets, like the home, is an area of real problems for many families and sometimes prevents their students from receiving assistance. Remember that when you start talking about sophisticated investments, most financial aid people can get lost rather quickly. This is because they are not trained in investments and finance. When financial aid was first conceived it was meant for the extremely poor. We did not run into the larger middle class that is now eligible in many cases to receive help.

What is considered in other real estate and investments?

Stocks (mutual funds)
Bonds
Land contracts
Trust funds
Securities
Real estate

In each case it is important to determine a current market value for each asset and then calculate what is owed on that asset. Note that you are not being asked about insurance, art objects, antiques, or jewelry that you may collect as a hobby, but only about those items which you consider to be investments or that the creators of the formula consider to be investments.

Stocks

In the case of stocks that are regularly traded on one of the major markets, it is relatively easy to get the current value by consulting *The Wall Street Journal,* a broker, or perhaps your local newspaper. Some people feel it is necessary to adjust the value by the cost of selling stocks including brokerage commission and capital gains taxes. These are individual judgments and not recommendations.

Many people who only own a few shares of stock are not really aware of what their investments are worth. If you own stock in a small, privately owned corporation, then determining the market value is more difficult. If the corporation is that small, there may not even be a market for the stock. In that case you can probably improve your aid chances by filing as a business or farm and showing your percentage of ownership. If you own stock in your employer's corporation ask your employer about the value of the stock. As a principal owner, your employer would be the one to buy the stock back, usually to maintain control of the company. If no one would buy the stock, then it may have a very small value. For example, a man came into the office one day and could not figure out why he was not getting more aid. He had listed as an asset some $50,000 in stock in a small corporation. When asked about this investment he informed me that he had been trying to sell this to the company owners but they would only pay him $20,000. It was hard to get him to understand that even though he thought his stock should be worth $50,000, the real market value was $20,000. This is what he should have listed on his Financial Aid Form. This one change would have increased the student's aid eligibility by almost $1,800.

If you have debts against stocks, be sure to include those. It will help to prepare a worksheet to figure out the net worth of the stocks you own (see the worksheet example in this section). The most common debt against stock is probably margin for those people that are actively trading in the marketplace. Margin is a loan against the value of the stock, usually made by the stockbroker to enable the stockholder to purchase more stock. If you are involved in this, I strongly urge that you check your records to find out how much you owe. Most people overestimate the value of their stock and underestimate what they owe on it, thus decreasing their chances for financial aid. Another common way to incur debt against stock is to pledge them as collateral for a loan. Be sure that you report any loans of this kind as debts against the stock.

Worksheet to Calculate Net Worth of Stocks

Company	Number of Shares	×	Price	=	Market Value
_____.............	_____		_____		_____
_____.............	_____		_____		_____
_____.............	_____		_____		_____
_____.............	_____		_____		_____
_____.............	_____		_____		_____
Total market value					_____

Less debts against stock:
1. Margin account _____
2. Collateralized loans _____
3. Other _____
Total debts against stock _____

Net worth of stock portfolio _____

Some shrewd people over the years have recognized that the financial aid system does not take into account consumer credit, or what you owe on credit cards to stores or other businesses. So they borrow against stock to pay off their consumer debts, thus reducing their assets and increasing the amount of aid they may qualify for. To look at this in more detail we will consider a case study.

Chapter 8: Parents' Contribution from Assets

The Brink family has had a large consumer credit debt in the last few years. These debts have been incurred and increased in part because of the ease of using credit cards, in part because of inflation, and in part because the Brinks want to put some of their money into investments. To simplify the case we will look only at their consumer credit and their assets in the form of stock.

Consumer credit for the Brink family:

Master Charge	$ 685.93
Visa	463.41
Department stores	391.13
Sears (appliances)	1,095.38
Finance company	2,453.09
Airline credit card	911.06
Total consumer credit	$6,000.00

Normally this debt is not taken into account in the financial aid formula unless there is some specific reason why the family has incurred these expenses (such as a major tragedy). Looking at the Brink's stock portfolio we notice the following:

Company	Number of Shares	Price of Stock	Market Value
XYZ Company	100	$76.50	$ 7,650
Fox Mutual Fund	50	52.80	2,640
Conglomerate, Inc.	375	9.00	3,375
Summer Ice Cream, Inc.	60	36.75	2,205
Total market value			$15,870

If the Brinks report their stock with no debt against it, they are not getting any credit for the amount of money they owe on the consumer debts. On the other hand, if the Brinks borrow $6,000 against the stock, whether at the bank or through their broker in a margin account, then their situation would be different. They would now report their stock as follows:

$$\text{Current market value} - \text{Debts} = \text{Net worth of assets}$$
$$\$15{,}870 \quad - \quad \$6{,}000 = \quad \$9{,}870$$

The Brinks should then use the $6,000 to pay off their consumer debts. This relatively simple procedure of reducing consumer debt by borrowing against collateral (the stock) would cause the Brinks' net worth in financial aid terms to reflect a truer picture of their situation. In this example under the formula in use during the 1981–82 year, this one change could have increased their aid eligibility by $300 a year.

Remember that those are 300 tax-free dollars. The additional benefit would be that the Brinks could make one payment on their loan to the bank or to the broker that was holding their stock instead of many payments to all of their creditors.

Once again we see that looking for ways to properly represent yourself on the form is one of the big keys to obtaining assistance. The implicit assumption in the current aid formula is that people will pay off their consumer debts before they accumulate assets. Therefore, all those credit-card, finance, and store debts are not considered.

Another family like the Brinks was the Wilcoxes. Mr. Wilcox was infuriated that he should be penalized by the financial aid system because he had managed to accumulate assets in the form of stock holdings. So he took his spare cash and a reasonable amount of margin on his stocks and bought paidup life insurance on himself against which he could quickly borrow if needed. Since the financial aid application forms have not asked for the value of life insurance policies (and are not likely to because of the complexity involved) Mr. Wilcox effectively removed those dollars from consideration. His original account with his broker was worth $50,000 in cash and stock. He borrowed $25,000 and invested that in paid-up life insurance. The net result was to reduce his portfolio value by $25,000 while maintaining the size of his estate.

Original situation:

$$\text{Current market value} - \text{Debts} = \text{Net worth}$$
$$\$50{,}000 - 0 = \$50{,}000$$

New situation:

$$\text{Current market value} - \text{Debts} = \text{Net worth}$$
$$\$50{,}000 - \$25{,}000 = \$25{,}000$$

This reduced Mr. Wilcox's family contribution by over $1,400. The disadvantage of doing this is that, like a gift to a charitable institution, the deduction of interest such as a margin account comes out after line 31 on the federal income tax form. So it has the effect of reducing your taxes but not your gross income, and therefore, your family contribution is increased. In Mr. Wilcox's case, he figured all this out carefully to his best advantage before making any decision. He approached his financial aid plan much as he does his tax planning.

Bonds

Bonds are the next major item to be considered among the assets after stocks. Many people who own bonds think in terms of their face value.

Chapter 8: Parents' Contribution from Assets

In other words, if the bond is due in 1985 and will pay $1,000 at that time, people will list its value as $1,000. This is not likely the case. Bonds, both tax-free and taxable, have constantly changing values. If you are familiar with the bond market, you can probably find the information you need in *The Wall Street Journal* or your local paper. If you are not sure, you may wish to ask a broker about the current value of your bonds. To give an example of how important this can be let's go back and look at the Brinks' situation as it relates to bonds.

When Mrs. Brink's father died he left her 10 Chrysler bonds with a face value of $1,000 each which were due in the 1990s. If the Brinks did not check on the current value of these bonds when filing the form, they might, as many people do, list the amount as $10,000. Assuming that there were no loans against the bonds, this would all pass through the formula and they could be requested to pay over $500 a year from this one resource for their child's education. If, on the other hand, the Brinks filed for aid at the same time that Chrysler Corporation was in trouble and interest rates were skyrocketing (thus making bonds less valuable), then we can see how important it is to check the value of whatever you report on the Financial Aid Form. Suppose that the Chrysler bonds were trading at 45 according to the paper. This means that people were willing to pay the Brinks $450 for each bond in the hope of receiving interest and the $1,000 when the bonds come due several years from now. Thus the 10 bonds really had a market value of $4,500. If the Brinks had reported this instead, they would have reduced their family contribution by over $300 a year for their student(s).

Both of these last two ideas seem to have only a small effect on the total family contribution (only a few hundred dollars). But if you add these things together, they can have a substantial impact on the financial aid available to the Brinks' children. Frequently these are the kinds of errors that can make a substantial difference to you in getting the assistance you need or want.

Land Contracts

Land contracts are another common area for error in reporting on Financial Aid Forms. Numerous families that have sold properties on land contracts have made the substantial error of improper listing on the Financial Aid Form, thus preventing their students from getting aid.

It is a good idea to review what a land contract is. Briefly it works as follows: Assume the Davis family is selling their home and the buyer would like the Davis family to help with the financing in the amount of $20,000. The financing of the sale might look something like this:

Sales price	$90,000
Sources of money:	
First mortgage held by the bank	$50,000
Buyer's cash	20,000
Land contract or second mortgage held by the Davis family	20,000
Total financing package	$90,000

Obviously the Davis family would expect to be paid interest on the $20,000. The Davis family and the buyer would agree on an interest rate, and the buyer would make regular monthly payments to the Davis family. The face value of the land contract is $20,000 for the Davis family, but that is not necessarily the real value.

If the Davis family sold their house several years ago they might well have agreed to an interest rate of 7 percent on the regular payments and a period of 10 years for repayment. How would they list the value of the land contract if they sold the house five years ago? There are three ways that people in the Davis's position have listed land contracts on forms, and in my opinion, only one of them fairly represents the Davis's situation.

   1. List the property's market value under other real estate as if it were owned and had never been sold. This makes some sense because theoretically the Davis family still has a claim against the property in the form of their second mortgage or land contract. Realistically, though most second mortgages and land contracts are paid off, this would unnecessarily inflate your assets and reduce the amount of aid that your student(s) is eligible for under the financial aid formula.

   2. A second way that families have handled this kind of situation is to list the face value of the land contract. Thus, in the case of the Davis family, even though they had been receiving payments for four years, they would be listing the value of the land contract or second mortgage as $20,000 under other real estate and investments. This is also unrealistic and unnecessarily inflates the value of your assets, thus reducing the aid possibilities. Another form of this same mistake occurs when people total all the payments, including interest, that they have left to receive and enter that figure. In the Davis's case this might be around $17,000, and it would again inflate their assets and decrease their aid eligibility.

   3. The best way to list the value of the land contract or second mortgage is to determine its actual current market value. If you had to sell it, what would you get paid for it? Believe it or not, there are actual markets for land contracts and second mortgages in many areas. The Davis family might approach a banker or a real estate broker to get some help directly. A person who deals in these kinds of investments could help determine the actual value of their note. Recently, when they tried

Chapter 8: Parents' Contribution from Assets

to sell their $20,000 land contract at 7 percent on which they had already received four years of payments, the Davises learned that they would have done well to get $11,000 for the contract. This in part reflected the high interest rates currently being charged. Mortgage rates were double the 7 percent that the Davises were receiving. Once a value had been established by determining what the land contract might actually sell for, then the Davises were in a position to list that under investments.

It is important to note that just the difference between listing the value of the land contract at $20,000 and the real value of $11,000 would lower the Davis's family contribution by almost $500 a year. Remember this $500 a year over the four years of an academic program would add up to $2,000 increased aid eligibility.

In an actual case, a student was not qualifying for any federal Basic Educational Opportunity Grant (BEOG) money because his parents had listed the land contract improperly. When the error was corrected and the true value of the land contract entered on the form, the student qualified for several hundred dollars in BEOG assistance. The family not only qualified for more BEOG but also received increases in other forms of aid. Even though I work with financial aid all the time, it still surprises me what dramatic shifts in aid a few small changes can make if parents correctly fill out the form to properly represent themselves.

Trust Funds

After land contracts the next investment reported is trust funds. People who have trusts need to be sure that they are properly entered on the form. Several years ago it was rare that the family of a financial aid applicant had a trust of any kind. But as more and more people are qualifying, this occurs with greater frequency. Once again, the secret is to list the real value of the fund or the family's share of the fund. To date, financial aid has considered a trust to be available resources for the family and for the student. To list the value of the trust or your portion of the trust, you have to determine the worth of that asset in the same way that we have all other assets. Total the current market value and subtract any debts, and you have the approximate value of the trust. Remember ownership interest may be different from distribution. For example, a client receives occasional payments from his sister's trust. He has no rights to the trust assets. Therefore, he would have to put a zero for trust funds.

Other Securities

Other securities that we have not covered would be listed under real estate and investments in much the same way. The important thing for the filer to remember is to establish the true market value of the security before listing it. A few errors in this area can greatly change the amount of aid.

Real Estate

The listing of other real estate in this section is also a place of frequent error. If you have a lake cottage or condominium, or land that has no business association, then it should be listed here along with any debts against it. On the other hand, if you are in the business of rental properties and file the proper business tax returns, then you should list your other real estate as a business. The same is true if you own land that is a farm. Be sure to list it as such. There are great advantages to listing these properties under business and farm and not under real estate when you are applying for financial aid.

The case of one family comes clearly to mind. The Johnsons were in the rental-property business. When they originally applied for aid they reported their three houses as other real estate.

Johnson's Real Estate Rental Properties

House	Market Value	Debt
1	$ 45,000	$ 30,651
2	60,000	49,789
3	45,000	24,560
Total value	$150,000	
Total debt		$105,000

Net worth = Total value − Total debt
$45,000 = $150,000 − $105,000

Listed incorrectly as real estate, these houses cost about $2,500 a year in additional family contribution and excluded the Johnsons from some state and federal aid. When it was discovered that the houses were really a business and the listing was changed, the related contribution was reduced to about $1,000. This increased the family's aid eligibility by a little over $1,500 a year. All of the above properties were rental properties as they had properly listed their home elsewhere. Relisting the properties as a business, after the error was discovered, made it possible for them to pay their college bill at the college of their student's choice with assistance from the government.

Another case is the Victors. They owned a cottage on a lake which they had used for summer fun for many years. As the price of raising two children and inflation caught up with them, they had turned the cottage into an all-year rental property. They were working on turning the

Chapter 8: Parents' Contribution from Assets

garage into a second rental unit at the time that we talked. Once again, it was clear from their tax return and from their efforts that this former cottage was a business and not their vacation home. When the property was shifted from other real estate and investments to business and farm, the victors became eligible for substantially more aid.

Review your investments and other real estate carefully when completing the financial aid forms to be sure that you have them in the correct place and that you are really representing yourself in a fair manner.

BUSINESSES

Businesses are the next area to be considered. This is one place where you can gain additional help if properly handled. It is to your advantage to list as many of your assets in this category as possible. The reason for this is that less of these assets are considered in calculating the aid eligibility.

For example, suppose we have two men each of whom have assets in addition to their homes of $50,000: Mr. Jones has $50,000 in stocks, bonds, and other investments; and Mr. Cory has $50,000 in a business. If everything else is the same, Mr. Cory's family contribution could be $1,600 less per year than Mr. Jones's.

While it will be explained how this works in greater detail later, suffice it to say for the moment that it is to your benefit to list as many of your assets as you honestly can under the business and farm questions. People who have stock in closely held corporations may want to list the value as a business as opposed to an investment in stock. You may well be asked to submit supplementary information about the business and farm to the financial aid office, so be prepared to respond to that request.

The major reason why Mr. Cory could have less family contribution for the same assets is the recognition that businesses require cash and capital to operate. To provide for this, there is a separate formula that is used on businesses and farms. If you have anything that you could remotely call a business or farm, it may well be to your advantage to read the sections in Chapter 13 on business and farms and consider listing that item as such on the form that you file. This is particularly true if you have stock in a small company. If we assume that you have $45,000 of stock in a small company, there are two ways you could list it. One way would be as an investment. The other method would be to report it as a business of which you own some percentage. The difference would be about $1,400 a year in family contribution for you. Your student could potentially be eligible for 1,400 more dollars in federal and state assistance if you listed the asset as a business instead of as stock.

A couple of suggestions that are important in this area:

1. Be sure that you include all the debts of the business as well as all the assets. Once again, do not inflate assets, but rather provide as realistic a picture as you can for the aid process.

2. List only your share of the business. If you get carried away and list the total business or farm when you only own a share, you will cause your assets to increase and your student's aid eligibility to decrease.

FARMS

Farms are another important area. If you have a farm, be sure that you do not list it under other real estate but rather under business and farm. (This assumes that it is a working farm.) Be careful if you live on the farm that you separate the home value out of the farm value and treat it separately. For example, if your home with a couple of acres around it has a value of $40,000, and your farm has a value of $200,000 including the house, then you should list your values as follows:

Home............................	$ 40,000
Farm............................	160,000
Total value	$200,000

Many people make the mistake of listing it as follows:

Home............................	$ 40,000
Farm............................	200,000
Total value	$240,000

By counting the home twice, once as a part of the farm and once separately, they have increased their assets by $40,000 and probably increased their expected family contribution by over $1,100 a year. If you own a farm be sure when you complete the forms that you are very careful about how you list your home and farm.

CASH

Cash is the next area to be considered in the assistance picture. Once again, it is important to be realistic. If you are filing the form in January, try to use a figure that honestly represents your situation. If you have just received a big Christmas bonus that you have not yet used to pay for Christmas shopping (and therefore you have considerably more cash than normal), it will increase your assets and thus reduce your aid. Recently every extra $1,000 you report in cash causes you to contribute between $50 and $60 more per year. Other cash items could include cash on deposit, certificates of deposit, money market funds, and so forth.

Look at our earlier example in which Mr. Cory has a business worth $50,000. If we assume that he also has $10,000 in cash that is really for the operation of the business, then we can see the difference in the effect of reporting this. There are two options: (1) Mr. Cory can report the $10,000 under cash; or (2) Mr. Cory can report the $10,000 under the business thus increasing the value of the business to $60,000. If Mr. Cory elects the second choice, he will have additional asset protection in his business and will save himself about $275 a year in family contribution under the 1981–82 formula.

Many people are not aware of the advantage in listing assets under the business and farm category. As more families understand this effect, many are taking a second look to be sure that they are assessing their situation accurately.

Maybe you will be using your cash to make a large purchase. If you are purchasing something that will show up in the form somewhere else as an asset, particularly under other real estate and investments, then it does not make a big difference. However, if the cash is about to be used for a purchase that will not show up as an asset on the form (cars, furniture, paintings, jewelry, and so forth), then you may wish to wait and complete the form after you have made the purchase. See Figure 8–1 for other "free" assets. In the same example, if Mr. Cory had the $10,000 cash on hand to buy a new station wagon, he would save himself over $500 a year in family contribution under the 1981–82 formula if he went ahead and purchased the new car before completing the form, thus reducing his cash assets. However, it would be unwise to purposefully try to spend cash just to increase aid eligibility. Yet, if you are in the process of making a purchase, it can work to your advantage to go ahead and do so. Be sure you have paid your full estimated income taxes before completing your form.

Another idea is the one that was suggested earlier for assets. If you have a large amount of consumer debts, you may wish to use some of the cash to reduce these debts. Thus you save on the high interest cost and you do not have that asset considered in the formula. Again, you should do this sparingly and with good family financial planning. If done properly, this will help you in many ways, including financial aid.

NET WORTH

In order to determine how much your family will be asked to contribute from assets toward the cost of your student(s) education, the

Calculation of Net Worth

Home equity	Less mortgage plus other debts			= Net home worth
				+
Other real estate and investments	Less debts			= Net worth other real estate and investments
				+
Business or farm	Less debts	Net worth of business or farm	Special treatment	= Value of business or farm to be considered
				+
Cash				Cash
				Total assets to be considered, as net worth

net worth of all the assets is calculated based on the information that you provide on the forms. (See Calculation of Net Worth.) Thus, the home value has the mortgages and debts subtracted from it to come up with a net worth. The same is done for other real estate and investments. The net worth of your business or farm is also calculated, but then it is run through an additional step of "special treatment" to determine how much of that value should be passed on into the main formula. Cash, of course, is considered in its full amount unless you have listed it as an asset of a business or farm. When all these figures have been derived it is possible to determine the net worth of the family for purposes of the financial aid formula under uniform methodology.

It is important to note that there are a number of items of some value in people's homes that are not considered in determining net worth. Individual schools may elect to consider these, but as a rule, many of them are never even asked about. These include things like art, collectibles, jewelry, and oriental rugs. Of course, if you buy them primarily for investment, it is your obligation to report them as such and treat them as investments. However, if you buy them as furnishings for your home or as part of your life-style, very few colleges will ask about them.

Chapter 8: Parents' Contribution from Assets

FIGURE 8–1
Assets Not Usually Considered by Formula (unless you list them as investments)

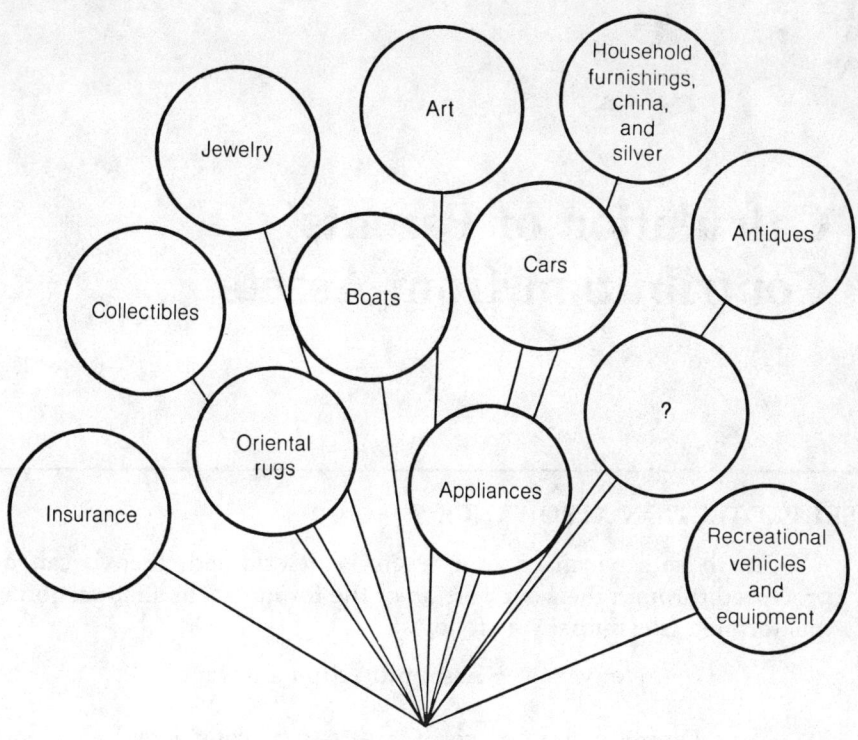

Fun-filled free balloons

Chapter 9

Calculation of Parents' Contribution from Assets

ASSET PROTECTION ALLOWANCE

Once the net worth of your assets is determined, then it can be processed through the asset portion of the formula. The first portion of this formula is essentially as follows:

$$\text{Net worth} - \text{Asset protection allowance} = \text{Discretionary net worth (assets to be considered)}$$

This immediately raises the question of what is the asset protection allowance. This is an allowance that varies with age and is an attempt to make provisions for retirement and emergencies (see Table 9–1). Theoretically the amount should be sufficient to purchase an annuity at age 65 that when added to social security benefits would provide a moderate standard of living. This amount is far greater for older people that are closer to retirement than it is for younger parents. Recently the amount ranged from $25,000 for a 42-year-old two-parent family to $56,800 for 65-year-old two-parent family.

How does this asset protection allowance affect a family contribution? Suppose that we have two families in otherwise similar circumstances except for the age of the parents.

	Age	Assets	Asset Protection Allowance
Mr. and Mrs. Williams	40	$50,000	$25,000
Mr. and Mrs. Olson	65	50,000	56,800

TABLE 9-1
Asset Protection Allowance

Age of Older Parent	Two-Parent Family	Age of Older Parent	Two Parent Family
40	$25,000	53	36,500
41	25,700	54	37,700
42	26,400	55	39,300
43	27,100	56	40,600
44	27,900	57	41,900
45	28,600	58	43,600
46	29,400	59	45,000
47	30,200	60	46,800
48	31,300	61	48,600
49	32,100	62	50,500
50	33,200	63	52,400
51	34,400	64	54,400
52	35,500	65 or over	56,800

Source: Reprinted with permission from *CSS Need Analysis: Theory and Computation Procedures for the 1981–1982 FAF.* Copyright © 1980 by College Entrance Examination Board, New York.

Parents' contribution from assets for Mr. and Mrs. Williams could be as high as $1,410 but for Mr. and Mrs. Olson it would be zero. It is easy to see that the older you are, the less that you are expected to give from the same pool of assets. This is why at many of the workshops, when the forms ask for the age of the older parent, we always stress that this is not a time to pretend to be young. If you are 50 when you fill out the financial aid application, you might as well face the fact and not put down 49. It can only help you to get more aid. It turns out to be worth about $60 a year in family contribution under the formula. Thus, if you by accident listed the younger parent and that person is three years younger than the older parent, you probably cheated yourself out of about $180 of aid eligibility.

Single parents also have an asset protection allowance. However, its spread for the same period was from $18,400 to $36,400. Similar to married couples, if you understate your age when you file, it will cost you each year in student eligibility.

The asset protection allowance has a large impact, and it has been recently and substantially adjusted. Now many older parents who did not expect to get help with their children's education find they can qualify for such assistance. It would not be that difficult for a couple in their late 50s or 60s to have a net worth of over $100,000 and substantial income and still have a child eligible for aid at a number of the more expensive schools. Because of the special treatment that a business or farm receives, if two thirds of the assets were in a business or farm, they could have assets totaling $160,000 plus a good income and still be eligible for some assistance. Many families in this situation think they are not eligible for aid, and so they do not bother to apply. This is a mistake.

With the net worth determined and the asset protection allowance subtracted out, it is now possible to figure what portion of your assets will actually be considered available to help with college costs. After the asset protection allowance has been subtracted from net worth, a maximum of 12 percent of the remaining assets are considered available to help with college costs as an income supplement.

(Net worth − Asset protection allowance) × 12%
= Income supplement

Returning to the cases we were looking at earlier.
Mr. and Mrs. Williams:

(Net worth − Asset protection allowance) × 12%
= Income supplement
($50,000 − $25,000) × 12%
$25,000 × 12% = $3,000

This figure then is assumed to be available at the maximum rate of 47 percent and would yield a family contribution from assets of $1,410 for the year for all students in the family.

Follow the same procedure for the other family, the Olsons, who were considerably older and, therefore, had a considerably larger asset protection allowance. This would yield the following results:

Mr. and Mrs. Olson:

(Net worth − Asset protection allowance) × 12%
= Income supplement
$50,000 − $56,800 × 12%
$0 × 12% = $0

In all cases we have mentioned that the maximum rate is 47 percent. This can be significantly less, down to a rate of 22 percent, depending on the size of income and the amount of assets after multiplying the assets by the 12 percent factor.

To get the total parents' contribution, the parents' contribution from assets and from income are added together. This sum, added to the student's contribution, makes the total family contribution. The formula for aid eligibility again is as follows:

Total cost − Family contribution = Maximum aid eligibility

Chapter 9: Calculation of Parents' Contribution from Assets

Remember, the family contribution is composed as follows:

Parents' contribution = Parents' contribution from income
+ Parents' contribution from assets

Family contribution = Parents' contribution + Student's contribution

Fortunately for you, you do not have to do these calculations. However, if you can understand what is happening, you are in a much better position to complete the form correctly. The more accurate you are on the form and the more you know about how the information is used, then the more tax-free dollars you are likely to help your student obtain.

Chapter 10

Student's Contribution from Income

STUDENT INCOME

The first portion of the student contribution that will be considered is the expectation of summer savings. This is the amount that the student is expected to save in the summer before school starts. Many schools have their own expectations of what students should save during this period, and you should verify what the expectation is at any school that you are considering. The generally accepted expectations have been as follows:

Summer before freshman year	$700
Summer before sophomore year	900
Summer before junior year	900
Summer before senior year	900

A better way to describe this expectation is that the student would save the amount listed and be able to bring that resource with him or her to school in the fall. There are many who argue that these amounts should be increased because of inflation and increases in the minimum wage. I have my reservations. It is particularly difficult for some students to earn that amount of money for freshman year. If you remember the object is to save and bring your $700 to the opening of school (or at least have it available), those numbers do not seem so small.

Chapter 10: Student's Contribution from Income

FIGURE 10-1
Dependent Student for Fall of 1982

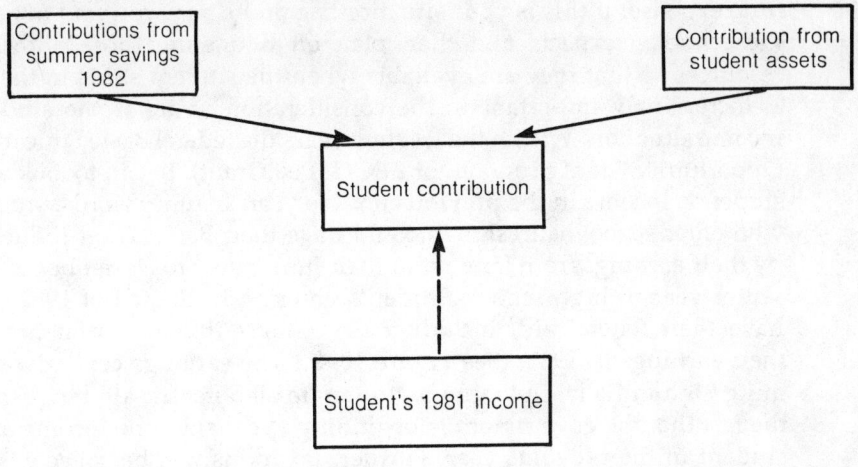

Many students are disappointed about how hard it is to save that money, especially if they want to work away from home where living costs cut into their savings. Another real difficulty today is that students either need or think they need a car, and this consumes a great deal of their income. And, of course, there are expenses for social activities, travel, and all the other things that young people find to spend money on. Students who are serious about contributing to their education need to budget carefully so that in the fall they will have saved enough to make their share of the payments.

If for some reason the student cannot or will not be able to work during the summer, be sure to talk this over with the financial aid office in advance. Some schools can and will make adjustments; others simply cannot change the expectation. In my experience the main reason for changing an expectation was certifiable. For example, the student may have to take care of the children in the family or nurse an ill parent.

If the family decides to travel or take a vacation together that prevents the student from working, then the parents should be prepared to put up the additional money to cover the student's expected earnings. Many parents feel these summer vacations are important for their student. They would rather come up with the expected savings themselves and provide their child with additional opportunities. This is perfectly legitimate as long as you have the resources and do not expect the state government, federal government, and/or the institution to help pay for the difference. People who own their own small business or farm often have trouble with these summer expected earnings. They may count on having the services of family members for free or at least for little expense. If this is your situation, again be sure you find out what the school(s) expects and then plan on budgeting those additional resources so that they are available when the student starts in the fall.

Increasingly important in the consideration of aid is the student's income situation. Within the last few years the federal Basic Educational Opportunity Grant program, or BEOG (Pell Grant), began to look at the student's income in the previous taxable year. In other words, students who enter school as freshmen could have their Basic Grant influenced by their earnings from January of their junior year to December of their senior year in high school. Students entering in the fall of 1982 could have their federal aid, including Pell Grants (BEOG), influenced by their earnings in 1981. (See Figure 10–1.) The earnings ceiling was set quite high initially. But more important to all potential aid recipients is the fact that the government is beginning to consider the income of the student in the previous year. Further, tax forms will be collected on a number of students to verify their previous year's income and taxes. This implies several things:

1. Students should be keeping good records of their financial affairs including a record of their tax papers. This is often a big weakness among students and will cause them difficulty if they are asked to provide that information.

2. It is wise to investigate if the previous year's income is going to impact aid and how much. This is a changing area and one that is hard to predict, but it is one that you should be aware of for now and for the future.

3. If students are employed in occupations that pay well but which have tremendous expenses associated with them (such as working in the Alaskan oil fields), then a record should be kept of the expenses required. This would help to justify not considering part of that income available for college expenses.

Nontaxable income has been considered in the uniform methodology for a long time. Students that are or will be receiving social security and/or veterans' benefits should plan to use the benefits for college costs. In most cases 100 percent of what they receive will be expected to be available to meet college costs. In low-income situations the formula allows a portion of the student's social security benefits to go to the maintenance of the family and the home. Frequently students that are eligible for these benefits will be surprised at how low their aid packages are. Aid eligibility is really affected by social security.

If we turn to the case of Carlos and assume that he has $2,500 a year available to him from the Social Security Administration, then his picture might change drastically.

	Without Social Security		With Social Security	
Charges for the year....................		$6,300		$6,300
Books, supplies, travel, etc.		700		700
Total cost........................		$7,000		$7,000
Less:				
Parents' contribution..................	$2,800		$2,800	
Student's contribution from assets......	1,000		1,000	
Student's summer savings	700		700	
Social security	0		2,500	
		− 4,500		− 7,000
Maximum aid eligibility.................		$2,500		0

You can see clearly that Carlos' parents were not expected to contribute more nor was Carlos, from summer earnings or from assets. The social security made all the difference. Students who receive social security often think that they will not have to use this for college and can, therefore, take on a car payment or something of that kind. Review your situation carefully if you are eligible for social security payments. If you are eligible, it may mean that you can afford to consider all kinds of schools since the payments will undoubtedly cover a large portion of the bills. This was made particularly clear recently when a student received both veterans' benefits and social security benefits that more than covered the cost of her education at an expensive private school. The mother pointed out that if the husband were still living they could never have afforded a private school without financial aid.

If you are not sure about social security benefits but believe that they may be available to your student, check with your social security office. Social security has been one of the best forms of aid available. This should be investigated during the student's junior year in high school or early in the senior year so that you have this information when you are making college choices and considering financial aid offers. There will be more on the effects of social security in Chapter 22.

Before we leave the subject of the student's income, it is important to remind you that this is an area that is currently changing. The two major formulas—the uniform methodology used by most schools and states and the Basic Grant Educational Opportunity (Pell Grant) formula—treat this factor differently.

Chapter 11

Student's Contribution from Assets

Probably one of the biggest surprises to many families when they become involved with financial aid is the treatment of the student's assets. Student's assets are treated in much the same way that parents' assets are treated to determine a net worth. The difference is that once the total net worth has been determined, it is assumed that 35 percent of the total assets will be available for the next year in college. The students reporting varying amounts of assets will be expected to make the following contributions.

Student's Assets	Expected Contribution for College Costs the Next Year
$ 500 × 35%.....................	$ 175
1,000 × 35%.....................	350
1,500 × 35%.....................	525
2,000 × 35%.....................	700
2,500 × 35%.....................	875
5,000 × 35%.....................	1,750
10,000 × 35%.....................	3,500
20,000 × 35%.....................	7,000

If a student has a large amount of savings, it can have a dramatic impact on the student's contribution (and thus the family contribution) and substantially reduce the maximum aid eligibility.

It is worthwhile to see what happens to a $1,000 savings account if withdrawals are made at a rate of 35 percent per year for four years.

Chapter 11: Student's Contribution from Assets

(This assumes that no deposits are made and excludes the impact of interest.)

Student's Contribution from Savings Account

	Savings	Student's Contribution
Freshman	$1,000.00 × 35% =	$350.00
Sophomore	650.00* × 35% =	227.50
Junior	422.50* × 35% =	147.88
Senior	274.62* × 35% =	96.12
Balance remaining	178.50*	

* Excluding interest.

Given the substantial impact of student assets on the financial aid eligibility, what are some of the strategies that can be used to maximize aid?

1. *Do not* give money to your children. Many parents think that this is a good way to prepare their children for money management later in life and to provide for their education. If you have $1,000 in the parents' name, you will not be asked to contribute more than $56 from that asset in the freshman year. If you give that money to your child, then the student would be expected to pay out $350 the first year. Over the four years, if the $1,000 was in the parents' name, the parents would not have to contribute more than $224 from that asset. If the money was in the child's name, the student would be expected to contribute $822. Assuming that you were qualifying for aid, this $1,000 would reduce your student's eligibility for aid by $598 over the four years using the current formula. (See Table—$1,000 over Four Years.)

$1,000 over Four Years

	Parent Contribution	Student Contribution	Difference
Freshman	$ 56	$350	$294
Sophomore	56	228	172
Junior	56	148	92
Senior	56	96	40
Total	$224	$822	$598

2. If you have money in *joint accounts* with your children, parents should pay the taxes on the interest to establish that the asset is theirs. Suppose you have been advised by an accountant, attorney, or banker that you can avoid some income taxes by creating a joint account with your children and letting them pay the income taxes on the interest.

Since the children are reporting the income, it would be assumed that it was their asset. Therefore, it would be considered available at the rate of 35 percent a year for their educational cost. For a few dollars in tax savings you may substantially reduce your aid eligibility, and if the account is large enough, you might totally eliminate yourself from any kind of need-based aid. You may even wish to consider the impact of holding that money in your business or farm accounts.

$5,000 Reported Three Different Ways (effect on family contribution)

	A Business or Farm	B Parents	C Student
Freshman	$141	$ 282	$1,750
Sophomore	141	282	1,138
Junior	141	282	739
Senior	141	282	481
Total	$564	$1,128	$4,108

The table shows the impact of reporting the same dollars in three different ways. Column A assumes that the $5,000 is reported as a business or farm asset in a business whose net worth is less than $135,000. Column B assumes that parents report the $5,000 as their savings and that they are in the maximum contribution bracket for financial aid. Column C assumes that the money is reported as a student's asset. The difference in aid eligibility could be substantial. If you were likely to qualify for aid anyway, putting the money in the business account instead of the student's account could increase the student's aid eligibility by $1,600 the first year; that is, the $1,750 the student would have to contribute out of the $5,000 less the $141 the parents would have to contribute if they listed it as a business asset. If you attempt to discuss this with your lawyer, banker, or accountant, please remember that the aid dollars you can qualify for are tax-free dollars. That can make a big difference in your calculations.

3. If your children already have substantial savings from gifts or from their own industriousness and the money is really theirs to use, it isn't wrong that those dollars should be spent for college. However, if you are still interested in maximizing the aid situation, you may choose to do the following:

a. Use the student's savings to pay for the freshman year in college.
b. Save the parents' contribution in the parents' name. This means that the application for the next year would not reflect any student's assets, thus providing increased aid eligibility.

Chapter 11: Student's Contribution from Assets

For example, let's look at the case of Cathy Smith. Over the years Cathy's parents gave her money which she saved along with her own earnings. This money was intended for college expenses, and Cathy is willing to use it. But she and her parents feel that they should be entitled to some help in the form of financial assistance. Further, the Smiths feel that Cathy's small aid offer is due in large part to their own frugality in the past. Likewise, Cathy feels that she has been frugal with her earnings, unlike many of her friends who have spent every penny that they earned. The Smith's financial aid award originally looked something like this.

School charges	$6,700	
Personal expenses, books, travel	800	
Total cost		$7,500
Less family contribution:		
Parents' contribution	$3,800	
Cathy's summer savings (freshman)	700	
Cathy's contribution from assets ($5,000 in savings)	1,750	
Total family contribution		6,250

Cathy's total aid eligibility for her freshman year was $7,500 less $6,250 or $1,250.

$$\text{Total cost} - \text{Family contribution} = \text{Aid eligibility}$$
$$\$7,500 - \$6,250 = \$1,250$$

But if the parents had put the $5,000 in their names, they would have qualified for an additional $1,500 aid for Cathy. Their situation would have looked like this.

Total cost		$7,500
Less family contribution:		
Original parents' contribution	$3,800	
Increase due to $5,000 more savings	282	
Cathy's summer savings	700	
Cathy's contribution from assets (remember this was transferred to parents)	0	
Total family contribution		4,782
Total aid eligibility		$2,718

Cathy's aid eligibility increased by almost $1,500.

But suppose that Cathy and her parents did not feel that moving the $5,000 was an honest representation of the situation. They could still use the suggestions in *a* and *b*. In other words, their payment for the first year would come as follows:

Cathy's contribution from assets	$5,000
Cathy's summer savings	700
Parents' contribution	550
Total family contribution	$6,250

This would allow Cathy to honestly report no savings when she applied for future aid as a sophomore. The parents could have saved the money that they would have normally spent on the freshman year and used that to help Cathy in her sophomore, junior, and senior years. Assuming everything remained the same, Cathy would have $900 more aid eligibility for her sophomore year than she would have if they had not used the whole $5,000 in her freshman year. Over the course of the three remaining years if everything remained the same, Cathy would receive an additional $1,800 by using her savings in the first year. And Cathy's parents would have more savings since they would not have to spend so much the first year.

One suggestion that has been made in an attempt to derive the best of both worlds is to write a note to your child lending him or her money at no interest. The child would then earn the interest on the money and pay taxes on it in a lower bracket. However, for financial aid purposes the money would belong to the parents. Before considering such a scheme, check with a tax adviser or attorney about the legality of such a situation in your case. If it would work for you, you could save tax dollars while maximizing financial aid dollars.

It is very apparent that the student's contribution from assets is one of the major areas of impact on the family contribution. With careful planning and some thought about the true benefit of various tax tips, you can save yourself a great deal of trouble and help your student have more aid eligibility. Most people who have attended the seminars have been surprised to find out how fast students' resources are used in the formula. The 35 percent rate seems high to many. Now that you know what it is and that it is better to have money in the parents' account, you can plan accordingly. Remember, if there is no chance of qualifying for aid at all, follow the advice of tax advisers. But keep in mind that there are more and more people qualifying. If you are on the edge of having some aid eligibility, every little bit that you can do to decrease your family contribution will increase the amount of aid for which your student is eligible.

If you believe after reading this chapter that the aid system penalizes those industrious students who work, you may be right. I do not believe that those who designed the formula intended it that way, but the effect is there. Students who do not work and save are likely to get more aid than those who do. Hopefully, when schools package aid awards, they take into account the industriousness of students like Cathy Smith and give them a better aid package. On the other hand, increased federal control of aid may mean even less flexibility in the area of student contribution.

Section IV
GENERAL STRATEGIES

Chapter 12
How Many Will Be in School?
Chapter 13
Using Your Income Taxes in the Aid Application

Chapter 12

How Many Will Be in School?

All people concerned with college cost should be aware that the potential to receive aid increases dramatically with the number of children in college. Maybe your family cannot qualify for aid when the first child starts school. But don't forget to apply later in the educational cycle when you may have two or three children in school. It is always better to have some assistance part of the time rather than no assistance at all. (By the way, for children to be considered "in school," they generally must have at least half-time status at an accredited college or university.)

Parents' Contribution

First, it is important to understand how the theory works. When the parents' contribution was determined in earlier examples, we assumed that they would have only one student in college. When parents have more than one student in college, some slight adjustments are made in the actual formula. Then the resulting parents' contribution is divided between their students.

For a family of four with two children in college, we must first determine the parents' contribution and then divide it by two—the number of children they have in college.

Parents' contribution + Student's contribution = Family contribution

$$\frac{\text{Parents' contribution}}{\text{Number in college}} + \text{Student's contribution} = \text{Family contribution}$$

Remember that when there is more than one in college the parents' contribution is modified slightly before it is divided by two (or the number in college if more than two). This modification is essentially a reduction in the amount of the standard maintenance allowance. The assumption is that the fewer people living in the home for nine months a year, the less it costs to run the home in terms of food and other variable expenses.

Case Example

Looking at a family of four, what happens if one child is attending college?

Total taxable and nontaxable income*		$44,200
Less allowance:		
U.S. income tax (four exemptions)	$10,312	
FICA (social security)	2,140	
State and other taxes (assume 9 percent)	3,978	
Medical and dental expenses	0	
Employment allowance	2,400	
Standard maintenance allowance (one in college)	10,850	
Total of all allowances for a family of four		29,680
Parents' available income		$14,520

* Family of four with two parents working, one student in college, second parent earns $9,000.

Using a recent formula and assuming that the parents do not have sufficient assets to be considered in the calculation, these parents would be expected to contribute $4,300 toward the cost of their one child in college.

The same family with two attending college would look as follows:

Total taxable and nontaxable income		$44,200
Less allowances:		
U.S. income tax (four exemptions)	$10,312	
FICA (social security)	2,140	
State and other taxes (assume 9 percent)	3,978	
Medical and dental expenses	0	
Employment allowance	2,400	
Standard maintenance allowance (two in college)	9,640	
Total of all allowances for a family of four, two in college		28,470
Parents' available income		$15,730

Assuming that they did not have sufficient assets to be considered in the calculation, the total parents' contribution for both children would be

Chapter 12: How Many Will Be in School?

expected to be $4,900. To obtain the contribution per student, the adjusted parents' contribution is divided by the number of students that will be attending college.

$$\frac{\text{Parents' contribution}}{\text{Number in college}} = \text{Parents' contribution per student}$$

$$\frac{\$4,900}{2} = \$2,450$$

The parents would be expected to contribute $2,450 per student.

Impact on Aid

The impact on the aid eligibility is tremendous when the two situations are compared with school cost to compute aid eligibility.

	School			
	A	B	C	D
School cost	$9,000	$7,000	$5,000	$3,000
Parents' contribution (from income with one student in college)	4,300	4,300	4,300	4,300
Aid eligibility considering only parents' contribution from income	4,700	2,700	700	0

Now it is possible to see what happens when the second student enrolls in school.

	School			
	A	B	C	D
School cost	$9,000	$7,000	$5,000	$3,000
Parents' contribution (from income with two students in college)	2,450	2,450	2,450	2,450
Aid eligibility considering only parents' contribution from income	6,550	4,550	2,550	550
Increase in aid eligibility per student when the only factor changed is the number of students in college	1,850	1,850	1,850	550

The more students that you have in college, the more aid eligibility each student is likely to have at a given institution. The impact can be quite dramatic. For example, if the same family were considered with three students in college, the parents' contribution would be reduced by the uniform methodology from $2,450 to $1,850 per student. This means that based on the parents' contribution from income alone, the student would have aid eligibility at all schools, A through D, in increasing amounts.

Apply for Aid for All Students

Unfortunately, many families are unaware of this phenomena. Therefore, they either do not apply for aid, or if they do, they apply only for the new student entering college. Thus they deprive the family of the potential for additional tax-free assistance for their older student. Many times when a family applies for financial aid for an expensive school, we have discovered that their children in less expensive institutions may also be eligible for large amounts of assistance. If you believe that you should apply for aid at one school because it is too much for your budget or because you think that you might qualify, then send aid forms to all the schools that your children may be attending. The payoff may be more than you expect.

Apply Every Year

This remains true even if you have tried this in the past. Remember, each year changes in the formula as well as changes in the number of students in college can make substantial differences in the amount of aid eligibility. As the formula continues to adjust for inflation, it is extremely important that you apply each year, especially if you have more students in college.

Strategies

The financial aid effect of the number of students in college is obviously important. Therefore, it is often not good planning to let a potential college student out of the nest. Many families are rushing their young people into independent status when they would actually receive more aid as a family if the student continued to be considered part of the family. (An independent student is one who files for assistance on his or her own income and resources only.) For example, if a family with three children in college at schools A, B, and C encouraged one to go independent, the parents would not have improved their financial situation much.

Total parents' contribution for three in college from examples previously listed:

$$3 \times \$1,850 = \$5,550$$

Chapter 12: How Many Will Be in School?

Reporting only two in college, the family contribution would be as follows:

$$2 \times \$2{,}450 = \$4{,}900$$

The third student in college only costs the parents $650, assuming schools are fully awarding:

$$\$5{,}550 - \$4{,}900 = \$650$$

And, encouraging one student to go independent may end up reducing the aid eligibility for the other two students in the family. This subject will be discussed more in the chapter on independent students (Chapter 21).

Planning

The number of students in college is important, and you can often do something to influence it. A common misconception is that if one of the parents would like to pursue further education, it should be done before or after the children are educated. However, since any full-time student in the family may count, it could work to your advantage to attend college at the same time as your children. Some parents find that the cheapest time for them to attend school is when the children are in college because they themselves become eligible for financial aid. In one family both parents are going to school. By planning and working together, they make it possible for their children to attend college on almost complete assistance. They have maximized their aid eligibility. They are receiving a substantial amount of tax-free income in the form of financial assistance to their children who otherwise would not be eligible. In addition, they are getting aid themselves. Parents are often surprised that they can qualify for assistance along with their children, although this is not common.

To make this situation a little clearer, consider the case of the Babcock family. He is a professional man (lawyer, doctor, accountant). She does not work for compensation but is involved in community service activities while her children are in school. When they are finally out of the nest she plans to return to the university and earn her master's degree. There are three Babcock children—ages 20, 18, and 16. At the time that the eldest child, Wentworth, Jr., applied for college, the Babcocks did not believe that they would qualify for assistance. When the second child began to consider college they were very concerned about the cost of having two children in expensive private schools at the same time. And Sarah (age 18) really wanted to go to a private school. Mrs. Babcock could see her dreams of completing her degree fading into the background. She figured that by the time they got the youngest child, Kenneth, through school there would not be enough money left for her education.

This is the Babcock's general financial structure. The Babcocks report a taxable and nontaxable income of $65,000. They own a home in which they feel they have $50,000 equity, and they have approximately $25,000 in investments. They attempt to keep a cash reserve of about $10,000 in their savings and checking accounts. Over the years they bought many fine antiques and purchased life insurance to provide income in case of Mr. Babcock's death. Thus, the estate could be considerably larger than the few assets we listed for financial aid purposes.

The Babcock family*

Taxable and nontaxable income		$65,000
Assets:		
Home equity	$50,000	
Investments	25,000	
Cash	10,000	
Net assets		85,000

*Family size, 5; number in college, (?).

At the encouragement of some friends the Babcocks sought out financial planning help to qualify for aid. They found that the smartest thing to do would be for Mrs. Babcock to go back to school when the oldest (Wentworth, Jr.) enters his junior year and Sarah starts her freshman year. Thus there would be three full-time students in the family. In order to help them with their plans, we estimated what the financial aid eligibility might be at several different schools based on the

Total taxable and nontaxable income		$65,000
Less allowances:		
U.S. income tax (five exemptions)	$19,670	
FICA	1,588	
State and other taxes	5,850	
Medical and dental expenses	0	
Employment allowance	0	
Standard maintenance allowance (family of five, three in college)	10,380	
Total allowances (family of five)		37,488
Parents' available income (for a family of five, three in college, one parent working)		$27,512
Parents' assets:		
Home equity	$50,000	
Investment equity	25,000	
Cash and bank accounts	10,000	
Net worth for financial aid purposes		$85,000

Chapter 12: How Many Will Be in School?

information above. First we must determine the Babcocks' available income and net worth for financial aid purposes. (See table at bottom of p. 92.) Mr. Babcock, age 50, is the older parent which means an asset protection allowance of $33,200 in the 1981–82 formula.

Net worth − Asset protection allowance = Discretionary net worth
$85,000 − $33,200 = $51,800

Discretionary net worth × 12% = Income supplement
$51,800 × 12% = $6,216

The resulting parents' contribution is computed as follows:

Parents' available income + Income supplement
$27,512 + $6,216 = $33,728

The amount of $33,728 generates a parents' contribution of $13,350. Thus, on a per student-basis, the Babcock parents would be expected to provide:

For one student $12,200*
For two students .... 6,375 each*
For three students .... 4,450 each

*Total varies from $13,350 due to changes in maintenance allowance.

Should Parents Go to School?

The impressive thing in the case of the Babcocks is that if Wentworth, Jr., and Sarah were going to schools which cost $8,000 or more and which had policies of meeting the needs of the families in full, then Mrs. Babcock might just as well go to school. Wentworth, Jr., and Sarah would receive substantial amounts of aid if their mother also attended.

Assuming that each child, Wentworth, Jr., and Sarah, had a student contribution of $900 a year, it is possible to see what their aid eligibility might be at different institutions.

Family contribution = Parents' contribution + Student's contribution
= $4,450 (assumes three in college) + $900
= $5,350

	School			
	A	B	C	D
School cost	$9,000	$8,000	$7,000	$6,000
Family contribution (with three in college and student contribution of $900	5,350	5,350	5,350	5,350
Aid eligibility per student (I)	3,650	2,650	1,650	650

But if Mrs. Babcock did not go to school full time (so that there would only be two in school) and we assume the same student contribution, then the situation would be as follows:

Family contribution = Parents' contribution + Student's contribution
= $6,375 (assumes two in college) + $900
= $7,275

Note that adjustment has been made for small change in family standard maintenance allowance.

	School			
	A	B	C	D
School cost	$9,000	$8,000	$7,000	$6,000
Family contribution (with two in college and student contribution of $900)	7,275	7,275	7,275	7,275
Aid eligibility per student (II)	1,725	725	0	0
Increase in aid eligibility per student with shift from two to three students (I-II)	1,925	1,925	1,650	650

If Wentworth, Jr., and Sarah attended institutions that cost $8,000 or had total cost budgets in that amount and were fully awarding their students, then Mrs. Babcock could use twice the savings per student, or two times $1,925, for a total of $3,850. Her education would not cost the family any more in cash flow dollars.

Check School Policies

It is important that as you consider these options, you verify the policies of the schools involved. Many schools meet the full aid eligibility of their students, but some do not—and more may not in the future. A word to the wise—investigate before you make all your final plans.

"Stopping Out"

"Stopping out" in the educational community means taking a period of time off from school—usually a year. Depending on how the students are arranged in your family, it could work for or against you to have a child stop out. For instance, if your eldest wants to wait a year before going to school and this will increase the overlap with younger children, then you may want to consider the positive financial aid impact of such a decision.

Chapter 12: How Many Will Be in School?

Strategies When Filing for Aid

On most financial aid forms there is a question about how many students you will have in college. Give this careful consideration. If you believe that there will be three (even though only two may finally attend), it is usually best to put down three and then notify the financial aid office once the final decision is made. If you put down the smaller number first, you may find that by the time the third person decides to attend, all the available funds have been given out.

Formulas Do Not Distinguish Cost of Schools

Remember that if you have one student going to a community college, one to a state university, and one to an expensive private school, as far as financial aid is concerned, they are all equal and all in school. The formula does not distinguish between the costs of schools, or at least it did not through the 1970s. (If you volunteer the information of what schools your other students are attending, the financial aid office may consider that information in making the awards.) But there is an interesting phenomena that can actually reduce your family contribution in total by counting multiple students. Assume that the McDonalds will have three children in college next year and that the parents' contribution is $5,000 per child using the uniform methodology. Logically, it would appear that the McDonald's parent contribution should be $15,000 for all three students. The students have no savings, but they do have different savings expectations from their summer work because of their years in college.

Dwight, senior summer savings: $900.

Sarah, sophomore summer savings: $900.

Lee, freshman summer savings: $700.

	Resources			
	Dwight	Sarah	Lee	Total
Parents' contribution (by formula)	$5,000	$5,000	$5,000	$15,000
Student's contribution	900	900	700	
Family contribution	5,900	5,900	5,700	
Total college cost	3,000	4,800	9,600	
Aid eligibility	0	0	3,900	

Assuming the school Lee attends fully awards the aid eligibility, what should the actual parents' contribution be if the children do their share:

	Dwight	Sarah	Lee	Total
College cost	$3,000	$4,800	$9,600	
Less aid eligibility	0	0	3,900	
Student's summer savings	900	900	700	
Actual parents' contribution	2,100	3,900	5,000	$11,000

If Lee's school fully awards and the students contribute to their total cost from their summer earnings at the expected rate, then the parents, instead of having a total contribution for all three children of $15,000, will only have an expectation of $11,000. Some colleges might consider the cost of the schools that Dwight and Sarah attend and suggest that the McDonalds have available $4,000 more for Lee ($15,000 − $11,000). But this would be an individual school policy. In most cases the parents would only have to provide the $11,000 unless Dwight or Sarah chose a more expensive school.

$80,000 Income Receives Aid

It is difficult to emphasize how strongly the number in college can affect a family's whole financial aid picture. I have seen people with incomes in the $80,000 range receive aid at schools costing $7,500. These families also have substantial assets, but as we have already seen, that does not prevent them from getting aid. These high-income families, usually have a number of family members in college.

Professional Schools Count

It is not uncommon for families to have one child in medical school, one in law school, one in an undergraduate institution, and one still in high school. In that case, mother may even be going to school too. Such a family could have an extremely high income and still qualify for assistance, especially under state and federal programs. If your family situation is something like this, at least apply for aid and find out what you may be entitled to under the various programs.

More Students, More Aid

For most people, having more in school simply qualifies them for more aid. If you are already qualifying for assistance, you may qualify for more if you add additional students to your list. If you are not sure whether to count a student, list the student anyway and put a note in the explanation section. You will receive notification if the decision is made not to count one of the students you have listed. Don't be afraid to let the financial aid officer make the decision if you are not sure. If you do not at least try to count that student, you may miss substantial benefits.

A Case of Large Assets

The McFerrins couldn't figure out how they were going to pay for their daughter Catherine to attend the private college of her choice. When we reviewed the forms they filled out, it did not appear that they would qualify for any help under normal guidelines. They listed two children on the aid form—Catherine and her sister Mary, a junior in high school. But on the admission application, they listed an older child, Gregg. The parents stated that Gregg did live at home and helped in the family business. They also said that he was going to attend a community college full time in the fall. This would have two effects on the McFerrins: (1) it would reduce their income because they would have to hire help in the family business and (2) it would cost them money for tuition, books, fees, transportation, and other expenses. After we put Gregg on the financial aid form and changed the number in college to two, it was evident that Catherine would receive assistance from the state and the college. This made it possible for her to consider the private college.

The McFerrins' situation looked something like this. They owned a home in which they had an equity of about $30,000; they had about $10,000 cash in the bank; and they owned a business with a value of approximately $100,000. Their taxable and nontaxable income was about $36,000. We figured the situation originally as follows:

The McFerrin Family*

Total taxable and nontaxable income		$36,000
Less allowances:		
U.S. income tax (five exemptions)	$ 6,600	
FICA	1,588	
State and other taxes	3,240	
Standard maintenance allowance	12,800	
Total for all allowances		24,228
Parents' available income (one in college and one parent working)		$11,772
Parents' assets:		
Home equity	$30,000	
Business adjusted from $100,000	45,500	
Cash and bank accounts	10,000	
Net worth for financial aid purposes		$85,500

* Family size, 5; number in college, 1; age of oldest parent, 48; asset protection allowance, $31,300.

Mr. McFerrin is 48 which means the asset protection allowance is $31,300.

Net worth − Asset protection allowance = Discretionary net worth
$85,500 − $31,300 = $54,200

Discretionary net worth × 12% = Income supplement
$54,200 × 12% = $6,504

Parents' contribution is then computed from the total of:

Parents' available income + Income supplement
$11,772 + $6,504 = $18,276

The amount of $18,276 generates a parents' contribution of $6,055. Catherine clearly would not get assistance at schools costing less than $7,000 with that kind of parents' contribution plus her own contribution of $700 for a total of $6,055 + $700 = $6,755.

When her brother was listed as being in school, the parents' contribution for Catherine changed to $3,350, plus her $700, or $4,050 for the family contribution. This made Catherine eligible for almost $3,000 in assistance at a school costing $7,000.

Maximize Your Aid

Think about your situation carefully, and do the best you can to maximize it. It is important to be honest on financial aid applications. In my experience many families like the McFerrins cheat themselves out of substantial resources. Plan ahead carefully when considering the number in college.

Which Assets Should You Use?

Where do parents get the cash to pay their contribution beyond educational loans (which are described in Chapter 16). If you borrow against or liquidate assets, be sure they are those assets that appear on the financial aid form. That way you can reduce the parents' contribution for the next year and thus hopefully get more assistance.

Earlier we mentioned the McDonalds who had three children in college, Dwight, Sarah, and Lee, and needed $11,000 to pay the actual parents' contribution. Assuming that this would put a strain on the family budget and that they were planning to get all or part of this from assets, it is important that they consider the impact of different choices.

Good and bad items to borrow against while applying for aid are listed below. The good list will show on your financial aid application and, therefore, help to get more aid. The bad list will have no effect on your application for financial aid.

Chapter 12: How Many Will Be in School?

Good	Bad
Stocks	Insurance
Bonds	Cars
Land contracts	Jewelry
Real estate	Credit cards
Cash	Personal loans
	Relatives
	College payment plans

If the McDonalds borrow the money from any of the items on the "bad" list, it would not help them get more financial aid in the future. On the other hand, if they borrowed the money from items like those on the "good" list, the impact would reduce the parents' contribution per student by as much as $206.80 (or $620 for the whole family) for the following year and thus help them qualify for more aid. When they file for financial aid the next year, they would show the asset encumbered by a loan in the amount of $11,000.

A family that followed this practice carefully while educating a number of children could reap substantial rewards for their good planning in the form of tax-free financial assistance that could be dramatically increased. In the case of the McDonalds, if the parents did this for two or three years, the total expected parents' contribution according to the current formula could drop by as much as $2,000.

Planning

Again, the key is *planning* for your particular situation. Like tax planning, a carefully worked out strategy is the best way to reap the maximum rewards for you and your family in the financial aid game.

Chapter 13

Using Your Income Taxes in the Aid Application

What most directly affects the amount of aid is the amount of income reported on line 31 of Form 1040. The higher the income, the larger your family contribution is likely to be; the lower the income, the less that you are likely to contribute. Thus, the student(s) will have more aid eligibility.

Because the federal government is more involved in the aid system, the formula is more dependent on the U.S. Income Tax Form 1040. Some people now realize this and try to maximize their aid situation by adjusting their taxable income from year to year. Good accountants and tax people can help you shift your taxable income between years to your advantage in the financial aid system. It takes some preplanning—the financial aid dollars awarded in the fall of a student's freshman year are based on the income earned and reported from January 1 of the junior year in high school to December 31 of the senior year in high school. Thus, a person who wished to maximize aid would have to start with the tax year beginning in January of the junior year in high school.

If you prepare your own tax form, you may be able to play around with it to see what options are available to you. If you have someone else prepare your taxes, as has been said before, arrange to get together with that person early. Explain the aid opportunity and discuss what tax strategies you can use to maximize aid eligibility. The earlier you meet and plan, the better your chances of meeting all deadlines for the forms. We have mentioned before that the financial aid forms should really be completed only after the tax form is done. Further, because you want to resolve the financial aid issue and because some schools and states run out of or are low on money, you want to apply for financial aid as early as you can. This probably means that you should plan to have your taxes done no later than the end of January. This is not easy. However, people who have been to financial aid workshops have found that the rewards are well worth the extra effort.

Your tax preparer may not like the idea of trying to do things for financial aid reasons, so be prepared to discuss this with him or her. Emphasize the differences in strategy: taxes and aid are, for practical purposes, inversely related. Let them know that you are trying to maximize financial aid and, therefore, are interested in planning a tax strategy that will work. Show them the financial aid forms with any references to IRS Form 1040 so that they can make appropriate suggestions. Discuss the trade-off in taxes that you are making. Don't do something for financial aid reasons that would ultimately increase your taxes more than the potential gain in tax-free financial aid dollars. The important thing to remember is that the aid dollars are tax-free.

Over the years people have tried all kinds of things, some of them good and some of them bad. Following are some of the items that make up line 31 on your tax form and a discussion of some of your possibilities. If one does not apply, skip to the next. Remember that the key is to have line 31 as small as possible. Many people make the mistake of working on items that come after line 31, such as deductions for interest expenses, insurance, gifts, and so on. These things help to minimize tax liability, but do not help with your financial aid because they do not affect line 31—adjusted gross income.

Business Income (or Loss)

This is one area where people can shift income around and thus help themselves to receive more financial aid. Business assets receive favorable treatment because they are taxed at a much lower rate for financial aid purposes than are other assets that you might list. Now you can also use business income to help with increasing your financial aid. You may want to proceed with certain expenditures (that are needed but optional) which would lower your net income in the business immediately but would potentially help you by making it more profitable.

To get a clearer understanding, remember that for a student who will begin college in September, the tax years that will be considered (based on current practice) are as shown on the four-year financial plan (Table 13-1).

TABLE 13-1
A Four-Year Financial Plan

	Class in School			
	Freshman	Sophomore	Junior	Senior
Calendar..................................	September 1982–June 1983	September 1983–June 1984	September 1984–June 1985	September 1985–June 1986
Federal tax year considered for financial aid...	1981	1982	1983	1984
Earning year.............................	January 1981–December 1981	January 1982–December 1982	January 1983–December 1983	January 1984–December 1984
Number of months between beginning of earning year to end of financial aid year......	30	30	30	30

Chapter 13: Using Your Income Taxes in the Aid Application

Thirty Months

Given the fact that there is a 30-month period between the time you first earn a dollar that counts toward financial aid and the last time your student's financial aid is affected by that dollar, it is important that you plan to do things carefully to affect your income the correct way. See Table 13–1 in this section showing time considerations for a four-year financial plan. For example:

Year A	January of sophomore year in high school to December of junior year in high school	Take profits, does not affect aid.
Year B	January of junior year in high school to December of senior year in high school	Minimize income to increase aid.
Year C	January of senior year in high school to December of freshman year in college	Continue to minimize income to increase aid.

Not everyone can shift substantial amounts of income around, but there are strategies that can be used to help. For those who have the potential to move income around through deferred gains and losses, the returns can be significant in terms of increased financial aid. This kind of planning needs to be done carefully to consider the ultimate tax and aid consequences. But to neglect it may be to overlook a potential harvest of tax-free dollars.

Real Estate

One family, the Scotts, invested heavily in real estate in the year before their child was to enter school. They did not expect this new enterprise to be profitable for two or three years because of needed improvements, heavy interest, and depreciation expenses in the first year. They figured out that the loss in this area would offset their joint earnings and thus reduce their adjusted gross income (line 31). Their son could then obtain more financial aid. They did not know how much more it would help them to transfer their personal assets (cash and securities) into the business account as well.

Scott Case I

In Table 13–2, you will see the Scott family listed in four different ways with their choices for investment and earnings distribution.

The family's primary wage earner (Mr. Scott) has a taxable income of $50,000 a year. Mr. Scott is an executive with a medium-sized manufacturing firm. The Scotts have a family of five (two parents plus three children); they have about $50,000 equity in their home; and including their home equity, their net worth is about $90,000 (in financial aid terms).

The Scott Family*

Income from wages		$50,000
Nontaxable income		0
Adjustments to income		?
Assets:		
Home equity	$50,000	
Investments	25,000	
Cash	15,000	
Net worth		$90,000

* Family size, 5; one child in college, age of older parent, 50, asset protection allowance, $33,200.

It is important to realize that a net worth of $90,000 in financial aid terms might really represent a net worth of substantially more, perhaps $250,000, if everything were included. Initially we will consider each case as if the Scotts have only one child in school. We will assume that the student's contribution is only the expected summer savings of $700.

Case I—No Changes

In Case I the Scotts have done nothing to change their situation. They have not taken advantage of what may be available to help them in

TABLE 13–2
Four Different Projections for the Scott Family

Case	Wages Earned	Taxable	Parents' Available Income
I	$50,000	$50,000	$18,742
II	50,000	40,000	14,004
III	50,000	35,000	11,552
IV	50,000	35,000	9,152

Case	Home Equity	Investments	40 percent of Business	Cash	Net Worth	Income Supplement
I	$50,000	$25,000	$ 0	$15,000	$90,000	$6,816
II	50,000	10,000	10,000	5,000	75,000	5,016
III	50,000	0	16,000	0	66,000	3,936
IV	50,000	0	16,000	0	66,000	3,936

Case	Parents' Contribution for One Child	Student's Contribution	Family Contribution
I	$9,477	$700	$10,177
II	6,404	700	7,104
III	4,744	700	5,444
IV	3,616	700	4,316

terms of investments that would reduce taxes and increase financial aid. Essentially they report $50,000 in income on which they pay approximately $12,370 in federal taxes and $4,500 in state and other taxes. Since Mrs. Scott is not working, there is no allowance for her income. This results in $31,258 in allowances against $50,000 in income, leaving $18,742 to be considered in the formula for the family contribution. In terms of assets the Scotts have their house (as already mentioned), $25,000 in some traditional equity investments, and about $15,000 in cash for a net worth of $90,000. Since Mr. Scott is 50, his asset protection allowance is $33,200, so only $56,800 of the $90,000 is considered by the formula. This provides an income supplement of $6,816. This $6,816 plus the $18,742 will, when run through the formula, yield a parents' contribution of $9,477. This, together with the student's contribution of $700, will yield a family contribution of $10,177.

Parents' contribution + Student's contribution = Family contribution
$9,477 + $700 = $10,177

So at most schools the Scotts' older daughter Pamela, who is the first one to be going to college, would not qualify for need-based assistance since total costs currently are usually under $10,177.

Case II—Investment in Real Estate

In Case II, the Scotts invest in real estate. But, they have a $10,000 loss on the real estate operation in the first year. Some of this is an actual loss in hard dollars, and some of it is a loss in the form of depreciation.

This $10,000 loss adjusts the Scotts' gross income; their taxable income is now only $40,000. This reduces federal taxes to about $8,008 and state and other taxes to about $3,600. The total allowances would be $25,996, leaving parents' available income at $14,004.

The Scotts' assets in Case II show up as only $75,000. The $50,000 remains in the house, $10,000 remains in investments, and $5,000 in cash. However, of the $25,000 invested in the real estate operation (only 40 percent of the first $45,000 is counted), $10,000 is listed and $15,000 is protected as if it did not exist. This reduces the income supplement to $5,016. The parents' contribution under these conditions turns out to be $6,404, and the family contribution is $7,104. At today's high prices this would get some aid at more expensive schools. But the Scotts want to find out if they can do more for Pamela.

Case III—Larger Real Estate Investment

In Case III, the Scotts want to see what the effects would be if they make a still larger investment in real estate. Suppose this time they have a $15,000 loss from the real estate operation for an adjusted gross income of $35,000. The estimated taxes on this are $5,910 for the federal and $3,150 for the state. The total allowances become $23,448, and the parents' available income is reduced to $11,552. In the assets area, the house remains with its equity of $50,000, and the business shows a value of $16,000, or 40 percent of the total $40,000 that the Scotts invested. No cash shows but that is because all funds are in the business accounts. Thus, the total net worth for financial aid purposes is $66,000, and $3,936 is the income supplement used to figure the parents' contribution. The parents' contribution works out to be $4,744, which, when added to the student's contribution, changes the family contribution to $5,444. This is a figure that would qualify for assistance at many private colleges.

Case IV—Addition of Small Business

In Case IV, the Scotts are interested in seeing what would happen if instead of investing only in real estate they bought a small business. That way Mrs. Scott would also become part of the working force in the family. They could then take advantage of an employment allowance for her. Assume that of the total income, Mrs. Scott generates more than $4,800. In that case, the contribution would be $3,616 from the parents and $700 from Pamela, or a total family contribution of $4,316. This would allow the Scotts to receive help at a number of schools.

If Pamela was considering a school that cost $7,000, the Scotts would not receive assistance in Case I or II, but they would begin to get help in Case III and could get about $2,500 in aid eligibility in Case IV.

The effects would be even more dramatic when Pamela's brother, Robert, starts school next year. Table 13–3 shows the situation in all four cases if the Scotts have two in school, assuming one is a freshman and one is a sophomore. Notice the impact in total family contribution that the different cases can have. For example, the difference between Case I and Case IV with two children in college would be an increase in aid

TABLE 13–3
Expected Contributions by Scott Family with Two in College

	Total	Parents' Contribution for Each Child	Robert's Family Contribution*	Pamela's Family Contribution*
I	$10,046	$5,023	$5,723	$5,923
II	6,973	3,487	4,187	4,387
III	5,313	2,657	3,357	3,557
IV	4,185	2,093	2,793	2,993

* Robert is a freshman with a $700 expected summer savings; Pamela is a sophomore with a $900 expected summer savings (assumes no contribution from either student's assets).

eligibility for the two children of almost $6,000 ($5,862). The Scotts may be much better off in the long run using this route to finance their childrens' education. It would take a tremendous raise for Mr. Scott to net $6,000 considering the impact of federal and state taxes.

The aid eligibility table shows you the kind of aid eligibility that a student could have at different priced schools (see Table 13-4). You can see that a family with an income of $50,000 could be receiving aid at some low-priced public and private schools if they appropriately arranged their finances. Admittedly, the impact at the low-priced schools is not as great and it might not be worth the trouble. But if one child was considering a less expensive school and the other a more expensive school, it would certainly be worth investigating.

Thus the use of business income and loss, plus the added bonus of the asset protection for a business, can be a very effective way to change your financial aid picture. Real estate has been used as an example, but there are a number of other opportunities that would serve the same function.

Capital Gains and Losses

If you believe that you will be qualifying for financial assistance a relatively simple way to pick up some extra aid eligibility (at no real cost to yourself) is to look through your investments for anything that might qualify as a capital loss. You are allowed up to $3,000 a year off your adjusted gross income on Form 1040, and this may help you to qualify for some additional aid. There are a number of ways that you can work this out.

Split Losses and Gains

If you trade in the stock market regularly, you probably already know that you can split your losses and gains between years. For example, if your eldest child is in his senior year in high school, you may decide to take your losses up to $3,000 and hold on to your profits until January of the next year. This would help to reduce your income and thus help your student to qualify for more financial aid. You could follow that up with an investment in January that would give you a big write-off in the fall of the student's freshman year. Then you can help the student qualify for the sophomore year, but more on that later. It is even possible to take the loss and maintain your position in the stock if you plan far enough ahead and check with a broker or investment advisor. Suppose you perceive the stock or the market to be under a temporary reversal; it would be possible to take the loss and thus reduce income and increase financial aid while maintaining your position.

TABLE 13–4
Aid Eligibility Table for Robert*

	$2,000	$3,000	$4,000	$5,000	$6,000	$7,000	$8,000	$9,000	$10,000	$11,000
					School Total Cost					
I.........	0	0	0	0	$ 275	$1,275	$2,275	$3,275	$4,275	$5,275
II........	0	0	0	$ 800	1,800	2,800	3,800	4,800	5,800	6,800
III.......	0	0	$ 600	1,600	2,600	3,600	4,600	5,600	6,600	7,600
IV.......	0	$ 200	1,200	2,200	3,200	4,200	5,200	6,200	7,200	8,200

* Robert, a freshman, is the second child attending college.

Chapter 13: Using Your Income Taxes in the Aid Application 109

Another place you might look for a loss would be stocks or bonds you have as investments. Though many people hate to admit it, among the few stocks they own, there are bound to be some losers. If there is one, this may be the time to let this company help by taking your loss. There is often great reticence to do that, but the worth of a stock is only what people are willing to pay for it—the market price. Selling is frequently the hardest investment decision. Suppose you find that you have 100 shares of Hula Hoop Industries for which you paid $50 a share and which is now worth only $25 a share. Check with your broker and be sure that your appraisal of the company's worth (future prospects) is correct. If it is, sell it. Thus, you are recognizing a loss on paper which you had already incurred in fact.

Caution: This is not a recommended investment plan. You should seek investment and tax advice for such decisions. Tax laws are constantly changing.

Effect of Loss

The effect of the loss if generated is what is important. Consider the Miller family: one parent earns $30,000 a year, the other parent, $10,000 a year, and there are three children. The family income is, then, about $40,000 a year, and they pay about $8,080 in federal taxes and $3,600 in state and other taxes. They have $44,000 equity in their home, and they have about $16,000 in investments and cash. The parents' contribution as originally calculated for one child in school was $4,216. This amount combined with the students contribution yields $4,916. The Millers then realize that it might help them to write-off the bad deal that they made last year.

The Miller Family*

Taxable income from wages, two parents working	$40,000
Nontaxable income	0
Assets:	
Home equity	$44,000
Investments	12,000
Cash	4,000
Net worth	60,000

* Family size, 5; number in college, 1, age of older parent, 48; asset protection allowance, $31,300.

At their request a recomputation of their situation was made assuming that they would include a $3,000 short-term capital loss. Thus their adjusted gross income went down to $37,000—even though they still had $40,000 in income. The impact reduced federal and state taxes and the parents' contribution to $3,336, or $880 less than it had been before. Everything else stayed the same including contribution from assets. The result increased the child's eligibility for financial aid by $880 at schools costing $5,000 or more. This may not seem like a particularly large amount, but consider again this is tax-free aid eligibility. The family will retain whatever dollars were generated by selling the asset at a loss.

Many families fail to consider all these little devices. But a few hundred dollars here and a few hundred dollars there make the job of financing a college education that much easier. Once again, anything that you can do to reduce the amount on line 31, the better your chances of getting financial aid.

Farm Income or Loss

Most financial aid officers do not understand farming particularly well. Traditionally, the problem for farmers is that they have too many assets (at least on paper) and those prevent them from getting assistance even if their cash flow is zero. As you can see from Table 13–5, it is not

TABLE 13–5
Farm Values

Farm Value	Parents' Contribution*
$ 50,000	0
75,000	$ 198
100,000	528
125,000	858
150,000	1,188
175,000	1,611
200,000	2,105
225,000	2,692
250,000	3,394
275,000	4,797
300,000	6,207
325,000	7,617
350,000	9,027

* Assumes zero family income; family of five, with one going to college; parents' age 40; and no other assets.

the farm value alone that prevents some farmers from getting assistance (unless the farms have values beyond debts in the $300,000 range and above). Often, if the farm is at all profitable, that profit together with the addition of the farm value can make it more difficult to get aid.

Chapter 13: Using Your Income Taxes in the Aid Application 111

Protection of Assets

Some people actually buy farms to protect assets from the financial aid process. If paper losses are generated, this may help with substantial amounts of aid. Consider what might be done by someone with an income of $65,000 a year and two children who will be going to college simultaneously. Dr. Storm and his wife have two children who will both be in college next year. While they have a good income, they are interested in capital appreciation. They also want to avoid using cash to pay for college if they can find a way to get the government to help. After reviewing financial aid literature they decided to investigate the possibility of pooling all their assets to buy a farm. They realize that the farm will probably lose money the first few years, but they are optimistic that in the long run, the investment will pay off.

They remortgage their home (so that they only have $10,000 in equity) and combine all their investments. They pay $100,000 down on a $250,000 operating farm and sign a management contract with the farmer to operate the farm for them. They, of course, will have to provide the cash if there are losses, but the Storms feel that with the husband's income they should be able to handle this if they plan wisely. Just before purchasing the farm they were interested in finding out what the implications would be to their children and financial aid eligibility based on current practice and assuming that the farm might lose $30,000 the first year. A comparison showed the Storms their situation for the two children, one to be a freshman and one to be a junior, and what their predicted aid would be before the purchase of the farm and after the purchase of the farm. See Table 13-6 showing the effect of the farm purchase on aid eligibility.

You can see that there is a dramatic difference. You would have to check your affairs carefully and verify the financial process in use, but the work involved in such planning could pay off handsomely. Suppose the Storms' two children had selected private colleges where the costs were $8,000 a year for everything (see Table 13-7). The aid eligibility would then be approximately $11,400 for the two students. If this was fully awarded, then it would be equivalent to the husband earning an additional $21,000, assuming that he is in the overall 50 percent bracket including federal, state, and all other nuisance taxes. In addition, he would be holding the farm for appreciation. Note that the combination of tax savings and aid would cover $25,000 out of the $30,000 loss.

Again, this is not an attempt to point out investment strategies for anyone, but rather to make you aware that there are things that you can do that will help you qualify for financial aid eligibility. The same would work on a much smaller scale for lower-income families.

TABLE 13-6
Effect of Farm Purchase on Aid Eligibility for the Storm Family*

	Before Farm Purchase	After $30,000 Operating Loss the First Year
Income from Dr. Storm's salary	$ 65,000	$ 65,000
Income from investment	2,500	
Loss from farm		(30,000)
Total Income	67,500	$ 35,000
Assets:		
Home equity	40,000	10,000
Investments	60,000	
Cash	10,000	
Farm		100,000
Total	$110,000	$110,000
Parents' contribution per child	7,626	1,595
Freshman student contribution (only summer earnings)	700	700
Total family contribution	$ 8,326	$ 2,295

* For family of four, with two in college; age of oldest parent, 50.

TABLE 13-7
Aid Eligibility—Freshman

	School Cost						
	$3,000	$4,000	$5,000	$6,000	$7,000	$8,000	$9,000
Before farm	0	0	0	0	0	0	$ 674
After farm	$ 705	$1,705	$2,705	$3,705	$4,705	$5,705	$6,705

Other Ventures—Oil!

There are many other things that you might look out for as potential investments that could help improve the financial aid picture for you. One family went to a financial aid workshop and decided not to apply for financial aid. Their taxable income was so high that they did not think they had a chance. After they went to their tax preparer, they learned that one of their investments (in a limited partnership in an oil drilling venture) would dramatically reduce their income. We reworked their financial aid and found that they had a good chance of qualifying for substantial assistance.

Plan Ahead

Planning is the key to applying for financial aid. Go through the exercise of putting your family situation on paper. Then experiment

Chapter 13: Using Your Income Taxes in the Aid Application 113

with any choices that you may have to see what, if any, effect they will have on your taxable and nontaxable income. You may be surprised what you can work out for yourself. Often parents do not realize that this potential is there until it is too late to take advantage of it. Remember that even if you do not qualify the first time with the first child in school, you may well qualify in another tax year (or if more students enter school from your family). As we have said before, it may be nothing that you change that causes you to qualify, but rather a shift in the formulas that are used by the federal government, the state you live in, or the institution that the student will be attending. Families that never dreamed of help are getting substantial amounts today just because they took the trouble to apply correctly and plan appropriately.

Adjustments to Income

A whole different area that you could explore in your efforts to affect your taxable income is that of the adjustments to income. These include:

Employee business expense.
Moving expenses.
Payments to an Individual Retirement Account (IRA).
Payments to a Keogh plan.
Alimony payments.
Disability income exclusion.

The potential for income reduction is greatest with the IRA, Keogh, and alimony payments unless, of course, you moved last year or have a great deal of business expense which you can legitimately deduct.

IRA and Keogh

If you are eligible and you have not done so already, you may want to discuss with your advisors the benefits of an IRA or Keogh plan. The added benefit you get by removing that income from consideration for financial aid might make the program that much more attractive to you. This is especially true if you face paying for a number of years of

The Rowe Family*

Taxable income		$40,000
Nontaxable income		0
Assets:		
Home equity	$50,000	
Investments and cash	25,000	
Net worth		75,000

* Family size, 5; number in college, 1; age of older parent, 45; asset protection allowance, $28,600.

schooling. For example, the Rowes have an income of $40,000 a year and assets totaling $75,000, including $50,000 in home equity. With five in the family and one planning to attend school, the family contribution based on standard tax rates is $7,998. This can be dropped by almost $300 if the Rowes put $1,000 into an IRA account.

Their actual situation would work like this for the last $1,000 earned:

	Taxes	Family Contribution
Before Keogh or IRA.............	$352	$304
After Keogh or IRA..............	0	0

You can readily see that before the Keogh or IRA plan the family was left with:

$1,000 - ($352 + $304) = $344 of real spending money

By foregoing that amount of spending money, they are able to put $1,000 into either the Keogh or the IRA plan.

Financial Aid and Tax Planning Go Together

In all of your tax planning, use your knowledge of financial aid to maximize your situation for both educational benefits and tax benefits. It has occurred to me that a family may be well advised to take a substantial risk if they have children in college. If the payoff is as hoped, the returns can pay for college. If a loss is incurred, you can write it off against income. Thus both the tax system and the financial aid system can help you cover the risk involved.

If the financial aid system and the tax system continue in their present forms, there may be specialists to help you with investments and risk-taking. More will be developing in this area in the future. Chapter 24 will relay some possible areas.

Section V
AVAILABLE MONEY

Chapter 14
The Philosophy of Aid Packaging
Chapter 15
Sources of Aid
Chapter 16
Loans
Chapter 17
Packaging

Chapter 14

The Philosophy of Aid Packaging

Types of Aid and Packaging

What kinds of aid are available to students if they have aid eligibility? This is always a question since there are so many subjective factors for aid awards. Financial aid officers refer to "packaging" when they decide how much of various kinds of aid that they think you are either entitled to or that they have available to assign to you.

At each school there are different costs, and therefore, the same student will have different aid eligibilities at two different schools. The total cost at any specific college is made up of the following:

Tuition charges
Fees
Room
Board
Personal expenses
Books
Travel
Other

It is important to remember where the aid eligibility comes from (see Figure 14–1).

Total cost − Family contribution = Maximum aid eligibility

Table 14–1 shows how these calculations are made.

TABLE 14–1
Chart of Aid Eligibility at Different School Costs with Varying Family Contributions

Family Contribution	School Total Cost								
	$1,000	$2,000	$3,000	$4,000	$5,000	$6,000	$7,000	$8,000	$9,000
$1,000	0	$1,000	$2,000	$3,000	$4,000	$5,000	$6,000	$7,000	$8,000
2,000	0	0	1,000	2,000	3,000	4,000	5,000	6,000	7,000
3,000	0	0	0	1,000	2,000	3,000	4,000	5,000	6,000
4,000	0	0	0	0	1,000	2,000	3,000	4,000	5,000
5,000	0	0	0	0	0	1,000	2,000	3,000	4,000
6,000	0	0	0	0	0	0	1,000	2,000	3,000
7,000	0	0	0	0	0	0	0	1,000	2,000
8,000	0	0	0	0	0	0	0	0	1,000
9,000	0	0	0	0	0	0	0	0	0

Chapter 14: The Philosophy of Aid Packaging

FIGURE 14-1

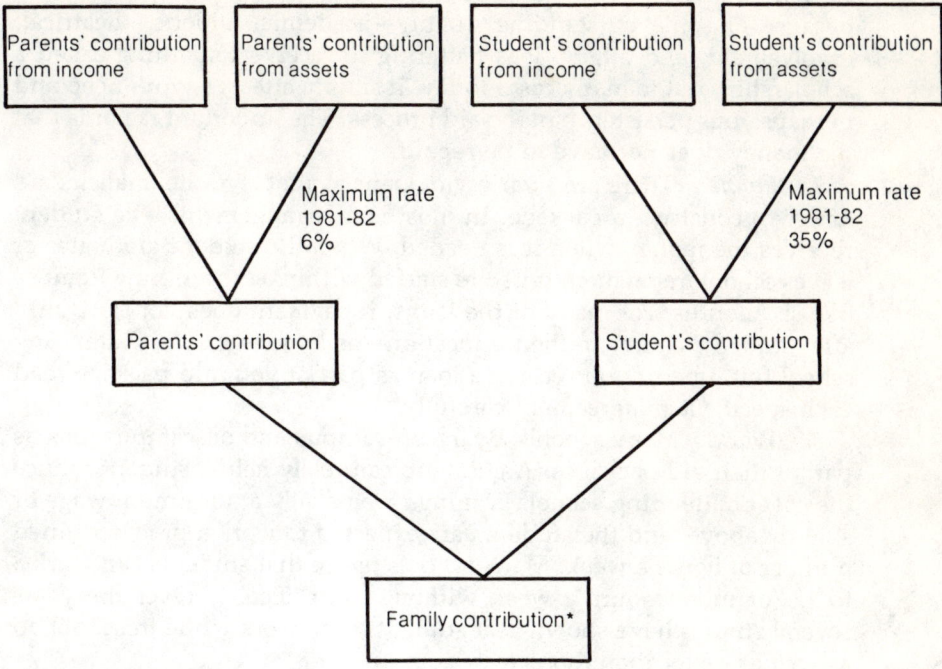

*Remember that two different children in the same family will probably have different family contributions because of differences in students' contributions.

TABLE 14-2
Basic Forms of Aid

	Sources of Aid			
Types of Aid	Federal	State	Institutional	Other
Scholarship and grants..............	Yes	Usually	Usually	Yes
Loans............................	Yes	Frequently	Usually	?
Work.............................	Yes	?	Usually	?

Once the aid officer has determined aid eligibility for a student at the aid officer's institution, then an award can be constructed. There are a number of resources that are available to an aid officer to construct a package (see Table 14–2). The three basic forms of assistance are:

1. Grants or Scholarships. This is gift money that helps to reduce or directly discount the bill that a student may have. If this money more than covers the bill, the student may get a refund to use for living expenses, books, and so on. These dollars are given out for a variety of reasons. Some are given out strictly on a need basis; some are given out as combination of need and scholarship; and others are given out because of some outstanding quality—academic, athletic, theatrical, involvement, and others. It is flattering to receive something called a scholarship, but in many cases today, it simply attests to your need and perhaps your persistence in the aid process. The important factor is that the money does not have to be repaid.

   2. Loans. There are a variety of loans available to the financial aid officer to construct a package. In most loan arrangements, the student receives the money when it is needed. When the student graduates or leaves school, repayment must be started within a certain time frame—like six months. For many of the loans, repayment does not start until after students complete their education—as long as they are attending school full time. If you receive a loan as part of your aid package read each specific loan agreement carefully.

   3. Work. Many schools award on-campus and off-campus jobs as part of their aid packages. A good job can really help a student reduce the cost of attending school. Earnings are usually at minimum wage or slightly above, and the students are expected to work a predetermined number of hours a week. Many schools figure that students can work 8 to 12 (or more) hours a week without any difficulty. Over the years several studies have shown that students who work while in school do as well or better than those who do not.

For these three types of aid there are essentially four major sources.

   1. Federal Government. We taxpayers are the largest aid program for private and public education. In fact, we have allowed our democratic printing presses to print enough extra money to subsidize education probably as much as any other industry in the country. The federal government has a tremendous program of financial aid including grants, loans, and work. Without this huge amount of assistance, many schools would not be able to help you with aid.

   2. State Governments. States have become involved in financial aid in different ways. Some states have particularly outstanding programs, and others are weak. Be sure to check your state programs; specifically:

   a. Is there a separate application?
   b. Can you use the money to attend out-of-state schools?
   c. Are there other special conditions (such as competitive examination)?

Aid officers are generally familiar with the details of the state aid programs in their own state. But they cannot be expected to know about programs in the other 49 states. Check with your high school or a

Chapter 14: The Philosophy of Aid Packaging

financial aid office in your state about how and where to get information on your state program. State aid generally falls into the category of grants, although there are some state loan programs apart from those programs that are really federal loan programs (more on this later). And there may be some state work programs.

3. Institutions. Public, private, and proprietary (privately owned) schools, colleges, and universities provide a tremendous amount of the aid available in this country. Some of the schools have endowment funds for this purpose; others simply take the necessary aid dollars out of the operating budget. Most institutions participate in grant programs, and many also participate in work and/or loan programs with their own resources. If you are seeking a considerable amount of aid, you may want to ask schools how much institutional money goes into the aid program and, further, how much of it is endowed. Unfortunately, with the spiraling inflation and the slow growth in endowment income for many institutions, these resources have not grown as fast as cost.

4. Other. There are many types of programs available on national, regional, and local bases that may be used to help with your financial aid. Some of these are well known like the National Merit Scholarship Program. Others you will have to ferret out with help from your high school guidance office, your pastor, schools financial aid offices, parents'

TABLE 14-3
Noncampus-Based and Campus-Based Aids

	Source of Federal Aid	
Type of Aid	Noncampus-Based	Campus-Based
Scholarship and grants	Yes	Yes
Loans	Yes	Yes
Work	No	Yes

TABLE 14-4
Basic Forms of Aid (Noncampus-based and campus-based)

	Source of Aid				
	Federal				
Type of Aid	Noncampus-Based	Campus-Based	State	Institutional	Other
Scholarship and grants	Yes	Yes	Usually	Usually	Yes
Loans	Yes	Yes	?	?	?
Work	No	Yes	?	?	?

TABLE 14–5
Potential Sources of Aid for Robert Jones

	Sources				
	Federal				
Types	Noncampus-Based	Campus-Based	Mythical State	Excellence University	Other
Scholarship or grant	Yes	Yes	Yes	Yes	Yes
Loan	Yes	Yes	No	Yes	No (none found)
Work	No	Yes	No	Yes	No (none found)

employers, and various other groups. Usually a student receives this kind of money because of his or her own work in finding out about the program and applying for the assistance. The financial aid officer then takes these amounts into account when building the financial aid package that the student will eventually receive. There are all kinds of other programs including scholarships, loans, and some small amounts of work; however for the most part, they are grant dollars that are given out at least in part on the basis of need.

Table 14–2 shows the three major types of aid and the four major sources of aid. Keep these factors in mind as you learn about individual programs so that you can put them in the correct framework.

Two Types of Financial Aid

When the aid officer decides how your aid eligibility will be met, there are many considerations to be made that help determine (1) what kinds of assistance you will be getting, and (2) from what source the dollars will be coming. To better understand the aid officer's situation, the table of sources and types of aid must be taken one step further. There are actually two types of federal aid. In the first type the decision to award is made off the campus; the second is awarded by the financial aid officer at the college and is called campus-based aid (see Table 14–3). In both campus-based and noncampus-based there are grant programs and loan programs. But only in campus-based aid is there a work program. Table 14–4 shows the five possibilities of aid sources. There are two ways this table may help you.

1. You may wish to make your own chart for your student, considering the state and school to which you are applying. Table 14–5 was done for a student, Robert Jones, who has applied to Excellence University, in a mythical state. You will note that there are 10 possible sources of aid for Robert. You may wish to fill out a matrix for yourself and find out what your possible options are (see Table 14–6).

TABLE 14–6
Potential Sources of Aid for Your Student

	Sources				
	Federal				
Types	Noncampus-Based	Campus-Based	Your State	Your School	Other
Scholarship or grant	———	———	———	———	———
Loan	———	———	———	———	———
Work	———	———	———	———	———

2. It may help to understand the difficulty that a financial aid officer faces when trying to fill your aid eligibility. In the case of Robert there are 10 possible sources of aid. Each has their own rules and regulations that must be checked to be sure the entire award is in compliance with all the restrictions placed on it by the various sources. This may help you to be more understanding when you ask an aid officer questions and there are no specific answers available.

Chapter 15

Sources of Aid

There are a variety of sources for the aid money that your student may receive. In the last decade there have been tremendous shifts in the proportions of the total national aid budget among the various sources. Under the Carter administration and the Democratic Congress, tremendous amounts of federal aid and federal control were pumped into the system. In the current political reaction to large government expenditures, there may again be major shifts amongst the sources of aid.

Federal:
    Pell Grant (BEOG, or Basic Educational Opportunity Grant)
    Guaranteed Student Loan (GSL)
    Parent loans
    Campus based
        Supplementary Educational Opportunity Grant (SEOG)
        National Direct Student Loan (NDSL)
        College Work Study Program (CWSP)
State
Institutional
Private

Specifically, what are some of the programs that aid officers choose from in meeting aid eligibility? In the federal programs probably their initial interest will be to see if your student is eligible for the BEOG program—the baseline or core of all the federal government programs. You apply for this separately when you fill out the financial aid application by agreeing to release your information to the Basic Grant Program. (This is the program mentioned earlier as being renamed the Pell Grant.)

PELL GRANT

The Pell Grant (BEOG) is awarded directly to the student by the federal government. It is called an entitlement because, like the GI Bill, every student applicant is assigned an index number which determines the aid entitlement. This entitlement may vary with school costs. The money comes to the student through the school, but the amount of the award is determined by a formula passed each year by Congress. (Chapter 23 deals with this grant in detail.)

Pell Grant Formula

The Pell Grant (BEOG) traditionally has had its own formula calculating eligibility. Thus, in recent years a student could have aid eligibility using the kind of formula discussed in the rest of the text but not qualify for a Pell Grant. Recent changes in the federal aid system have made the Pell Grant formula applicable to all federal aid programs. The Pell formula is sometimes referred to as the federal formula by professionals in the financial aid community.

One of the functions of this formula has been to provide a rationing system for federal dollars. Thus, based on projected need for Pell Grants and appropriations by Congress, the funds can be adjusted or rationed by means of the federal formula. Each year the availability of federal funds and the rationing system are major decisions that affect you and the entire educational community.

This formula more than any other is directly related to your income tax forms. The reasoning behind this has been ease of validation of the data that you provide on the aid application. In seeking consistency and ease of validation of the data, the Congress attempted to eliminate home equity from consideration in the formula. If this stands, it will make a significant difference in which families can qualify for aid. Imagine the family with $100,000 home equity and a taxable income of $24,000 that might not have previously qualified for educational assistance from the federal government. They may now be entitled to substantial help. Members of the financial aid community continue to seek a "fair and equitable" treatment of home equity.

Pell Grant—Student Eligibility Report

If you apply for federal aid in the form of a Pell Grant, you will be mailed a student Eligibility Report in triplicate that tells you whether or not you qualify for the BEOG. Like all financial aid correspondence, be very careful with all three parts of the form. You will need to turn them in to the school of your final choice so that the money you are to receive can be applied to your student account. If your student is considering several schools, you will want to make copies of the BEOG (Pell) SER (the Basic Educational Opportunity Grant Student Eligibility Report) that is sent to you and forward these to the financial aid officers at the schools which are being considered.

The Pell Grant consists entirely of grants or gift money. In recent years students have received up to $1,750 in grant assistance depending on their family income, assets, and the cost of the school the student attends.

A summary of the BEOG would be as follows:

1. It has its own formula, determined by Congress.
2. The range of aid is determined by amount of funds appropriated by Congress.
3. It is a grant or gift.
4. The amount may be affected by the cost of the chosen school.

GUARANTEED STUDENT LOAN

The Guaranteed Student Loan (GSL) is another major noncampus based federal program for undergraduate and graduate students. The G.S.L. program will be discussed in detail in Chapter 16. Suffice it to say that these are low-interest loans available to students to help with their educational cost. To apply for these loans, contact a local bank, savings and loan, credit union, or other thrift institution and ask for a Guaranteed Student Loan application. If for any reason you are refused, contact the financial aid office at the school to which you are applying.

PARENT LOANS

The concept of parent loans is a new one to the financial aid community. These are generally not packaged as part of an aid award but are supplemental. For more information see Chapter 16 on loans.

CAMPUS-BASED PROGRAMS

Among the campus-based federal programs there are essentially three major choices for the financial aid officer to consider in packaging an award. They are the SEOG, the NDSL, and the CWSP.

SEOG

The SEOG is the Supplementary Educational Opportunity Grant program. These funds are provided to help students with large aid eligibility to have sufficient grant assistance to meet part of the cost of their school. If the financial aid officer includes SEOG in your package, it is a good thing to have. Like BEOG, the SEOG is gift money; it does not have to be repaid upon graduating or leaving school. Recent inflationary price increases have caused a dramatic increase in the need for SEOG.

NDSL

NDSL, the National Direct Student Loan program, has been helping students for many years. The original concept was that the money would be loaned to students interest free while they were in school. Upon graduation students would repay the loan with interest at 3 percent per year. Because of high inflation and low interest rates, these funds have not become self-supporting as originally planned. Each year the government must pour hundreds of millions into this fund to keep it solvent at each school. These loan funds became famous early in the Carter administration when attempts were made to get delinquent accounts repaid. For years many students had been reaping the benefits of such loans and neglecting repayment. Repayment rates varied substantially among institutions. Recently the federal government has started to study the repayment rates of different schools before providing them with more funds to lend out. Each year there are debates in Congress about the NDSL program and about raising the interest rate (which was 3 percent for many years and was recently raised to 4 percent).

In years past many families did not want their students to take loans for college education. Because of the high inflation rate and low interest rates on the loans, few people object to these loans today. They are almost like gifts because the students repay them in less valuable dollars many years later. Again, we the taxpayers subsidize this give-away program, but if you are paying for it and qualify, you might as well take advantage of it. The financial aid officer will decide if the student receives these funds.

If the student is awarded an NDSL as part of the financial aid package, it should probably be accepted. When the student registers, it will be necessary to sign papers relative to the loan, including an affidavit saying that these funds are going to be used for educational purposes. Before the student leaves school or graduates, there will probably be another loan meeting to learn about repayment plans and schedules. As long as the student continues half-time education, deferments will probably be available. Thus, a student pursuing a law degree could conceivably borrow money in the fall as a freshman and not begin repayment until sometime after June of the seventh year. Of course, if the student left school in between for any length of time, repayment would have to begin.

CWSP

CWSP is the College Work Study program. Under this program the student is usually assigned an amount which can be earned during the school year. Schools have different methods of handling job assignments and pay scales. With a few exceptions the law requires that the working students be paid at least minimum wage. As minimum wage has been pushed upward rapidly by legislation, students have benefited by receiving much more income from the same number of hours of work. On the other hand, the increase in minimum wage has sometimes limited the number of campus jobs available. In one work study program students were assigned work in amounts equal to 10 hours per week for all 15 weeks of a semester. Thus, if minimum wage was $3.50 and the student was going to be working both semesters, the work study award (CWSP) could be calculated as follows:

$$\$3.50 \times 10 \times 15 \times 2 = \$1,050$$

Minimum wage × Hours per week × Number of weeks in a semester × Number of semesters = Total work study award

The amount in this case, $1,050, would be built into the aid award to help meet the aid eligibility.

Research indicates that students with jobs tend to do better in school. How much should a student work while trying to carry a full course load? There is no magic answer because there are so many variables including the student, the difficulty of the courses, the type of job, and the student's other involvements. It always seems criminal if a student tries to work so much that he or she cannot enjoy the fun and excitement of the campus activities that are such a major part of college.

Once the student has an amount of work assigned, the questions are always what kinds of jobs are open to students and how are they assigned. Again, schools vary substantially in their policies and practices in this area. Using our program as an example, we surveyed students on job skills and used this information to place students in jobs in conjunction with requests from the employers (departments). Generally, but not exclusively, the upper-class students got jobs as lab assistants, research assistants, and other office jobs; students new to the system received clerical, maintenance, and food-service jobs. These were not exclusive by any means. For example, some of the best students really liked the physical activity involved in maintenance work. If your student is awarded work study (CWSP), you will have to inquire how the system works at the school he or she is planning to attend—there are different systems at different schools.

Six Major Federal Programs

There are six major federal programs available to undergraduates—three noncampus-based and three campus-based—which are administered by the financial aid office.

Noncampus-Based	*Campus-Based*
Basic Educational Opportunity Grant (Pell Grant) (BEOG)	Supplementary Educational Opportunity Grant (SEOG)
Guaranteed Student Loan (GSL)	National Direct Student Loan (NDSL)
Parents' Loan Program (PLP)	College Work Study Program (CWSP)

Beyond federal resources the financial aid director can include state aid programs, institutional aid programs, and other aid sources such as local and national scholarship competitions. As was mentioned earlier, the state programs vary significantly.

STATE

While there will be no attempt to detail the state programs here, it is important to stress that these can be an extremely large sources of funds for any student who has aid eligibility. When advising students considering both in-state and out-of-state schools, I often suggest that they look at the difference in aid packages before making up their minds. In some cases, students who go to school out of state (with no state help) find that they get more loans and work study in their package of aid than the student who stays in his or her own state for schooling. It is not uncommon though for state grant programs to provide large amounts for need- and nonneed-based assistance to resident students who attend schools in the home state. Sometimes this money is given to equalize the cost of public and private education within the state.

It is difficult to stress just how important it is to investigate what your own state will do for you and what the rules are. Some states have agreements with other states so that a student can take home-state money and attend an institution in another state. Your high school guidance office will probably have information available on your state programs. Information on other states may be available to the counselor; ask to have this researched.

INSTITUTIONS

The kinds of resources available at institutions vary substantially between schools. Some schools have large financial aid endowments given by alumni, friends, and foundations; others have virtually nothing. It is not uncommon for private schools with an enrollment of 1,000 students to have financial aid budgets well in excess of $500,000, or $500 per student. Most schools have some kind of grant dollars in their financial aid resources. Schools also have their own loan programs and even their own work programs. Many of these resources can be used to complete an aid package. Often the aid officer has the most discretion in how these funds are used.

Most of the rules governing the use of institutional funds are generated by the institution and the athletic conference to which it belongs. Many schools have agreements with other schools with whom their athletes compete to award aid on the same or similar basis. This is supposed to help reduce "the buying of athletes," but it is difficult to monitor and there are always questions about what is appropriate.

While most institutions have not yet dealt with the reality of this, most institutional grants or scholarships are really just a method to discount the price of education to your student. As the student market continues to tighten, discounting (awarding grants and scholarships) will become more important. You will probably want to maximize your discount whether because of aid eligibility or because of other qualities such as academic or athletic excellence. The most effective way that I know to do this is to let the school know what you want. Suppose you are offered the following:

Institutional grant	$ 500
State grant	1,000
Loan	500
Work	1,000
	$3,000

Your aid eligibility is $3,200, or $200 more than the school is offering. You might write to the admissions or financial aid office, particularly at a small school, and suggest that you will consider the school if the package is as follows:

Institutional grant	$ 800
State grant	1,000
Loan	500
Work	800
	$3,100

The worst the school can do is say that there is no room for negotiation. However, if they really think that the slight difference (out of a budget of several million) will cause your student to enroll, they may very well succumb to your pressure for a further discount. In a sense you are simply offering less and asking for a larger discount. The use of institutional funds is a very misunderstood area by financial aid officers, admissions people, college administration, faculty, and parents who receive these moneys. What is truly a discounting technique is cloaked in some mysterious discussion of social responsibility. Be aware that there may be flexible dollars that your persuasion could bring in your direction. You will never know if you don't ask.

PRIVATE

One of the things that you should consider for your student is if either the company(s) you work for or club(s) that you belong to have scholarship or grant money available. Many of these dollars go untapped every year because people do not bother to check with their personnel office to see what kinds of benefits may be available to their students. Similarly, many people worked for or contributed to scholarship funds for organizations that they belong to. What about you? Have you investigated these opportunities thoroughly?

Many local groups have scholarship and aid programs, including the American Association of University Women, Jaycees, Rotary clubs, teacher associations, and small foundations. These are all worth checking into and completing the application process. Start by asking the high school counselor what local scholarships are available. Reportedly there are books out to help with this search—check your local library for the resources they have available. Some of the programs you come across will not be based on your income. So much the better.

There are some well-known national programs, but most of these are academically based scholarships, and your high school counselor will probably recommend that your student start this process early if it is applicable.

Institutions always like to see you bring outside scholarships with you because it reduces the need to use institutional dollars for a student. For example, assume the family contribution is $2,000 and the total cost of the institution is $5,000. Then the aid eligibility is $3,000.

$$\text{Total cost} - \text{Family contribution} = \text{Aid eligibility}$$
$$\$5,000 - \$2,000 = \$3,000$$

If you bring a $1,000 scholarship with you from a local source and have a $1,000 state grant or scholarship, then the school only needs to find

Chapter 15: Sources of Aid

$1,000 in aid from its own resources to help you attend. In other words, your resources total $4,000.

Family contribution	$2,000
Local scholarship	1,000
State grant or scholarship	1,000
	$4,000

Total cost − Resources = Demand on institutional resources
or remaining aid eligibility
$5,000   − $4,000   = $1,000

Schools vary on how they handle the remaining aid eligibility. It would help your student greatly to have reduced the remaining aid eligibility down to $1,000, since the school has a much better chance of helping with $1,000. Thus, outside grants and scholarships can be extremely helpful in meeting your full aid eligibility.

Chapter 16

Loans

There are four major loan programs that most undergraduate students are likely to get involved in. These are:

National Direct Student Loan (NDSL).
Guaranteed Student Loan (GSL).
State Direct Student Loan (SDSL).
Parent Loan Program (PLP)

NDSL

The NDSL, as discussed in Chapter 15 requires that you file an aid application and have aid eligibility; it is awarded to you by the financial aid office. The GSL and the SDSL are actually different forms of the same loan program, but the funds come from a lending institution in the case of the former and directly from the state in the case of the latter. The GSL, or Guaranteed Student Loan, will be discussed first.

The GSL was a program to help families and students meet the expected family contribution. Originally, if your income was below approximately $30,000, the federal government would pay the interest on the loan while the student was in school. When the student left school or graduated, then interest would begin at the rate of 7 percent.

Chapter 16: Loans

Like the previously discussed NDSL, there was a one-time, nine-month (now six months) grace period after leaving school or graduating before the student must begin repayment.

In October of 1978 the Middle Income Assistance Act was passed. This removed all income limits from this loan fund, meaning that any student—no matter what the family income—could get this loan interest free while the student was in school. Taxpayers were to pay the interest for any student who wanted to take this loan. This, of course, meant that at last there was a desirable loan program for every student who wanted aid in the form of loans.

Students suddenly found that they could borrow up to $2,500 a year, or a maximum of $7,500 at zero interest while in school to be repaid at the rate of 7 percent. This has now been raised to a maximum of $12,500, to be repaid at 9 percent, and there are discussions of raising it further.

HOW IS THE GSL USED WITH AID?

Many families find that, despite revisions in the aid system, they are having difficulty coming up with the entire family contribution. Assume for example that they spend too much money on other family essentials because of inflationary prices. Further, assume that the family is supposed to contribute $4,000 toward the cost of education. Perhaps the breakdown is something like this:

Expected Contribution for the Brooks Family

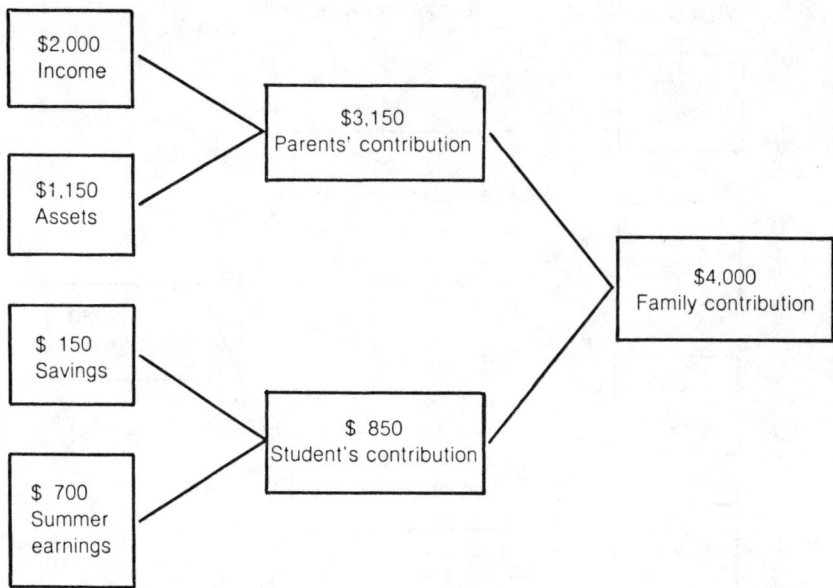

Difficulty with Family Contribution

In reviewing hundreds of families' personal financial situations, it became very clear to me that there are many ways for a budget to get out of kilter. Unexpected things happen to everyone. Some of these difficulties might be:

1. The summer job for the student falls through.
2. The water heater has to be replaced.
3. The pool requires major work.
4. The car has to be rebuilt or replaced.
5. The expenses of maintaining a younger sibling in the tennis circuit or orthodontist expenses are high.
6. An elderly parent requires assistance.
7. Unexpected medical bills.
8. Cash flow problems occur.
9. The formula is not a fair measure of family's situation.

Whatever the reason, many families do not feel that they can come up with the money projected as their family contribution. If there is, in fact, a major change in income, this should be reported to and discussed with the financial aid office at the school your student is planning to attend. They may be able to review the whole situation and create a new award.

The Brooks family that was supposed to come up with $4,000 for Florence may be able to provide only $2,850.

What Brooks Believe They Can Contribute

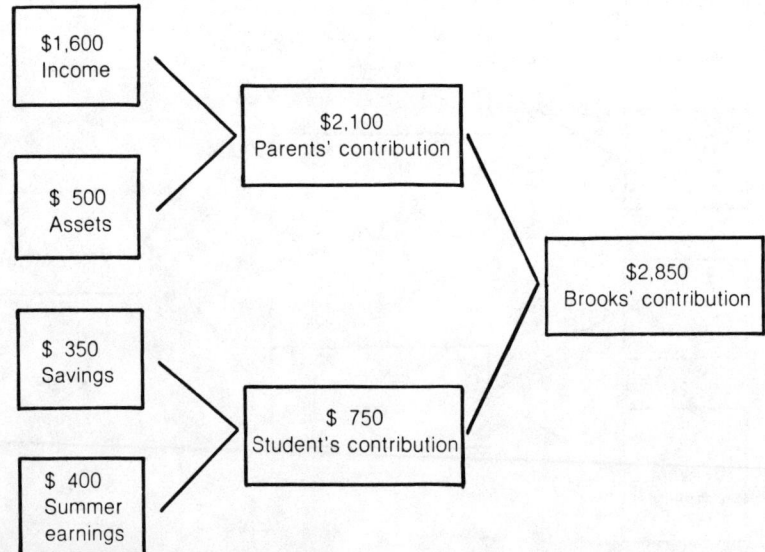

GSL Helps When Family Contribution Falls Short

Assuming that the Brooks' expected family contribution is $4,000, there will be a gap of $1,150 between what the school is going to expect the Brooks to provide and what they actually will provide—$4,000 less what they have, $2,850.

$$\underset{\substack{\text{Expected} \\ \text{family} \\ \text{contribution}}}{\$4,000} - \underset{\substack{\text{Brooks'} \\ \text{actual} \\ \text{contribution}}}{\$2,850} = \underset{\text{Gap}}{\$1,150}$$

This is where the GSL can be extremely useful. While the Guaranteed Student Loan is considered aid, it does not have to be used to meet part of the aid eligibility with the exception that all aid a student is receiving may not total more than the budgeted cost of attending school for the period under consideration. The Brooks' situation:

Cost of school	$7,500
Less expected family contribution	4,000
Aid eligibility	3,500
Less total aid	3,369
Unmet aid eligibility	131
Unmet family contribution (Gap)	1,150
Minimum requirement—GSL	1,281

Theoretically, they can borrow anything they want to up to $2,500 and use it to replace the family contribution. This is because the family contribution is greater than the $2,500 limit. Many families in circumstances like the Brooks would only borrow the $1,150. But many other families would borrow more, figuring that it is hard to beat having the interest paid by the rest of the taxpayers.

The Brooks might be rightfully hesitant about taking on another loan of between $1,000 and $2,500 with two more children to educate. When they file for a GSL they will be pleased to find that the *student* is incurring the responsibility for repaying the loan, not the parents. *Thus, Florence Brooks is taking on financial responsibility for her own education.* When Florence graduates, leaves school, or anytime before or after that, the Brooks may give money to Florence to help her reduce or pay off her loan commitment. If Florence decides to continue on in graduate school, then she could again defer payment and even borrow additional funds until she has completed her program or left school.

Loan Dollars Are for Educational Purposes

If Florence borrows more than the $1,150 that she apparently needs to help fund the family contribution, then she needs to be aware of the following:

1. The dollars she has borrowed were borrowed for educational expenses and should only be used for that purpose. New stereos, trips to visit roommates, and presents for parents are not legitimate uses of these dollars.
2. If Florence still has some of the Guaranteed Student Loan funds that she borrowed in January of her freshman year at the time she applies for aid for her sophomore year, then she should be careful not to list the amount of the borrowed funds as savings if she will use the funds to pay for the balance of her freshman year.

The latter is a common costly mistake made by students who have Guaranteed Student Loans. If Florence reports an extra $1,000 in her savings account, it will reduce her aid eligibility by $350 for the next year. Florence should subtract out any funds that came from the Guaranteed Student Loan and report the remaining balance as her savings. In this way her aid will be calculated on her true savings and not on her borrowing.

GSL Limits

The limits of the GSL are important (see Table 16–1).

1. As previously mentioned, your student's Guaranteed Student Loan, plus other aid, cannot total more than the school's budget cost. This appears to be more of a problem when there is a low family contribution (high aid eligibility).

TABLE 16–1
Calculations of Maximum GSL

	Cost of School			
	A	B	C	D*
	$9,000	$7,000	$5,000	$3,000
Family contribution.................	2,500	2,500	2,500	2,500
Aid eligibility	6,500	4,500	2,500	500
Aid................................	6,350	4,500	2,000	1,000
Unmet aid eligibility...............	150	0	500	(−500)†
Unmet aid eligibility plus family contribution............	2,650	2,500	3,000	2,000
Maximum GSL	2,500	2,500	2,500	2,000

* For School D the family cannot borrow more than the $2,000 limit because they would be exceeding the total budget. The other families are limited by the $2,500 maximum and could be further limited by the actual lender that they were working with.
† School D overawarded the student perhaps a special scholarship.

2. It takes some time to process a GSL in most areas. If you are going to need or want this kind of assistance, be sure you apply for a GSL in plenty of time. Families should plan on a processing time for a GSL of 6 to 10 weeks. In many areas you may apply beginning April 1,

Chapter 16: Loans

for the fall. Thus a senior in high school may be well advised to apply as soon as the student knows what school he or she will be attending.

3. Like everything else about financial aid, the GSL has to be reapplied for every year, and the student has to be reapproved.

4. If your student borrows money for a full year and only goes half a year, or switches schools or programs in a way that may change the cost, then your student's eligibility for the GSL may change.

5. If your student leaves school, then the lending agent should be notified by both the student and the school.

Graduate Students

Graduate students can borrow up to $5,000 a year through the GSL program to a maximum of $25,000. This can be of substantial help if older children wish to go on for professional schooling.

Change in Situation

To help clarify the GSL, look at the case of John Price. John is one of four children from a family with a comfortable income of $40,000 a year and some assets. After the original awards from several schools, John's father was laid off as part of the automotive-related layoffs. This, of course, radically changed the family situation. After consultation I encouraged John to inform his schools of all the details so that they could recalculate his aid awards.

John Price's GSL Maximum Limits

	A	B	C	D
Original Situation				
Cost of School	$7,500	$6,000	$4,500	$3,000
Family contribution	3,000	3,000	3,000	3,000
Aid eligibility	4,500	3,000	1,500	0
Aid and scholarship	4,400	2,500	2,250*	750*
Unmet aid eligibility	100	500	(−750)	(−750)
Unmet aid eligibility plus family contribution	3,100	3,500	2,250	2,250
Maximum GSL	2,500	2,500	2,250	2,250
Revised Situation				
Family contribution	$1,250	$1,250	$1,250	$1,250
Aid eligibility	6,250	4,750	3,250	1,750
Aid and scholarship	6,000	4,000	2,250	1,500
Unmet aid eligibility	250	750	100	250
Unmet aid eligibility plus family contribution	1,500	2,000	1,350	1,500
Maximum GSL	1,500	2,000	1,350	1,500

* Honor scholarship.

It is easy to see what happens to John's ability to use the GSL. The family contribution dropped from $3,000 to $1,000. This change, when carried through the whole process by the individual schools, also affected how much GSL John could be eligible for at any given school. Note that in the original situation some honor scholarships were apparently driving his aid above his aid eligibility. These honor dollars limit what else John Price can receive or borrow. Many times after a student's complete package has been worked out they will receive an honor award of some amount. Students often find it difficult to understand why the other aid should be affected or even reduced.

Following John's situation through you will see that schools react differently to John's changed situation. Thus, the amount of GSL that John can use varies. The maximum loan may not be available at the most expensive schools because these school(s) made John and his family a much better aid offer.

	School			
	A	B	C	D
Original GSL limit	$2,500	$2,500	$2,250	$2,250
Revised GSL limit	1,500	2,000	1,350	1,500
Change	(1,000)	(500)	(900)	(750)

If John had previously applied for a $2,500 GSL, believing he would attend School A, he would have to change his application. Some families expect to go ahead and use the extra $1,000 to help them through their difficult situation. This, unfortunately, would not work as it would make John's total aid more than the cost. Thus, the GSL at school A for his changed situation is:

Aid	$6,000
GSL	2,500
Total aid	$8,500
Less cost	7,500
Overaward	$1,000

and this GSL amount has to be reduced to $1,500 so that an overaward does not occur.

Aid	$6,000
GSL	1,500
Total aid	$7,500
Less cost	7,500
Overaward	0

Multiple Loans

Schools have different policies on NDSL and GSL loans that are created locally. One such school policy is that a student may not have both a GSL and an NDSL. There are many good reasons for this type of local institutional policy. It avoids having a student pay back on two sets of loans after graduation. Further, it keeps the volume of total loan dollars for any one student as low as possible. The biggest difficulty that this causes for families is that the GSL can replace the NDSL, but the NDSL cannot necessarily replace the GSL. Further, in most cases the student is being artificially limited by the school in the amount of money that he or she can have.

Consider the Berger family and their son, Max. The Bergers had planned on Max using the Guaranteed Student Loan to help with his educational cost because their growing business was absorbing all the cash they currently had available. In the future they planned to help Max repay the loan. Max's aid was as follows:

School cost		$7,000
Less family contribution		3,500
Aid eligibility		$3,500
Aid award:		
State grant	$1,000	
Work	1,000	
Grant	700	
NDSL	700	
Total		$3,400
Unmet aid eligibility		$ 100

Since the Bergers had planned on borrowing $2,500 from GSL sources, in addition to the $700 National Direct Student Loan, they had planned on a total of $3,200 in loans. If they can only use one loan fund or the other at some institutions because of internal policy, then the most that they can borrow under GSL is $2,500, and under NDSL, $800 ($700 NDSL assigned plus $100 in unmet aid eligibility). Either way the school has severely limited the Bergers' options. The cost of the school policy in loan dollars to the Berger family for one year would be:

	GSL	NDSL
Expected limit	$2,500	$ 800
Cost to Bergers in lost loan dollars of using only one loan fund	700	2,400
Total	$3,200	$3,200

It is important as you make your final choice of schools to be sure that local institutional policies (such as the loan policy of allowing only

NDSL or GSL, but not both) do not hamper you or make your aid situation more difficult than it should be. If Max Berger wishes to go to school under the circumstances, the best thing for him to do is to take the GSL and to forget the NDSL. Unfortunately, the school will be depriving him of the extra $700 or $800 in lower-interest money (NDSL, 4 percent; GSL, 9 percent). Recent legislation has eliminated much of the need for such concerns by schools. Consolidation of education loans will be made possible. Thus, if a student has multiple-loan sources, it may be possible to eliminate multiple-loan payments.

Use the GSL if Possible

Many families who should be considering the Guaranteed Student Loan are not even aware that it is available to them. This is one form of aid that has for the last two years been open to almost everyone. This means that even if the family income was $1 million a year, the student could still use these loans.

Financial aid officers report that there are tremendous increases in the volume of applications for these loans as people have learned that you do not have to reveal your income or answer all the questions on the various aid forms to take advantage of these opportunities.

As some parents have pointed out to me, it is almost foolish not to use the Guaranteed Student Loan. Where else can you get interest-free and low-interest money? Such recognition is putting tremendous demands on the system. Some state lenders have had to regularly delay loans while they have gone into the bond market to seek the needed capital to cover the obligations. This often has delayed the approval of loans. This is a case where the early bird gets the worm. Those who come later will, in all likelihood, receive their money, but it may be many weeks or even months later.

Changes Possible

Because of the high cost of the loan subsidies being paid by the taxpayers, there are some discussions in the Congress and in the educational community about putting income limits back on the GSL or increasing the interest rates. Be sure to find out what, if any, restrictions there are on these loans before you incorporate them into your plans.

Protect Yourself

If you decide to borrow through the GSL program, it is important to be aware of the rules and safeguards. A student borrowing the money is stating that the funds borrowed are to be used for educational expenses.

The best suggestion is to have the check made payable to the student and the school, and use it for payment of tuition and other expenses. This gives the student proof in the form of a paper trail that the actual dollars borrowed from the taxpayers (government) are being used for legitimate educational expenses. While there has been little verification to date, many in the financial aid community have expressed concern over the use of these funds. It will probably not be long before someone in Washington decides to launch an investigation. To prevent future difficulties for yourself, it would be wise to keep a good record of what happened to the borrowed funds.

Some families have wisely handled this by opening a separate account and writing down the reason for each withdrawal from that account. The history might look as follows for a family who borrowed $2,500 in two installments, one in September and one in January.

Record of Angela's GSL Expenditures

Date	Reason	Deposit	Withdrawal
September 1	Received first GSL check	$1,250	
5	Tuition payment added to $1,000 summer savings for first of three terms		$ 450.00
18	Book expenses for English Composition, History of Civilization, Intro. to Biology		78.95
28	Books and supplies		25.73
October 10	Personal expenses and supplies		75.00
December 1	Ticket home		198.00
3	Advance payment on tuition for winter term		400.00
January 3	Received second check	1,250	
8	Tuition payment plus $600 from mom and dad		450.00
9	Books		96.00
March 8	Tuition payment for spring term with $750 from folks		700.00
28	Final withdrawal from bank (used for books for spring)		26.32
		$2,500	$2,500.00

Obviously, not all of Angela's expenses would be reflected in her record, but that is not important. What is important is that she has a record that indicates that she spent all the money she borrowed for educational purposes. If she or her parents simultaneously bought her a new stereo, a car, or a trip to the Bahamas for Christmas, it is not important.

However, if careful records are not maintained, it could appear that the money borrowed for educational purposes was actually used for a stereo, car, or trip. To avoid problems later, keep good records if you borrow these funds. Wherever possible have proof that the dollars were used for what they were intended.

Strategies for Using GSL

Despite all the precautions, the Guaranteed Student Loan is still a great opportunity, especially for the successful family. There are a number of strategies that can be employed to use the dollars to the best benefit of the student. In the case of Angela, suppose that her parents could easily pay the full tuition. Instead of doing so, her parents encouraged her to take the loan. Her parents then bought for her an equivalent amount of bonds due to mature within the year after Angela expected to finish school.

1. Many bonds have an established maturity date and full cash value at maturity in dollars.
2. The bond interest would be far better for the small amount of $2,500 than he could hope to get for Angela through their local bank.

Angela's situation looked like this over the four years.

		Debts	Assets
Year 1, freshman	Loan for $2,500	$2,500	
	Father gave three bonds due in year 5 at coupon rate of 5 percent*		$2,500
Year 2, sophomore	Loan for $2,500	2,500	
	Interest on three bonds purchased in year 1		150
	Father gave three bonds due in year 5 at coupon rate of 4 percent*		2,500
Year 3, junior	Loan for $2,500	2,500	
	Interest on three bonds purchased in year 1		150
	Interest on three bonds purchased in year 2		120
	Father gave three bonds due in year 5 at coupon rate of 6 percent*		2,500
Year 4	No loan		
	Interest on bonds from year 1		150
	Interest on bonds from year 2		120
	Interest on bonds from year 3		180
Year 5	No loan		
	Interest on bonds from year 1		150
	Interest on bonds from year 2		120
	Interest on bonds from year 3		180

* Bonds bought at discount ($3,000 face value for $2,500).

Note: If Angela qualified for other aid, the bonds should be held in father's name to avoid inclusion in Angela's student asset base.

At the end of year 5 Angela will have received the following:

Year 1 bonds mature	$ 3,000
Year 2 bonds mature	3,000
Year 3 bonds mature	3,000
Interest from all bonds since year 1	1,320
Total receipts	$10,320
Less total debt	7,500
Net	2,820

Angela will have to decide whether she should pay off her loan at 7 percent or pay it off all at once and keep the profit of $2,820. Either way at virtually no cost to himself, Angela's father has helped her to develop a tidy little nest egg. This would be particularly true if she reinvested the $10,000 at 12 percent and paid off the loan out of her earnings. (There has been no attempt to take out brokerage commissions or account for interest on interest.) You can see what a potentially terrific tool the Guaranteed Student Loan can be as long as Angela uses the actual dollars borrowed for her education. Her father might have chosen any number of investments. Bonds appeared at the time to be safer than the volatile stock market.

If Angela's father had not put aside the money each year and bought the bonds, then Angela might have graduated with a substantial debt of $7,500 and no way of paying it off until she got a job. This would have been unfortunate for Angela.

It does not take much to imagine the dramatic increase that Angela could have generated if she pursued a graduate professional program for three years and thus all interest would have been waived as long as she continued as a qualified student. For example, if she took her $10,000 and could average 12 percent a year, she could have over $14,000 by the time she completes her graduate program, still owing only $7,500 at 7 percent. She might have even more if her parents continued to let her borrow for graduate study and then made a gift to her each year. As a graduate student, Angela could borrow through the GSL program up to $5,000 a year. In special programs there could be additional funds available. Creative financing leads to unlimited possibilities.

More GSL Ideas

Some families with a number of children in school have found that if the children pay for a portion of their own education using the GSL, then the same amount of money can be attractively invested in long-term certificates with savings and thrift institutions. For example, if you have one graduate student at $5,000 and two undergraduates at $2,500, the total amount of money that you have available because the children borrowed would be $10,000. In the current interest market, some attractive long-term rates have been available for that amount of money. Since this is money that you would normally have spent, it will not matter that it is not easily accessible and, therefore, protected for loan repayment. It is important to remember the gift tax laws if the amount invested for the children in the parents' names begins to get large.

One parent I worked with puts the money in a money market fund that offers Visa and checking. He uses the money to pay college bills but earns maximum interest until the check clears. With three children in school, he figures he picks up an extra few hundred dollars in interest.

Financial Guardians

It has struck me as curious that people responsible for the children of others, particularly bank trust officers and attorneys, do not help young people take advantage of the kind of financing open to them through the GSL, thus preserving intact a large share of the estate that their parents or grandparents may have left them. One young woman graduated with nothing—not even the money for a bus ticket home. The officer in charge of her trust had simply paid the bills and never considered ways of preserving the principal. With careful management the young woman could have graduated with almost $10,000 available to her and a very low interest loan. She could have made the choice to pay off the loan or keep the loan and invest the principal.

Where to Apply

How do you get one of these Guaranteed Student Loans? The first place to apply for a Guaranteed Student Loan is from your bank, savings and loan, credit union, or other thrift institution. Over the years some banks have gone back and forth on the decision to participate in the program. Plan early. Find out if your bank does participate and whether or not your student would be considered for a loan. Some banks limit loans to students of regular customers. This makes sense because many banks see the processing of these loans as a service that they provide for their "good customers." By planning ahead you may find a thrift institution that will make a loan and also have time to meet the institutional, bank, or credit union requirements. Incidentally, parents have been very complimentary of credit unions in providing Guaranteed Student Loans.

The Application

The application form itself is not really difficult. It consists of a few questions designed to help the lender keep track of the borrower, such as the names of relatives, records of other loans that the student may have, and a notarized statement about the purpose of the loan. Once the student has completed the loan application, then it is forwarded to the school for processing. *Remember, the loans are made to the students and not to the parents.* Parents do not even have to cosign for the loan.

Processing Delays

There is frequently a delay in the school's processing of a GSL application, especially during July, August, and September. In some cases from the time a loan application arrives at a school, it could be several weeks before the school processes it and forwards it on to the next step in the approval process. Once again, the message is plan ahead. If you can, start the loan application in April or May before the September when your student will need the funds.

What if You Are Refused?

Some people are refused by banks or unable to find a participating bank. In this case you should check with the financial aid office at the school the student is planning to attend. There are usually alternatives to banks; for example, in many states the schools will accept your application for an SDSL, or State Direct Student Loan, if you have been refused by the banks. To obtain an application, contact the financial aid office at the school. The application process is very similar to the Guaranteed Student Loan. The state has to seek the funds in the bond market, which sometimes can create added delays beyond the processing time delays already mentioned. On the other hand this system assures that almost every student can get an SDSL or GSL if they feel they need it.

The SDSL

There are virtually no differences between the GSL and the SDSL. In both cases the student is doing the borrowing. In both cases repayment does not begin until after a student completes full-time study or leaves school. In both cases there is a one-time, six-month grace period before a student needs to go into repayment. The interest rates have been paid by the taxpayers while the student is in school. When the student goes into repayment, the rate will be at either the old 7 percent or the new 9 percent rate, and the taxpayers will pick up the difference between that and the current interest rates.

Why Banks Participate

Many people wonder why a bank would participate in a loan at 9 percent except as a public service. But the banks make out all right. They have a guarantee from the federal government that they will receive an interest rate that fluctuates with the open market rates (according to a formula). Like the Chrysler loan, all this money is theoretically guaranteed to the bankers—not only the interest rates but the principal as well—should the student borrower default. It will be interesting to see how this system works in a few years when several billion dollars are outstanding.

Potential Changes

There are many changes being contemplated now in Congress. As has been stressed before, good financial practice includes a great deal of planning. You will have to investigate what changes have actually occurred when you are making your preparations and plans for college cost.

Higher Interest Rates

An obvious consideration for Congress would be to raise the interest rate from 9 percent to some more current figure, considering the continued expected inflation rate. A Congress that continues to promise a free lunch must continue to print more money and thus drive the inflation cycle even higher. It would not be unreasonable to raise the interest rate for repayment to near-market levels and still have the loan be an excellent deal for students.

Another idea that has been discussed is to put an income limit back on the loans. This would apply particularly to the State Direct Student Loan, but as in the past, it might mean that students above a certain family income would have to pay the interest while in school. This, of course, makes the whole loan process much less attractive to the borrower.

Use the GSL or SDSL if You Can

In conclusion, Guaranteed Student Loans (GSL and SDSL) are a great asset in financing an education. You should make every effort to use them as part of the total package to finance your student's education.

Chapter 16: Loans

Remember, the key to financial aid is investigating and planning ahead to be in the best position to take advantage of the resources available.

PARENTS' LOAN PROGRAM

The Parents' Loan Program (PLP) was first authorized by Congress in the fall of 1980. Under this program, parents of students should be able to borrow up to $3,000 a year per student at 9 percent interest (a total of $15,000). The major points in the Parent Loan Program as originally authorized are as follows:

1. The loans are made directly to the parents of students and are the *liability of the parent*. In the other loan programs that have been discussed, the loan is made to the student (NDSL, GSL, and SDSL).
2. Repayment begins within 60 days. This means that even if the government is willing to pay a portion of the interest, you will not have the money to work with as long.

There are a number of exciting possibilities for the planner in financial aid if the Parents' Loan Program does become fully operational.

Ease of Payment

Using the Parents' Loan Program will allow you to even out the cash flow problems that often occur in financing a college education. Some schools are very creative about understanding the financial problems of families. They provide services to allow for, in effect, time payments. But this is not true at many schools, and the Parents' Loan Program will provide that kind of flexibility. Table 16–2 shows that with a 9 percent

TABLE 16–2
Repayment of $3,000 at 9 percent*

Number of Months to Repay	Approximate Monthly Payment
12	$262.35
24	137.05
36	95.40
48	74.66
60	62.28
72	54.08
84	48.27
96	43.95
108	40.63

* Money borrowed in September of freshman year.

interest rate, $3,000 can easily be broken down into 12 monthly payments of less than $265. This should help with cash flow problems. Of course the longer the repayment period, the smaller the payments, and thus the more helpful the Parents' Loan Program will be to parents with cash problems. Table 16–3 shows estimated payments at higher interest rates should the rates be raised.

TABLE 16–3
One-Year and Five-Year Repayment Schedules for $3,000 at Various Percentages

Annual Percentage Rate	Approximate Monthly Repayment of $3,000	
	Over One Year	Over Five Years
10	$263.75	$63.74
11	265.14	65.23
12	266.55	66.73
13	267.95	68.66
14	269.36	69.80
15	270.77	71.37
16	272.19	72.95
17	273.61	74.56
18	275.04	76.18
19	276.47	77.82
20	277.90	79.48
21	279.34	81.16

Nonliquid Assets

Many families have nonliquid assets—those that cannot easily be converted to cash. If you own 100 acres of land worth $100,000, you cannot necessarily sell off three acres every time you want $3,000. Further, there are all kinds of tax consequences that sometimes mean it would be better to wait and sell at a different time. Or installment sales may slow up the flow of funds that you need to help pay for college education. If you find yourself unable to come up with the suggested resources even after reviewing your situation carefully, then the Parents' Loan Program may be a good way to bail yourself out. Traditionally, home equity has been a real problem for people. Families that have accumulated a large home equity cannot get their money out except by selling their home or by remortgaging the property; neither one is a very attractive prospect. The Parents' Loan Program is perfect in this case.

A Major Financial Resource

Like the GSL, the Parents' Loan Program may offer all kinds of possibilities for the shrewd financial planner. For example, a parent can have the student borrow the maximum amount through the GSL and the parent can borrow the maximum allowed through the Parents' Loan Program. Thus they save their own funds for investing. If they can generate a return of 12 percent, then over the four-year period (assuming that the education loans were at 9 percent), the family can retain $4,694 excluding tax considerations (see Table 16–4). This reduces the cost of education substantially.

TABLE 16–4
Investment of GSL and PLP Loans

	New Loan	Annual Cumulative Loan	Annual Interest Income at 12 percent	Annual Interest and Principal on PLP Expense at 9 percent Sept.–Aug.*	Total Annual Principal Payment*
Year 1:	GSL,$2,500............	$ 2,500	$ 660		
	PLP,$3,000............	3,000		$ 623	$ 411
Year 2:	GSL,$2,500............	5,000	1,320		
	PLP,$3,000............	6,000		1,370	948
Year 3:	GSL,$2,500............	7,500	1,980		
	PLP,$3,000............	9,000		2,117	1,534
Year 4:	GSL,$2,500............	10,000	2,640		
	PLP,$3,000............	12,000		2,864	2,175
Total principal on PLP...........			$6,600	$6,974	$5,068

* The first year of each loan includes only 10 months of payments.

Now see where we are:

Amount invested at 12 percent..............		$22,000
Interest received...........................		6,600
		28,600
Less:		
PLP annual payment....................	$ 6,974	
Amount owed PLP.....................	6,932	
Amount owed GSL.....................	10,000	23,906
Balance		$ 4,694

Thus, the 12 percent interest income off both loans—GSL and PLP—will just about cover 9 percent interest plus principal on PLP.

High Interest Rates

Even if the interest rates on Parents' Loans are raised to market levels, they may still be an easy way to expand your credit and protect your capital. Be sure to study the potential carefully and include this loan program (if it is available to you) in your overall tax and financial aid plans.

Guardians

Bankers, lawyers, and other guardians may be able to obtain a Parents' Loan for the student, thus conserving the estate until the young person has graduated from college and is in a better position to make critical financial decisions. Through the use of these loans, plus GSL, almost $20,000 of a student's estate might be protected until after college graduation.

Chapter 17

Packaging

Aid Packaging and How It Works

Each institution and sometimes aid officers within larger institutions have different ways of packaging aid in an attempt to ration out limited resources in a fair and equitable way. What is shown below is one system or method that might be in use someplace. Generally, the first step is to determine the student's aid eligibility at the school which is constructing the award. As was mentioned earlier, this may vary for two students in the same program because of different costs. For example, one might live in the same state as the school; the second might come from the opposite coast. Total cost then could look like this for three different students living different distances from campus:

College A	Student 1	Student 2	Student 3
Tuition	$ 5,000	$5,000	$5,000
Room and board	2,400	2,400	2,400
Books	150	150	150
Personal expenses	450	450	450
Travel	2,000	75	400
Total cost	$10,000	$8,075	$8,400

Assuming that all three students had exactly the same family contribution of $4,500, they would again have different aid eligibilities.

Total cost − Family contribution = Aid eligibility

Student 1:

$10,000 − $4,500 = $5,500

Student 2:

$8,075 − $4,500 = $3,575

Student 3:

$8,400 − $4,500 = $3,900

It is easy to see why financial aid can end up being so individualized.

With the aid eligibility for a student established, the financial aid director can then see what the "entitlements" are. What things may already belong to the student because they are determined outside of the school? An example of the process might go like this:

	Student 1	Student 2	Student 3
Aid eligibility	$5,500	$3,575	$3,900
How much BEOG is the student entitled to	600*	1,000*	0*
How much state assistance is the student entitled to?	0†	1,500†	1,500†
Outside scholarship that the student has won	0‡	200‡	0‡
Total aid so far	600	2,700	1,500
Remaining aid eligibility	4,900§	875§	2,400§

*The BEOG (Pell Grant) may work out differently for families even though they have the same family contribution under the uniform methodology.
†It is assumed that since student 1 has $2,000 in travel expenses he or she is from out of state.
‡Only student 2 has outside resources to help with college costs.
§Note the differences in the remaining aid eligibility which is to be met all or in part by campus-based federal funds (SEOG, NDSL, CWSP) and institutional funds.

Assume that the financial aid officer decides to allocate $900 to student 1 from campus-based federal funds and to make a work study assignment to each of the students. Now the situation looks like this:

	Student 1	Student 2	Student 3
Remaining aid eligibility(A)	$4,900	$875	$2,400
SEOG	900	0	0
CWSP (College Work Study Program a campus-based program)	1,000	500	1,000
Remaining aid eligibility(B)	3,000	375	1,400

College work study is awarded in different ways on campuses. Many feel that every student should have some self-help and would add it in at this point. The amounts chosen are completely arbitrary except that $1,000 equals about 10 hours work per week for 30 weeks or two semesters at $3.35 an hour, and $500 equals 5 hours per week.

Remaining aid eligibility (B) must be met with a combination of institutional grants, NDSL loan, unmet aid eligibility (or a recommendation that the student take a Guaranteed Student Loan). This is where the resources of the institution can greatly affect what the student receives, from all gift assistance to nothing. To give you an idea of what might happen, some figures have been put in place, but in no way should they be interpreted to represent a pattern for institutions giving financial aid. This is the area where institutional policy and the judgment of the financial aid officer take over.

	Student 1	Student 2	Student 3
Remaining aid eligibility(B)	$3,000	$375	$1,400
NDSL	1,000	0	600
Institutional grant	1,500	300	600
Unmet aid eligibility	$ 500	$ 75	$ 200

Thus, the total awarding for each student is as follows:

	Student 1	Student 2	Student 3
Total cost	$10,000	$8,075	$8,400
Family contribution	4,500	4,500	4,500
Aid eligibility	$ 5,500	$3,575	$3,900
BEOG	600	1,000	0
State	0	1,500	1,500
Outside	0	200	0
SEOG	900	0	0
CWSP	1,000	500	1,000
NDSL	1,000	0	600
Institutional grant	1,500	300	600
Total aid	$ 5,000	$3,500	$3,700
Unmet need (Aid eligibility − Total aid)	$ 500	$ 75	$ 200

Below, you can see that the three students have three different aid packages of grants, loans, and work:

	Federal Noncampus-Based	Campus-Based	Mythical State	Excellence University	Other
Student 1:					
Grant	$ 600	$ 900	0	$1,500	0
Loan	0	1,000	0	0	0
Work	0	1,000	0	0	0
Student 2:					
Grant	$1,000	0	$1,500	$ 300	$200
Loan	0	0	0	0	0
Work	0	500	0	0	0
Student 3:					
Grant	0	0	$1,500	$ 600	0
Loan	0	$ 600	0	0	0
Work	0	1,000	0	0	0

The actual types of aid that your student will receive in an aid package from a given institution will depend on a multitude of factors. They are hard to predict until the total cost for your student, the family contribution for your student, and the aid policies for the institution are considered. Your efforts should be on getting yourself entered properly on the aid forms. Let the professional aid officers decide what your student's types and amounts of aid should be when they package.

Like tax planning, planning ahead can help you maximize your aid eligibility and thus increase your potential for tax-free dollars. Institutions vary in their aid packaging philosophy, and you will want to ask questions about that.

1. Is need the only criteria?
2. Does past academic record influence aid?
3. Will the school make up a shortfall in state or federal dollars?
4. Is aid guaranteed for all four years as long as you can demonstrate need?
5. How much self-help (loan and work) is expected out of a student—$1,000, $1,500, or more?

Section VI
SPECIFIC STRATEGIES

Chapter 18
Divorce

Chapter 19
Gifts to Students

Chapter 20
Small Trusts

Chapter 21
Independent Students

Chapter 22
Social Security and Veterans' Benefits

Chapter 23
Pell Grant (BEOG)

Chapter 18

Divorce

There are many misconceptions about how divorce is handled in financial aid cases. In general, aid is based on the financial situation *of the parent with whom the child resides.* This situation has evolved in part because of the difficulty of dealing with both parents at once. A very few schools will ask for the other parent's (natural parent) income and asset information as well.

AID IS BASED ON CHILD'S HOME

Aid is based on the home in which the student lives. To better understand this consider the case of the Taylor family. Originally there was Mr. and Mrs. Richard Taylor and children, Roland and Susan. When Mrs. Madeline Taylor divorced Richard, she received custody of the children except for some vacation periods. When Mrs. Taylor came to a financial aid workshop she was concerned that she would never be able to get her former husband's financial information, and therefore, she did not think that her children could get financial aid. She was extremely relieved to find that since the children lived with her she could file for financial aid on her own income and assets including, of course, any payments that she received from Richard (her ex-husband). Thus, Mrs. Taylor and the children were considered as a family unit. When Mrs. Taylor completes the forms she should use a household size of three. She can do this even though the tax exemptions go to Mr. Taylor because of the large amount of child support that he is paying.

Financial Aid and Tax Status

Many parents that are separated and divorced think that the financial aid "family" must be consistent with the tax "dependents." *This is not true.* It is frequently the case that a student's primary residence will be with one parent while the other parent, not living in the home, is providing the majority of the support and, therefore, is entitled to take an exemption for that student for tax purposes. Under financial aid the student is considered part of the family where he claims residence.

Stepparent's Income

Now assume that Mrs. Taylor is considering marriage to a Mr. Wilson. Mrs. Taylor is interested in knowing what the effect would be on financial aid for Susan and Roland. The answer is that when she marries Mr. Wilson, financial aid would start considering his income and assets as part of the income and assets in the home in which Roland and Susan live. This is shown in the exhibit in this section as the Financial Aid Family after Remarriage. Like many parents in this

---

Original Family
Mr. and Mrs. Richard Taylor, Roland and Susan

Financial Aid Family	*Other Parent*
Mrs. Taylor, Roland, and Susan	Mr. Taylor

Tax Deductions
Mrs. Taylor 1   Mr. Taylor 3

*Financial Aid Family after Remarriage**

Mr. Wilson
Mrs. (Taylor) Wilson
Roland Taylor
Susan Taylor

*Assumes:
1. Mr. Wilson contributes more than $1,000, or
2. Lives in the home with the children more than six weeks, or
3. Deducts them on income tax.

---

situation, Mr. Wilson felt this was unfair; he did not think that he should have to support another man's children through college. This is a difficult argument to counter. The way that this is usually resolved is to figure out how much Mr. Wilson will actually have to help, and then let him make his decision.

Chapter 18: Divorce

Yours, Mine, and Ours!

Another example would be the Post Family (see Figure 18-1). The parents, Ivan and Jane Post, were divorced some time ago. Recently when Jane Post became the international account representative for a growing firm, it was decided that the children would live with Ivan Post

FIGURE 18-1

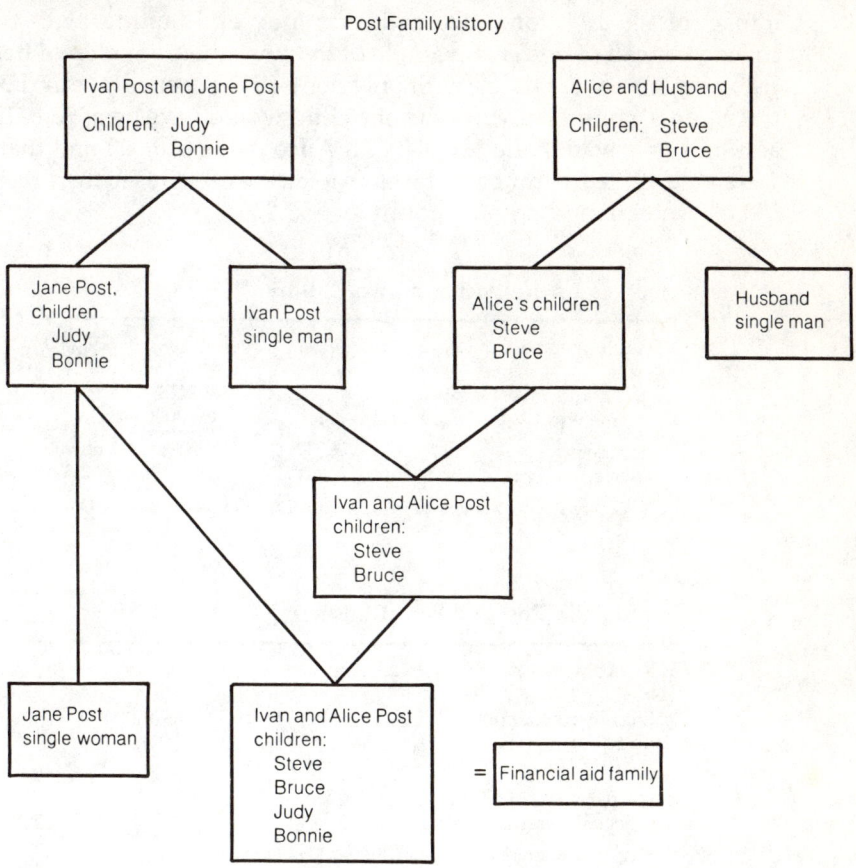

Post Family history

and his new wife, Alice, and Alice's two children, Steven and Bruce. Ivan Post came to the office not long after he and Alice had agreed to accept custody of Judy and Bonnie from his ex-wife. He was concerned and wanted to know how we were going to straighten out the financial aid for the children starting college next year, one child of Alice's by her first marriage and his daughter Judy. While this was complicated to Ivan and Alice, as far as financial aid was concerned the new family consisting of two parents, Ivan and Alice Post, and four children, Steven, Bruce, Judy, and Bonnie, would be considered one family. The aid for the two students planning to enter college would revolve around the family income and asset situation that existed for that new family unit. Ivan was pleased and relieved to have this straightened out since it meant that they had a good chance of qualifying for financial aid.

Ivan Post's concern was so great that it was decided to calculate the impact of the additional two children, Judy and Bonnie, with two in college instead of one (see example of the two situations shown here). If Ivan and Alice were living with only her two children, Steve and Bruce, the parents' contribution for the one child would have been $2,871. This assumes that Ivan made $20,000 and Alice made $10,000 and that they were able to file their income taxes as a family of four. Further, they had $10,000 in cash and a home equity of $50,000.

Ivan and Alice Post and Two Children*

Taxable income		$30,000
Assets:		
Cash and investments	$10,000	
Home equity	50,000	
Net assets		60,000
Expected parents' contribution		2,871

*Family size, 4; number to be in school, 1; age of oldest parent, 42.

Ivan and Alice Post and Four Children*

Taxable income		$30,000
Assets:		
Cash and investments	$10,000	
Home equity	50,000	
Net assets		60,000
Expected parents' contribution per child		1,053
Total expected parents' contribution		2,106

*Family size, 6; number to be in school, 2; age of oldest parent, 42.

When Judy and Bonnie were added to the family the tax deductions increased as there were no support payments from Ivan's ex-wife. However, the expected parents' contribution decreased to $1,053 per child or a total of $2,106 for two attending college. In fact, the Posts would be paying less for college for two than they would have been with just one in college.

DIVORCE AND SEPARATION

Divorce and separation are interchangeable, for financial aid purposes. The financial aid office is unlikely to delve into the details of your legal arrangements with your ex-spouse. Perhaps the biggest indicator of marital status is the kind of income tax return you file. If you are separated but file a joint return, it will be your obligation to prove you are separated. (This does not include married people who file separate returns for tax reasons but live together at the same address.)

Get Information

Many people think that their divorce or separation situation is unique. To individuals I am sure that it is. But financial aid officers are used to seeing all kinds of family configurations, separations, remarriages, and so forth. If you have questions, try to lay out your situation on paper without emotion so that you can talk about the finances of the situation with an aid officer and get advice.

Financial Aid Is Not Judgmental

Much of the time people cloud the realities of the financial aid process with their own emotions. What is important for financial aid is that a couple is divorced, not that the 45-year-old father ran off with the 18-year-old babysitter. Financial aid is not in the business of making judgments of people, their values, or morals. Rather we attempt to take a picture of your situation as it exists on a given day. You must be open about your situation as well as your finances to receive help.

One young woman thought she was going to have to drop out of school because she could not afford to keep paying the bills. After much hard work trying to figure out why she was facing such difficulty, Cynthia blurted out in a mass of tears the fact that her parents were not really living together. They had separated sometime ago and maintained two separate households. She went on to explain her personal embarrassment at this as well as her family's. The family had clearly attempted to "pretend" that they were still together when filling out the aid form (as if in some way this was going to help the situation). In fact, they paid a tremendous price in terms of reduced financial aid—and in terms of the emotional price Cynthia was paying because the family unit was not dealing with the reality of the situation. Cynthia was finally helped to deal with the situation by an excellent counselor. And the parents refiled after I had several long discussions with them. Again, they were the losers in not having been open about their situation. The following year Cynthia's aid form showed her living with her father in a single-parent family receiving very modest support payments from her mother.

Disappearing Parents

In many single-parent families the other parent may have disappeared or no income and asset information may be available. This is not uncommon and will not (at most institutions) prevent the student from receiving assistance.

Jane Russell is in just such a situation. Mrs. Russell lives with her three children, Lucy, Mike, and Jack. She knows only that their father, Mr. Russell, has a good job, but she never hears from him. Her attorney advised her that it was not worth pursuing Mr. Russell. Mrs. Russell is concerned that her students will not be able to receive assistance because of the lack of information about Mr. Russell. She was very relieved to find out that his information would not be necessary.

WHERE SHOULD STUDENTS LIVE?

To better understand the financial impact of filing in the home in which the child lives, observe what differences there would be in the Stewart situation. Mike and Mona Stewart have been married about 25 years and have three children—George who is currently in college, Patti who is about to enter college, and Seth who is a sophomore in high school. They are considering separating and want to know the financial aid consequences of the following choices:

A. Remain as a single family unit.
B. Mona separate and leave the three children with Mike.
C. Mona separate and take Patti, leaving George and Seth with Mike.

Their financial situation is as follows (Mike and Mona are both 45):

Mike's income from teaching	$20,000
Mona's income from accounting	35,000
Home equity	40,000
Cash	10,000

The Stewarts assumed that the house would go to Mike and that Mona would take the cash. The expected family contribution varies considerably as you will see. The reason it varies so much is that when two households are created there are additional expenses which reduce the funds available for college expenses.

Situation A: Stewarts as Single Family*

Total taxable income............		$55,000
Assets:		
Cash......................	$10,000	
Home equity	40,000	
Net assets		50,000

*Family size, 5; number in college, 2.

Situation B: Mike and Three Children*

Total taxable income............		$20,000
Assets:		
Home equity	$40,000	
Net assets		40,000

*Family size, 4; number in college, 2.

Situation C: Mike and Two Children*

Total taxable income............		$20,000
Assets:		
Home equity	$40,000	
Net assets		40,000

*Family size, 3; number in college, 1.

Situation D: Mona and One Child*

Total taxable income............		$35,000
Assets:		
Cash......................	$10,000	
Net asset		10,000

*Family size, 2; number in college, 1.

Situation A. The family remains as a single unit with two parents, three children, and two in college—George and Patti. The parents' contribution would be:

Parents' contribution for George	$3,678
Parents' contribution for Patti................	3,678

Situation B. Mona separates taking the cash and leaving Mike with the three children and the house. Thus Mike would have a single-parent family of four—three children with two in college. Mike's contribution, assuming no assistance from Mona, would be:

Parents' contribution for George	$393
Parents' contribution for Patti	393

Situations C and D. Mona separates taking Patti and leaving Mike with two children, George and Seth, with one in college. Mona also has one in college. Again, there is no assumed contribution from Mona to Mike:

Parents' contribution (from Mike) for George	$ 973
Parents' contribution (from Mona) for Patti	3,375

When you review the cost of maintaining two separate homes, paying two sets of taxes, and so on, you quickly see that there is no real advantage to any choice. Of course the decision should be made on some basis other than a financial one. The above merely shows the impact on financial aid if the schools which George and Patti are planning to attend are fully awarding students.

EDUCATIONAL SUPPORT AGREEMENTS

One of the difficult problems for financial aid officers occurs because divorce settlements are sometimes worked out in direct contradiction to the best financial aid strategy. The case of the Kahns is a good example. The divorce decree said that Mr. Kahn would provide up to $4,000 a year in financial assistance *after* all financial aid was received by their son, Alex. When Mrs. Kahn applied for assistance for Alex on her secretarial salary, her parent's contribution was minimal. This, together with Alex's student contribution of $1,000, only gave an expected family contribution of $1,500.

Parents' contribution (Mrs. Kahn)	$ 500
Student's contribution (Alex Kahn)	1,000
Family contribution	$1,500

If the assumption is made that Alex will attend a school where the total costs are $7,500, then Alex should be eligible for $6,000 in assistance, including all kinds of aid (see Chapter 15 on aid sources). If Alex receives that much aid (according to the terms of the agreement as understood by Mr. Kahn), all that Mr. Kahn would have to do is replace the $1,500 family contribution and let Alex receive the rest in aid. However, the financial aid formula says that when Mr. Kahn contributes a dollar directly for education expenses, it is considered the same as aid. Therefore, if he contributed $1,500, the financial aid office might see Alex's situation as follows:

Parents' contribution (Mrs. Kahn)	$ 500
Student's contribution (Alex Kahn)	1,000
Court ordered (from father)	1,500
Family contribution	$3,000

Thus, the aid at a $7,500-total-cost school would be reduced from the original $6,000 eligibility to $4,500. Mrs. Kahn would still want Mr. Kahn to pay her $1,500 because she is not getting the full $4,000 from him, and the circle would continue until the situation ended up like this:

Parents' contribution (Mrs. Kahn)	$ 500
Student's contribution (Alex Kahn)	1,000
Court ordered (from father)	4,000
Family contribution	$5,500

The aid would then, of course, be reduced to the total cost less the family contribution.

$$\text{Total cost} - \text{Family contribution} = \text{Aid eligibility}$$
$$\$7,500 - \$5,500 = \$2,000$$

No One Benefits. Unfortunately, in this situation everyone feels cheated. Mrs. Kahn does not think that she should have to pay anything. Mr. Kahn does not understand why he should have to pay the $4,000 when originally his son's aid award called for an aid eligibility of $6,000. Alex is tired of the hassle going on between his parents, and the financial aid office is hassled trying to straighten out this matter.

Definitions of Aid

Another problem is what you define as aid. Are loans considered to be aid or not? Mrs. Kahn does not want to burden her son with loans and would like to get the most out of Mr. Kahn. Therefore, she does not want to count as aid any loans that Alex might take. On the contrary, Mr. Kahn's attorney wishes to protect his client from paying any more than he has to and believes loans should count as aid. These kinds of arguments can go around and around in circles. It is far easier if a family can agree on what the other parent's responsibility is in paying for college educational cost in a fixed dollar amount per year. In this case, the "other parent" refers to the parent with whom the child is not living at the time of filing.

In the case of the Kahns, if they had agreed specifically that Mr. Kahn would contribute $3,500 a year to college educational cost, then there would have been no argument from the beginning. When Mrs. Kahn filled out the financial aid form for Alex she would have indicated in the appropriate space that there was to be a contribution from the father of $3,500. This amount would have been added to Mrs. Kahn's contribution and Alex's student contribution to determine a total family contribution, which could then be subtracted from cost to determine aid eligibility.

Parents' contribution (Mrs. Kahn)	$ 500
Student's contribution	1,000
Mr. Kahn's contribution	3,500
Family contribution	$5,000

Total Cost − Family contribution = Aid eligibility
$7,500 − $5,000 = $2,500

This would have saved Mr. Kahn money. He would only have to contribute the $3,500 and would have avoided hassles for everyone as well as attorney's expenses.

Agreements that revolve around assistance do not make sense when the financial aid formulas say that all available family sources must be considered before aid is awarded.

Benefits of Lump-Sum Settlements

Recently I was advising a family that was divorcing and suggested that they agree on a lump-sum payment from the husband to the wife in lieu of anything for children's education. Thus the wife would not have to negotiate with the husband each year for the children's money and it would make the financial aid application much simpler. On the application for aid under payments from the other parent (the husband), there would be nothing listed. Thus nothing would be expected. The lump sum would show up under the wife's assets.

Check Divorce Agreement

There are many other crazy entanglements you can get into with divorce decisions that are written without knowledge or attention to financial aid practices and law. If you are already divorced, check your agreement before you start the financial aid application process. Negotiate in advance with your former spouse if necessary so that at the time you fill out the form, you know what your former spouse's contribution will be. Financial aid officers award moneys; they have neither time nor interest in legal battles that should have been settled long before.

Nonpayment

If you have an agreement for some amount, such as $200 a month while the student is in college, but you have not and do not expect to receive the payments, then do not list the amount on the form directly. Attach a letter of explanation or, if available, use the explanation section of the form. If you list the amount and the form is machine read, the amount will automatically be plugged in as available—even though you may not have a prayer of getting it. But do list it in a letter of explanation along with the reason why you do not believe that you will receive these educational support payments. This will help financial aid officers make judgments. If there is any question, they will get in touch with you.

The difference can be dramatic if we look at the case of the Jennings. Mrs. Jennings was divorced 10 years ago and has raised her three children by herself on her modest salary as a bank manager. She has an agreement that says her husband is to pay $200 a month for college expenses, but she has not received assistance from him in nine years. The last that she knew of him, he had become an alcoholic and was drifting. Her attorney advised her that there was no way to get money out of Mr. Jennings and that she should just consider the issue dead. When originally filling out the financial aid form Mrs. Jennings came to a section that asked if there was an agreement for educational expenses and if so how much. She responded that there was such an agreement and the amount was $200 a month. She then completed the form and sent it into the processor. When the Financial Aid Office reviewed her situation they saw the following:

Parents' contribution (Mrs. Jennings)	$1,000
Student's contribution	1,000
Contribution from father	2,400
Family contribution	$4,400

Since the school to which her student was applying only cost $5,000, the aid eligibility was only $600.

Total cost − Family contribution = Aid eligibility
$5,000 − $4,400 = $600

Mrs. Jennings was surprised and upset. She figured there was no way that she and her son could come up with $4,400 to make up the family contribution. After she came to the office we reviewed the situation in detail. Finally the fact came out that her husband had not been contributing. It was suggested that she amend the aid application and write a letter to the financial aid director at each of the schools to which her son was applying. The school with the total cost of $5,000 adjusted her situation as follows:

Parents' contribution (Mrs. Jennings)	$1,000
Student's contribution	1,000
Contribution from father	0
Family contributon	$2,000

Total cost − Family contribution = Aid eligibility
$5,000 − $2,000 = $3,000

The new increased aid eligibility and resulting award made it possible for Mrs. Jennings' son to go to the school of his choice.

PLANNING A DIVORCE

One of the more humorous moments at the financial aid workshops is when I tell parents that if they are planning a divorce they should come and talk with me about how to structure their arrangements. I have been surprised at the number of families that have taken up the offer. Here are some suggestions based on the current financial aid laws (1980–81):

1. Do not work out an agreement that provides for the parent not living with the student to pay the cost after financial aid. As explained earlier in this chapter, this does not work.

2. Do not require each parent to pay a specific amount. Parents often end up paying more than they would be required to under financial aid laws.

3. Consider making all settlements for college educational expenses between spouses. Thus, if Mr. Adams is divorcing Mrs. Adams, instead of agreeing to make any college payments, he might let that be her responsibility. Instead he could pay her a yearly sum or, better still, a lump-sum payment. Consider the impact of this. Suppose that there are three Adams children that will be going to school over a period of six years. If Mr. Adams provides assistance in the amount of $2,000 a year for educational costs and pays the money out as direct assistance as the children go to school, the net result will be to reduce any potential financial aid by that same $12,000, as we have already seen in the case of

the Kahns. Instead, if before the first child starts school, Mr. Adams makes a lump-sum payment to Mrs. Adams in the amount of, say, $8,000 what happens is that Mrs. Adams' assets would be increased by $8,000. Over the six years Mrs. Adams could be asked to contribute as much as $4,800 from these resources.

> From income: If a 9 percent interest rate is assumed on the $8,000 the maximum contribution from income would be about $340 per year.
>
> From assets: The contribution would be about $460. Thus, the total contribution annually would be a maximum of $800, or $4,800 for the six years that Mrs. Adams' children would be in school.

Assume that Mrs. Adams paid her parents contribution directly out of the $8,000 cash. She would end up with $3,200 when the last one finished school. The net result is that she would be $3,200 richer, and Mr. Adams would have paid her $4,000 less. They would be using the financial aid system to pick up the difference.

	Educational Support	Lump Sum
Total cost to Mr. Adams	$12,000	$8,000
Payments for education	12,000	4,800
Remaining amount (Mrs. Adams)	0	3,200

4. Another consideration is where the student should reside. Families may want to consider where they will qualify for the most aid in determining where the student will establish residence. If they will qualify for more aid with the student living with the mother, it may be better for them to agree to that and let the father make a small compensation payment directly to the mother. This will maximize the outside assistance. Remember that a few schools *do* look at the other parent's income as well. In those cases it is immaterial where the child lives.

5. State of residence could make a big difference because of state aid laws. In one family when we found out where the children were in school and planned to go to school, we did some calculations and divided the children up for the best aid situation, considering the sizeable state grants available. The result was a tremendous savings in educational cost to an already strained family. As the father pointed out after I suggested that he give custody to the mother for financial reasons, the children were free to visit whomever they wished during college breaks.

Divorce can do terrible things to young people, and I would certainly oppose divorce as a financial aid strategy. However, if you are in the process of separation or divorce, consider the financial aid planning implications along with your other considerations. Unfortunately, most people that offer advice in divorce matters are not aware of the big dollars that are available in financial aid and the importance of constructing agreements to take these things into account. When I started working with financial aid, I did not think that I would ever need to know much about divorce laws. I am sure that attorneys and divorce clinics do not expect to get involved in financial aid. Seek as much information as you can find. Your decisions should not be based on financial aid alone. However, it may be worth your while to integrate financial aid planning into your private solutions. The right decision may save both you and your former spouse money and open up more opportunity for your children.

Chapter 19

Gifts to Students

Each year there are students who cannot get the assistance from federal and state sources because of a variety of arrangements that have put money into the students' accounts. In many cases the student is fortunate and there is more than enough money available.

However, in a number of cases a well-intentioned relative excluded the students from financial aid to which they would otherwise be entitled.

Gifts from Relatives

Consider the case of the Small family. The grandparents are extremely proud of their three grandchildren. After many discussions with their tax advisors, they decide that they will give $3,000 each year to the grandchildren while they are in high school. The grandparents think that this is particularly important because despite the hard work of their son and his wife they do not seem to have accumulated the capital necessary to start the grandchildren off in college. While the grandparents are not wealthy, they are willing to make substantial sacrifices to be sure that their grandchildren have the educational opportunity that they so cherish as a right in this country.

It is not uncommon to have grandparents and other relatives who feel this way. There are many who feel education is so important that they will make tremendous sacrifices to see that the student can take maximum advantage of available opportunities. I admire this quality in people and hope that we can help them stretch their dollars even further.

In the Small's situation their older child, Marcia, plans to enter school. Mr. Small is a bank officer earning $30,000 a year, and Mrs. Small works as a real estate agent from which she nets about $12,000 a year. She is constantly hoping to improve her net earnings, but the cost of doing business seems to be going up faster than her commission income. A recent slump in the real estate market did not help either. Together, then, they have a taxable income of about $42,000 a year. They have some assets, primarily in the form of their house, life insurance, a couple of rental properties as part of the real estate business, and approximately $5,000 in the bank. Thus, their situation looks like this:

The Small Family*

Taxable income		$42,000
Assets;		
Home equity	$50,000	
Business (real estate equity)	40,000	
Cash	5,000	
Net assets		95,000

* Parents' age, 45; family of four.

FIGURE 19-1

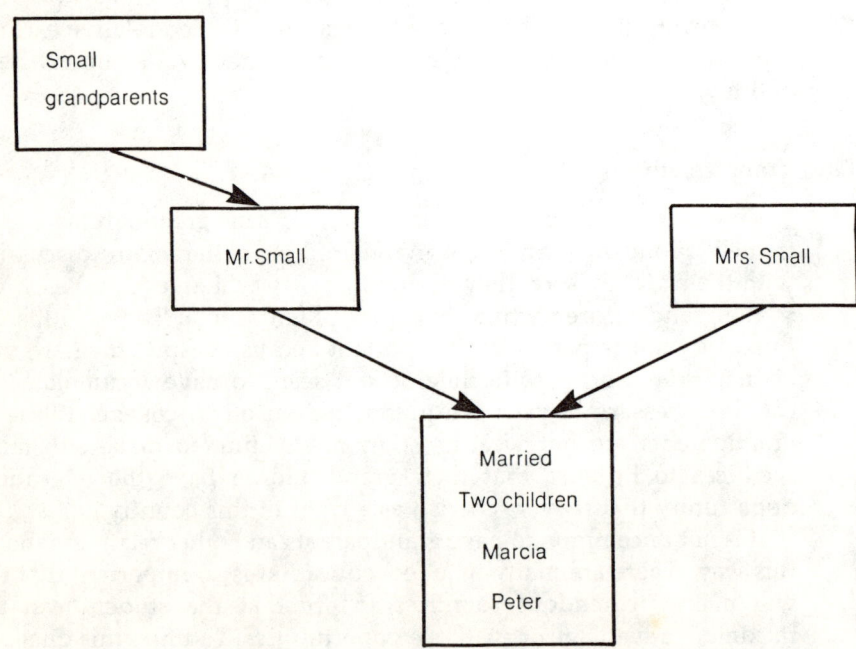

Should the grandparents give $3,000 a year to Marcia and Peter for educational purposes?

Marcia is interested in schools that cost between $5,000 and $9,000 a year. Their concern is not only for the first year. Marcia's younger brother, Peter, will start school in two years. In doing their figuring they assumed that the average cost of a year in school over the six-year period might be $9,000. They are not sure where they are going to come up with $36,000 for each child (4 × $9,000) or a total of $72,000. And the thought of their children going on to graduate school leaves the Smalls believing that they will be in the poorhouse forever. We compared their chances of getting aid under two different assumptions (see Figure 19–1).

In Case 1, the assumption is that the grandparents have given each child a total of $12,000 which they will have at the time they complete the application for financial aid as a senior in high school. Although the formula is based on the consumption rate for students' assets of 35 percent, we have assumed that the Small's money will be spent at the rate of $3,000 per year.

Case 1: The two children given $12,000 each by the grandparents.

Year	Marcia	Peter
1 (Year in school)................	College freshman	High school junior
Family contribution*............	$11,001	0
Aid eligibility..................	0	0
2 (Year in school)................	College sophomore	High school senior
Family contribution*............	10,151	0
Aid eligibility..................	0	0
3 (Year in school)................	College Junior	College freshman
Family contribution.............	6,377	$ 8,277
Aid eligibility..................	2,623	723
4 (Year in school)................	College senior	College sophomore
Family contribution.............	5,327	7,427
Aid eligibility..................	3,673	1,573
5 (Year in school)................	Graduate	College junior
Family contribution*............		10,069
Aid eligibility..................		0
6 (Year in school)................		College senior
Family contribution*............		Over $9,019
Aid eligibility..................		0
Total aid eligibility for the Small family:		
Marcia, year 3....................	$2,623	
Marcia, year 4....................	3,673	
Peter, year 3	723	
Peter, year 4	1,573	
Total	$8,592	

* The family contribution is calculated by using the formula. The Smalls of course, would only pay the $9,000 total cost of education.
  Assumptions:
  a. That all income and costs remain the same.
  b. That Marcia does not go directly on to graduate school but rather goes to work.

(cont. on bottom of p. 176)

Before we look at case 2 it may be helpful to show you the expected student contribution for Marcia. This assumes that the $12,000 gift from her grandparents was available to her when she applied for financial aid as a freshman.

Year	Marcia's Contribution from Assets ($12,000 gift)	Marcia's Summer Savings	Marcia's Total Expected Contribution
1	$4,200	$700	$4,900
2	2,730	900	3,630
3	1,775	900	2,675
4	1,153	900	2,053

Give It to the Parents of Students

Case 2: The grandparents give the $24,000 to the parents instead of to the grandchildren.

Year	Marcia	Peter
1 (Year in school)	College freshman	High school junior
Family contribution	$8,154	0
Aid eligibility	846	0
2 (Year in school)	College sophomore	High school senior
Family contribution	8,354	0
Aid eligibility	646	0
3 (Year in school)	College junior	College freshman
Family contribution	4,954	$4,754
Aid eligibility	4,046	4,246
4 (Year in school)	College senior	College sophomore
Family contribution	4,954	4,954
Aid eligibility	4,046	4,046

(cont. from p. 175)

Note:
i. The differences in the family contribution for Marcia and Peter are caused by the difference in their expected summer earnings and savings. In year 3, the formulas look like this:

Parents' contribution + Summer earnings + 35 percent of savings (gift)
= Family contribution

Marcia, year 3:

$$\$3,377 + \$900 + .35(\$6,000) = \$6,377$$

Peter, year 1:

$$\$3,377 + \$700 + .35(\$12,000) = \$8,277$$

It was assumed that Marcia had used $3,000 a year of her gift money for her freshman and sophomore years. Peter, on the other hand, had all $12,000 available and exposed on the financial aid form.

ii. Summer earnings expectancy may vary from institution to institution but in the past have been freshman, $700; sophomore, $900; junior and senior, $900.

Chapter 19: Gifts to Students

Year	Marcia	Peter
5 (Year in school).................	Graduate	College junior
Family contribution.............		Over $9,000
Aid eligibility...................		0
6 (Year in school).................		College senior
Family contribution.............		Over $9,000
Aid eligibility...................		0
Total aid eligibility for the Small family:		
Marcia, year 1....................	$ 846	
Marcia, year 2....................	646	
Marcia, year 3....................	4,046	
Marcia, year 4....................	4,046	
Peter, year 3	4,246	
Peter, year 4	4,046	
Peter, year 5	0	
Peter, year 6	0	
Total	$17,876	

Assumptions:
1. That all income and costs remain the same.
2. That Marcia does not go directly to graduate school.
3. That negligible additional income is generated by the money.
4. That the parents never have to dip into assets to spend for education. If they did do that, the family contribution would shrink correspondingly.
5. That the parents receive all $24,000 before Marcia starts school, in fact by the time they complete the original aid application in her senior year in high school.
Note: Total parents' contribution (Marcia and Peter have no assets other than summer savings):

Year 1, $7,454.
Year 2, 7,454.
Year 3, 8,108 ÷ 2 = $4,054 for Marcia; $4,054 for Peter.
Year 4, 8,108 ÷ 2 = 4,054 for Marcia; 4,054 for Peter.
Year 5, over 8,100.
Year 6, over 8,100.

It is impressive that the family would have total increased aid eligibility of over $9,000 in this simplified example if the grandparents give the money to the parents instead of to the grandchildren.

Total aid eligibility, Case 2 − Total aid elibibility, Case 1
= $17,876 − $8,592 = $9,284

Give It after the Students Are through College

Now look at the aid eligibility in Case 3 where the grandparents did not make any gifts until after the children had finished college.
Case 3:

Year	Marcia	Peter
1 (Year in school).................	College freshman	High school junior
Family contribution.............	$6,801	0
Aid eligibility...................	2,199	0

Year	Marcia	Peter
2 (Year in school)	College sophomore	High school senior
Family contribution	7,001	0
Aid eligibility	1,999	0
3 (Year in school)	College junior	College freshman
Family contribution	4,277	$4,077
Aid eligibility	4,723	4,923
4 (Year in school)	College senior	College sophomore
Family contribution	4,277	4,277
Aid eligibility	4,723	4,723
5 (Year in school)	Graduate	College junior
Family contribution		7,969
Aid eligibility		1,031
6 (Year in school)		College senior
Family contribution		7,969
Aid eligibility		1,031

Total aid eligibility for the Small family:	
Marcia, year 1	$ 2,199
Marcia, year 2	1,999
Marcia, year 3	4,723
Marcia, year 4	4,723
Peter, year 1	4,923
Peter, year 2	4,723
Peter, year 3	1,031
Peter, year 4	1,031
Total	$25,352

The family would have increased aid eligibility another $7,000 if the grandparents had totally withheld the gift.

Total aid eligibility, Case 3 − Total aid eligibility, Case 2
= $25,352 − $17,876 = $7,476

Total aid eligibility, Case 3 − Total aid eligibility, Case 1
= $25,352 − $8,582 = $16,760

In this case we have seen that well-intended gifts made at considerable sacrifice could end up substantially reducing the chances for aid eligibility and thus financial aid. In fact, if the grandparents did not give the gift, the children might receive 60 percent of the amount that the grandparents had planned to give in aid if all schools fully awarded the aid eligibility. (The $16,760 in increased aid eligibility in Case 3 is considerably more than 50 percent of the contemplated gift of $24,000.)

Planning

Even in families where gifts are being made for tax reasons the question should be asked, "What are the estate tax rates that would otherwise be paid on these dollars?" If they are less than 50 percent, it may be worth reconsidering and including some financial aid planning. I am not opposed to grandparents giving to their grandchildren whether out of generosity, to avoid taxes (particularly inheritance taxes), or for a host of other good reasons. However, if the primary emphasis is to help finance college education, it may be self-defeating. In general, it would probably be better to give the gift to the parents if they have a chance for qualifying for financial assistance. It would be easy to make the case more dramatic than the Smalls with their $42,000 a year income and $95,000 in assets. The lower the income and the assets, the more damage it would do to give the money directly to the grandchildren instead of to their parents.

Getting around Financial Aid. I know of at least one family where the grandparents simply made a gift to the children or grandchildren about the time that tuition was due. Thus, it never really showed up as an asset on the financial aid form. And since the family never knew they were going to get it, they could not list it as an expected contribution on the financial aid form. Thus, the occasional or incidental gift has no effect on the financial aid eligibility, whereas programmed giving has to be factored into the calculations.

Parents Saving Tax Dollars and Losing Financial Aid

It is not always grandparents who make this kind of gift. Sometimes it is a close friend or, more often, parents. There are many bankers and accountants who will advise you to save tax dollars by starting early to give to the children. This may look good on the surface, but consider the financial aid consequences if you think you might be eligible. It would be tragic to save a few tax dollars and then give up a large amount of tax-free assistance. As an example, let's look at a family that has been giving their children money. The Grass family were advised it would be a good idea for tax reasons as well as for educational planning to give their children money. The person advising them thought that this would also ultimately help them assure the educational goals of their children.

The Grass Family*

Taxable income............		$30,000
Assets:		
Home equity............	$40,000	
Investments............	10,000	
Cash	8,000	
Net assets................		58,000

* Family size, 5; number in college, 1; age of oldest parent, 40.

There are three Grass children—Martha, James, and Elizabeth. Mr. Grass makes about $25,000 a year as the manager of a car dealership, and Mrs. Grass makes about $5,000 as a teacher's assistant in the local school system (see table on The Grass Family). When Mrs. Grass started working she planned to put aside her earnings to help with educating Martha, James, and Elizabeth. The home equity is $40,000. They have a few stocks purchased from money that Mrs. Grass inherited when her grandmother passed away ($10,000) and savings of $8,000. The Grasses are 40 years of age. For purposes of the illustration, assume that Martha has picked a school that will cost about $7,500 to attend next year. Compare the aid that she might receive if the parents gave her $1,000 a year for the last four years, or if they kept that money in their own name, bringing their total savings to about $12,000.

1. The $4,000 in Martha's name:

Student's contribution = Contribution from assets + Summer savings
$2,100 = $1,400 (35% of $4,000) + $700(Freshman)

Family contribution
= Parents' contribution + Student's contribution
$4,348 = $2,248 + $2,100

Aid eligibility = Total cost − Family contribution
$3,152 = $7,500 − $4,348

2. The $4,000 in the parents' account:

Student's contribution = Contribution from assets + Summer savings
$700 = 0 + $700(Freshman)

Family contribution = Parents' contribution + Student's contribution
$3,111 = $2,411 + $700

Aid eligibility = Total cost − Family contribution
$4,389 = $7,500 − $3,111

The evidence is overwhelming. The parents should keep the money in their own name because the increased aid eligibility in the first year totals well over $1,200 ($1,237) for a school with a total cost of $7,500. These are tax-free dollars. Depending on your tax situation, they can represent the equivalent in taxable income of anywhere from $1,400 to $3,900 per year.

Joint Accounts

Some parents have joint accounts with their children. If you are in this situation and you have the legal power to withdraw the funds because the money is really yours (the parent), it may be far cheaper for you to pay the income tax on the interest than to give up the financial aid. In general financial aid officers look to see who is paying taxes in their determination of ownership. So, if you have a joint account with a child in the amount of $10,000, and you pay the taxes on the interest, then claim it as yours on the financial aid form. Obviously, if the money belongs to your child (that is, you cannot legally withdraw and spend the funds), then he or she should claim it on the financial aid form.

Education Accounts

There are a number of banks and savings and loans that have really pushed the idea of educational accounts—money that belongs to the student for college education purposes. These educational accounts usually belong to the student for tax purposes. You may save several hundred dollars in taxes while costing yourself several thousand dollars in financial aid.

One Man's Solution

One man informed me that he gets the best of both worlds (which leads me to suspect that it is either illegal or immoral). Reportedly he lends his children money at low interest and has them invest it in high yields. Thus he retains control of the principal amount for tax and financial aid purposes. But he passes the income and the taxes that go with it to his children, who use it to pay for summer vacations, and so forth. When the student files for financial aid he is supposed to list assets less debts. Theoretically the only thing that will show on the financial aid form is a little interest income. This man may find himself being questioned by a financial aid officer or the IRS.

The Message

Avoid putting money in your student's name if you think there is even a remote chance of qualifying for financial aid. Keep it in the parents' name—they have better asset protection.

Chapter 20

Small Trusts

In general small trusts (i.e., $50,000 and under) are treated as students' or parents' assets. This is the case even when the trust is not available for distribution for some years into the future, perhaps when the child reaches the age of 25. Thus, if you list an amount in trust for a student, it will be treated like cash and be assumed to be readily available.

Possible Avoidance

One client suggested that a possible way around this might be to leave a trust to all of his children to be distributed at the discretion of the trustees. Thus, none of the children could properly list any specific amount for a trust or intended distribution. The students would, therefore, presumably put down zero. This might avoid such amount being considered in financial aid. After seeing how much financial aid was available, the trustees could then disperse as they felt would be appropriate and needed.

Warning

In most cases, once you let the financial aid officer know that there is a trust involved, they may well have visions of big money and you may find it difficult to obtain the aid you need and desire.

If you are not sure what to do about a trust, list the smallest amount you think would be fair on the form and then explain in the explanation

Chapter 20: Small Trusts

section or send the Financial Aid Office a letter. If you later revise the student's situation upward, the aid may be reduced but that is easier than asking for more aid.

How Do Trusts Work in Financial Aid?

If a student has a trust account in the amount of $10,000, perhaps from a grandparent, parent, or other relative, it is the same as that student's having $10,000 in a savings account. Traditionally, the formula has asked the same 35 percent per year contribution from assets. This heavy demand on the trust fund sometimes comes as a surprise to those who know about the trust and why it was set up. For example, one young woman who had about $15,000 in trust left to her, supposedly to be available to her to help her get started in life, could not understand why she should have to use those dollars for education. It is not always easy to carry out the desires of a trust document and the proper procedure for financial aid.

Trusts of $50,000

To help with the understanding of how this works, three types of trusts will be reviewed. The first will be trusts of $50,000 or more. Trusts of this magnitude in a student's name virtually precludes the student from receiving any kind of aid at all. This is not all that bad because a trust of this size should be able to take care of the student's tuition even at the most expensive schools. In a few years, if prices keep going up, that will not be enough money for an education that may easily cost $15,000 a year. However, right now if we assume that the student had no parents' contribution and only summer savings in addition to the trust, his situation might look like this at a school that cost $9,000:

Year in School	Trust Beginning		Expected Contribution	Actual Trust Contribution	Student Summer Savings	Cost	Trust Balance
Freshman	$50,000	× 35%	$17,500	$8,300	$700	$9,000	$41,700
Sophomore	41,700	× 35%	14,595	8,100	900	9,000	33,600
Junior	33,600	× 35%	11,760	8,100	900	9,000	25,500
Senior	25,500	× 35%	8,925	8,100	900	9,000	17,400

You can readily see that if the total cost did not change the student would supposedly graduate with $17,400 in his or her trust account. In each year in the model as little as possible was used of the trust to add to the summer earnings, just enough to make $9,000.

In some cases trusts have restrictions about disbursement of income and principal. Suppose that this trust of $50,000 had a restriction on it that no more than $2,000 of the principal and income could be distributed in any one year. In that case there would be a real difficulty because the student would be unlikely to get financial assistance based on need, and yet there would not be enough funds available to take care of his educational needs. Perhaps the bank or other trustee would help by suggesting a Guaranteed Student Loan or Parents' Loan as possible alternatives (see Chapter 16).

Trust of $35,000

A medium-sized trust poses a different situation. Considering school expenses of $10,000 and the fact that the student may have no other contributions other than summer earnings, what are the demands on a trust of $35,000?

Year in School	Trust Beginning		Expected Contribution	Summer Savings	Cost	Actual Trust Contribution	Trust Balance
Freshman	$35,000	× 35%	$12,250	$700	$10,000	$9,300	$25,700
Sophomore	25,700	× 35%	8,995	900	10,000	8,995	16,705
Junior	16,705	× 35%	5,847	900	10,000	5,847	10,858
Senior	10,858	× 35%	3,800	900	10,000	3,800	7,058

Assuming that there were no other resources to help with the college education, the student would have been eligible for financial aid in the junior and senior years ($105 aid eligibility in the sophomore year). The situation would have been like this:

Aid eligibility = Total cost − Family contribution

Student's contribution
 = Trust contribution (savings) + Summer earnings

Parents' contribution = 0 (This was already assumed.)

Family contribution = Parents' contribution + Student's contribution

Family contribution = 0 + Trust contribution + Summer savings

Junior year:

Aid eligibility = $10,000 − [0(parents' contribution) + $5,847 (trust)
 + $900 (summer savings)]
 = $10,000 − $6,747
 = $3,253

Senior year:

Aid eligibility = $10,000 − [0(parents' contribution) + $3,800 (trust) + $900 (summer savings)]
= $10,000 − $4,700
= $5,300

Thus, theoretically the student would have been eligible for over $8,000 worth of aid in the junior and senior years.

Small Trusts

Small trusts of $10,000 or less act just like savings and have a tremendous impact on reducing financial aid even at comparatively inexpensive schools. The trouble with a trust is that the money is not very easily moved around where savings can be shifted from account to account to have it reflect what the money was intended to do.

Planning Your Estate

How trusts like this are used is important in a number of ways. If you know the financial aid situation, it may influence how you structure your estate or how grandparents are encouraged to structure their estates. Careful planning may help you to stretch limited dollars further, and to obtain some tax-free financing of your children's education.

To give you an example of how this works, in a recent discussion with a retired friend, I suggested that he not create an educational trust for his grandchildren, but rather that he leave the money to his children where it would have less impact on financial aid. He and his advisers decided that based on his $500,000 estate, it would be better to leave the money to his children. The advisers concluded that to put the money in an educational trust for the grandchildren would primarily serve to reduce their potential financial aid. (Estate plans should be reviewed after the grandchildren complete their education.)

Remember that trusts, whether in parents' name or students' name, are considered in financial aid. The difference is that assets in trusts under the parents' name are consumed at a lesser rate (6 percent) than under the children's name (35 percent).

The issue of parents leaving money to their children who have not gone to college is related. If one parent dies, it is often better to leave the money to the remaining spouse. Money left to students may jeopardize financial aid. The remaining spouse could use the funds to help pay the parents' contribution which in combination with financial aid may well send your child through school with much less direct expense than if you had left funds in the name of the student.

Does Your Children's Guardian Know about Financial Aid?

At the time you plan your estate, be sure that the person who will be administering the trust or estate is aware of financial aid laws. They should be prepared to help your child to take the best advantage of what is available. Recently I met a young lady who had been left a trust of about $30,000 after her parents were killed in an automobile crash. She had never applied for financial aid and was graduating without a penny to her name. Because I was interested, we reviewed her situation and found that if the trustee had been aware of financial aid policies and practices she could have been graduating with about $10,000. She would have been eligible for financial aid the last two or three years of college. Further, she could have taken some low interest loans and preserved her capital so that she would have set out into the world with some funds available. This kind of happening is not as rare as you think because most of the people administering this kind of trust for a young person just are not familiar with the current financial aid setup.

Plan Ahead

It is impossible to predict what the financial aid laws will be in the distant future. It is a guess that students' assets will continue to be taxed at a very heavy rate in all financial aid considerations. Knowing this should help you to structure your finances in order that your children can get the most assistance possible.

I am sure that someday in the not too distant future lawyers, accountants, and bankers will be learning more about the intricacies of financing an education. The cost of education is clearly one of the major expenses that families with children must anticipate and plan for. If they are to be effective guardians of your children's financial affairs, then they should be responsible for exploring and understanding every possible financial aid benefit that your child may be entitled to receive.

Check Your Estate Plans

Do you have instructions to your executors and successor guardians to use financial aid resources? These should include the G.S.L. and Parents' Loans as a good way of preserving capital for your children.

Chapter 21

Independent Students

Frequently students or parents ask about the advantages of going "independent." This is at best a tricky situation and somewhat difficult to define.

Most students apply for aid as dependent students. In other words, they apply for aid using their parents' income and assets as well as their own resources. This is the traditional way to finance a college education. Before financial aid, parents had to pay almost the entire bill. The dependent status of a financial aid student recognizes this as a three-way partnership—student, parents, and financial aid.

Definition

Some students, for a variety of reasons, are considered independent. (Many students would like to consider themselves independent of their parents at one time or another. Similarly, many parents would like to be independent of their students periodically.) It has been a subject of much debate what constitutes an independent student for financial aid purposes. Recently the questions that determine independence were as follows:

	Year 1		Year 2	
	Yes	No	Yes	No
1. Did or will the parents claim the student as an income tax exemption?	—	—	—	—
2. Did or will the student live with the parents for more than six weeks?	—	—	—	—
3. Did or will the student get more than $1,000 worth of support from parents?	—	—	—	—

For a student to apply for financial aid based on his or her financial situation rather than that of the parents, the student would have to answer *no* to all of these questions. Many schools have their own additional hurdles to qualify for instititutional funds if a student claims independence.

Is Independence Important?

Why is this even an issue? If a student can successfully claim independence, the aid for that student will be determined based on that student's income and assets alone, using a formula for independent students. When a student might otherwise not qualify for aid or at least not substantial aid, the payoff is potentially substantial if school policies do not cause trouble.

For example, consider the case of Sheldon Maxwell. Sheldon's family did not believe that they would qualify for aid because of their high income. Since Sheldon had been living on his own meager resources for the last tax year and planned on doing the same in the next tax year, the Maxwells and Sheldon believed that he might qualify as an independent student. The Maxwells had to check their tax records to see what if anything they were planning to deduct for Sheldon in the last tax year. It was decided between Sheldon and his parents that because they had not provided support, had not provided him with living arrangements, or deducted him from their taxes that Sheldon should file as an independent. The only time Sheldon really came to visit was for Christmas, Thanksgiving, or other major holidays and then only rarely did he stay overnight.

As an independent student, Sheldon could receive a substantial amount of financial aid because of his low earnings and low assets. It is rumored that many students attempt to use this at state universities as a means of getting and increasing financial aid.

Things to Be Considered

There are a number of important concerns to be considered if a student is thinking about going independent.

1. Is the student truly independent or are you just stretching a point? Particularly at private institutions you may find a great deal more checking, including the collection of past income tax records and notarized affidavits of nonsupport.

2. While the obvious impact may be greater aid for the student, often a review of the entire family's situation and consideration of future planning for aid may show that the total aid for the family will be reduced if one student goes independent.

3. There is always the real possibility that the requirements for independent student status could change and become more severe as a method of rationing financial aid dollars. These requirements are frequently reviewed, which makes it difficult to plan on receiving aid as an independent student.

4. Some schools have their own policies to discourage the applications of independent students. For example, one school requires a minimum of $1,500 contribution in addition to summer earnings. This means that the student with no savings had a built-in requirement for a GSL of that amount.

5. Independent students who earn money during vacation periods are expected to provide a much greater share than dependent students.

Look at these points one by one if you are considering this option for your student.

Planning for Independence

It is relatively easy to do your tax preparation with or without the student included. However, be sure to include the lost tax dollars when considering the benefits of this option. This decision must be made before you file your taxes for the preceding year. Since the other questions relating to support and how many weeks the student lived with you also cover a longer period of time, you can see that this is a long-term decision.

December of Junior Year in High School

If a freshman student is going to truly qualify as independent, the decision needs to be made in December of the junior year in high school (see Figure 21–1). This is the only way that all of the following tax year would be truly independent for the student. Remember that you would most likely file for the fall of the freshman year in January of the senior year in high school.

If students even contemplate independent status, where will they live for the remainder of high school—January and beyond of the junior year and all of their senior year in high school? If students think that they will wait and go independent later, it only gets more difficult. It

FIGURE 21-1
Decisions on Independence Must Be Made Twenty Months in Advance

```
                    Initial tax year of independence
      1978  |             1979
      Dec   | Jan  Feb  Mar  Apr  May  Jun  Jul  Aug  Sept  Oct  Nov  Dec
       1      2    3    4    5    6    7    8    9    10   11   12   13
   Junior year in                                       Senior year
   high school                                          in high school

                          1980
                 Jan  Feb  Mar  Apr  May  Jun  Jul  Aug  Sept
                 14   15   16   17   18   19   20   21   22
               Senior year in                     Enter
               high school                        college
                                                  as
                                                  freshman
```

practically prohibits parents from contributing to educational cost because the $1,000 limit is easily reached.

Separate Residence for Students

Claiming the student on the tax return can be easily verified. The second question deals with how many weeks the student lives with the family. It was recently revised to be six weeks or more (from two weeks). This gives more leniency in this one area and will help some students to qualify as independent who would not have qualified previously. Clearly if the student is going to qualify as independent, a separate residence is a must. There are times in some families when this seems like a good idea anyway. For most families, however, this is a relatively drastic step not to be taken lightly.

$1,000 Support

Many families who have no problems foregoing the tax deduction or letting the student live elsewhere, but they cannot comply with the $1000 of support. Support means all kinds of things, including the obvious gifts of cash, shelter, clothing, medical and dental services. Helping a youngster with the purchase of a car and car insurance could be a real difficulty for many families and students—these expenses alone quickly exceed $1,000.

Chapter 21: Independent Students

In general to obtain independence, the student is going to have to be working and maintaining a separate life-style for almost two years. This is not as rare as you may think, but these students often choose to go to less expensive schools so that they can continue to support themselves. This situation most often occurs where there is family disintegration of some kind, not as a planned financial aid strategy.

Independence as a Financial Aid Strategy

Plan carefully if you wish to use independence as a financial aid strategy. Be aware that the definition of independent status might easily change, for example, requiring longer periods of independence. Therefore, you cannot plan too solidly on this as a strategy. If your student does choose this option, you will find that there is a wide variety of methods to handle independent students at different schools. Some schools will accept your claim; others will want as much proof as possible. One of the reasons for these differences is the amount of institutional money that you consume. If the school can fund your need easily out of its aid budgets, then you may not be hassled. Many expensive schools cannot afford large numbers of independent students because they consume volumes of aid dollars, particularly institutional aid dollars. Therefore, they check more thoroughly into your student's status.

Total Family Financial Aid Planning

What may help one student may have a negative impact on the total family situation. Here again financial aid planning comes into effect. Sometimes a student has been independent and I have encouraged them to declare themselves as dependent because the whole family would derive much greater advantage. A simple case might be as follows:

The Alderson family has an income of $40,000, equally divided between the two spouses. When the eldest daughter, Rachael, originally entered college she filed as an independent because she had been living away from home since early in her junior year in high school. While the trauma of the original separation had been difficult for the family, the parents were pleased when Rachael left her boyfriend and decided to go to school full time just as their son, Zachariah, was planning to start school. The question of concern was what was the best way to file. The choices were:

1. Rachael as independent, Zachariah as dependent.
2. Rachael as dependent, Zachariah as dependent.

There was no way to make Zachariah independent because he had lived at home the whole time. It was, however, easy to make Rachael dependent by answering any of the following questions Yes:

		Yes	No
1.	Will the student live with the parents for more than six weeks?	—	—
2.	Will the parents claim the student as an income tax exemption?	—	—
3.	Will the student get more than $1,000 of support from the parents?	—	—

Since most of the events have not occurred, the Aldersons only have to estimate that they will provide more than $1,000 to change Rachael's status. If in fact they do not spend that much, then the following year, assuming the rules for independent students do not change, Rachael could again file for independent status.

What is the advantage of Rachael's becoming dependent? Let us assume that the Aldersons, at age 47, in addition to their $40,000 income, have a home value of $90,000 with an equity of $69,000, and other investments and cash of $15,000 for a total financial aid net worth of $84,000. The first step is to construct the basic parental contribution in each case. We already know that showing two in school will work to increase the aid eligibility by approximately halving the parental contribution per student.

The Alderson Family*

Taxable income............		$40,000
Assets:		
Home equity............	$69,000	
Cash	15,000	
Net assets................		84,000

* Family size, 3 or 4; number in college, 1 or 2; age of oldest parent, 47.

The family contribution, assuming a family of three with only Zachariah in school, is about $8,000. If both children are considered dependent, the contribution for each child, Zachariah and Rachael, is about $4,100. This assumes Rachael files as a dependent and thus the Aldersons report four in the family and two in school.

In order to help the Aldersons plan, we would have to know whether the new family contribution for Rachael would be lower or higher than when she filed as an independent student and thus if she would lose or gain aid. Table 21-1 indicates what a difference it can make. How large it will be depends on how much aid Rachael will lose by filing as a dependent. Negatives have not been shown because if the value is zero

TABLE 21-1
Impact on Aid of Conversion of Rachael Alderson to Dependent Student (net gain in aid dollars for family)

Lost Aid for Rachael Because She Is Not Independent	Cost of School for Zachariah						
	$4,000*	$5,000*	$6,000*	$7,000*	$8,000†	$9,000†	$10,000†
$ 500	0	$ 400	$1,400	$2,400	$3,400	$3,400	$ 3,400
1,000	0	0	900	1,900	2,900	2,900	2,900
1,500	0	0	400	1,400	2,400	2,400	2,400
2,000	0	0	0	900	1,900	1,900	1,900
2,500	0	0	0	400	1,400	1,400	1,400
3,000	0	0	0	150	900	900	900
3,500	0	0	0	0	400	400	400

* For a school cost of $4,000 to $7,000:

Zachariah's school cost − Family contribution = Zachariah's aid eligibility

Zachariah's aid eligibility − Rachael's lost aid = Net gain for family

† For a school cost of $8,000 to $10,000:

Zachariah's school cost − Family contribution = Zachariah's aid eligibility

Zachariah's aid eligibility − Rachael's lost aid − Aid Zachariah would have had as single child = Net gain or loss

or less, then there is no reason to consider switching Rachael's status. Further, the table assumes that schools will meet the full aid eligibility. Because of the uncertainty of financial aid awards, it would be advisable to look for improvement of at least $1,000 before considering changing Rachael's status. If Rachael would lose $500, than Zachariah should be considering a school that costs more than $6,000 to make the exchange worthwhile. As you can see, as the cost of Zachariah's school approaches $8,000 and Rachael's loss by converting approaches zero, the maximum gain derived is a potential $3,400.

You will note that after $8,000 when the school already costs more than Zachariah's expected family contribution of $8,000, there is no additional gain expected. The reason for this phenomenon is that there is already an aid eligibility for Zachariah as a single child in school in a family of three without Rachael in the $8,000, $9,000, and $10,000 categories. This is shown as follows:

Parents' contribution + Student's contribution

$7,000   + $900 (assumes no savings)

= Family contribution
= $7,900

It is clear that one student's actions (Rachael) can affect other students in the family in terms of financial aid. It is a difficult planning process for the entire family, but careful attention should be paid to the options and an investigation of the latest financial aid rules should be carried out. The payoff for a few hours of work can be tremendous. If the Aldersons act properly and choose to have Rachael become a dependent student, they could be paid an additional $2,000 in tax-free financial assistance (which in their income bracket would be the equivalent of earning an extra $4,000 for the year).

In some cases instead of losing money in the form of aid, Rachael might do better herself and make the whole operation vastly more beneficial to the Alderson clan. Of course, if there were more children, the effects would be different in scope but the principle would work the same. It would be a good idea if every family could chart their financial aid course with skilled financial aid planners. Like tax preparers, the fees charged could be covered many times over by the benefits received.

Other Factors

There are some additional facts to consider when looking at the total benefits to the family. First, when Rachael rejoins the family, federal taxes would be about $400 less. Since these dollars would be available without any reduction in aid, they probably should be considered in the decision. Table 21–2 reflects this gain for the Aldersons, and makes

TABLE 21–2
Impact on Aid of Conversion of Rachael Alderson to Dependent Status (net gain in aid and tax dollars for family)*

Lost Aid for Rachael Because She Is Not Independent	Cost of School for Zachariah						
	$4,000	$5,000	$6,000	$7,000	$8,000	$9,000	$10,000
$ 500	0	$ 800	$1,800	$2,800	$3,800	$3,800	$ 3,800
1,000	0	300	1,300	2,300	3,300	3,300	3,300
1,500	0	0	800	1,800	2,800	2,800	2,800
2,000	0	0	300	1,300	2,400	2,400	2,400
2,500	0	0	0	800	1,800	1,800	1,800
3,000	0	0	0	300	1,300	1,300	1,300
3,500	0	0	0	0	800	800	800

* Assuming $400 in federal tax savings.

Rachael's change of status look even better. Note that it would probably become worthwhile even if Zachariah chose a lower cost school. Second, remember that it is quite difficult to go from dependent status to independent status but relatively easy to go from independent status to dependent status. So several years should be considered in the projection so that a decision can be made based on total estimated return. Third, if there is only one child left to go to school, it is quite possible that that child going independent is one of the best things that could happen in terms of financial aid.

Changing Regulations

One of the concerns about filing as an independent is the possibility of changing regulations. For years the financial aid community has debated how to define an independent student. As the federal government moved to take over the aid system, the Office of Education has also been involved in this debate. One of the policies often discussed in the past was the idea of looking at three years of history to determine a student's independence. This would mean that in order to qualify as an independent student for the freshman fall a student would have had to become independent of his or her parents in December or early January of the sophomore year in high school. This would hamper many students from achieving independent status, particularly as entering freshmen.

Using the GSL to Gain Independent Status

Changing to three years would effectively put a stop to students going independent by using the GSL to pay the parents' contribution. Some students have used the Guaranteed Student Loan very effectively to replace the expected parents' contribution in the first and second year of college thus allowing the student to apply as an independent during the junior year. Thus, if a freshman student had decided that it was the best thing to go independent, this process could be followed.

Since the student who we shall call Jock lived at home until after graduation from high school, he could not qualify as independent as a sophomore because he would have lived with his parents more than six weeks during his senior year. As a freshman, however, suppose Jock declined to let his parents help him at all after January 1, and suppose Jock used the money he borrowed through the Guaranteed Student Loan Program plus financial aid he would receive as a dependent student to pay his bills. This would allow him to function financially independent of his parents, thus falling below the $1,000 contribution from parents' limit, (assuming that they did not give gifts, pay car insurance, provide housing or other services that would total more than $1,000).

Jock would have to apply as dependent again for the sophomore year. Then as a sophomore he would have to use the Guaranteed Student Loan to again replace his parents' contribution so he could remain independent. This may not be as easy as it appears on the surface, especially if the family contribution is greater than the Guaranteed Student Loan limit and the student must attempt to get other resources to pay his bills.

As a sophomore, Jock could then apply for independent status as a junior, assuming that his parents were not deducting him for taxes, contributing more than $1,000, or providing him with a place to stay more than six weeks a year. The projected aid for the last two years would have to be substantial for Jock to take on all the difficulties involved in establishing independence. If the regulations were to change and require two years of past history as an independent student, Jock could not qualify until his senior year, so it would not be worth the trouble to try to establish independence.

Changes in GSL Could Limit Independence

Another shift could conceivably make the whole operation considerably more difficult. If the loan requirements are changed, as has been contemplated, they may require dependent students' parents to take some kind of parental loan before a Guaranteed Student Loan is approved. This would make it especially difficult for people like Jock to qualify. He would have no source of funds from which to draw additional resources without help from his parents. The GSL could then be effectively barred from use by students trying to establish independence. If a student like Jock had a large family contribution, he would have a hard time making it up without the help of a GSL. This is especially true since theoretically all student earnings can be counted in financial aid. Thus, the more Jock earned, the less aid he would get. He would be trapped in a financial circle that would never help him achieve independence.

Independent Student Who Works

The most obvious way to achieve independence is for a student to work for awhile before starting school, thus establishing the student as a separate economic entity. Again, the period of time must be substantial if the student really wishes to achieve independent status. It could be longer than the current two years if the rules for independence are changed.

Chapter 21: Independent Students

SCHOOL POLICIES

Some schools have their own policies to discourage students from going independent. While schools cannot change federal or state regulations, they can use discretion in awarding their own funds. Check with your student's financial aid office to see if your student qualifies as an independent. One school expects independent student to provide resources of $750 a semester plus summer earnings to qualify for institutional funds. Thus, if a student, Dawn, plans to apply for aid at Creditable College, she should get an estimate of her family contribution. If the family contribution is less than $750 a semester or $1,500 a year, then Dawn might be better off to file as a dependent for Creditable College where total costs are $6,000. Let us assume that because many members of her family will be in school the family contribution is $1,150 a year. Then Dawn's choices are essentially as follows:

As an independent student:

Cost		$6,000
Freshman summer savings	$ 700	
Other resources expected from Dawn	1,500	
Total resources from Dawn		2,200
Aid eligibility		$3,800

As a dependent student:

Cost		$6,000
Freshman summer savings	$ 700	
Parents' contribution	1,150	
Total family contribution		1,850
Aid eligibility		$4,150

If the school met full need or full aid eligibility, then Dawn would end up with $350 more assistance by filing as a dependent student. The reverse would be true if the school was fully awarding and not requiring other resources of independent students. Consider Dawn's case at Solid State University where the costs are $4,000.

As an independent student:

Cost		$4,000
Freshman summer savings	$700	
Other income and savings	0	
Total resources from Dawn		700
Aid eligibility		$3,300

As a dependent student:

Cost		$4,000
Freshman summer savings	$ 700	
Parents' contribution	1,150	
Total family contribution		1,850
Aid eligibility		$2,150

Clearly, if Solid State University was fully awarding, Dawn would do far better as an independent under this set of circumstances. She would receive $1,150 more aid eligibiity and thus probably that much more aid.

Investigate School Policy on Independent Students

If your student is considering independence, investigate the options at the school(s) being considered or attended. As has been said before, because it helped someone else's situation does not mean it will help you and your student. You will need to collect your own information and make your own decision based on your family situation. In most cases the problem is not whether to go independent, but rather to persuade a family member to go dependent.

The Carson Family*

Taxable income		$ 60,000
Assets:		
Home equity	$ 50,000	
Business	100,000	
Net assets		150,000

*Family size, 5 or 6; number in school, 2 or 3; age of oldest parent, 55.

Consider one additional family to see the effects of one of the children going independent. The Carson family has an annual income of $60,000 a year, a business with a worth of about $250,000 on which they owe $150,000, a home worth about $100,000 on which they owe $50,000, and three children who will be at private schools plus one at home. The children's situation is as follows:

Name	Year in School	Projected School Cost
Emily Carson	College sophomore	$4,000
Jordan (twin)	High school senior	7,500
Montague (twin)	High school senior	8,500
Colleen	High school sophomore	0

Chapter 21: Independent Students

Emily has always been a progressive, assertive young woman. She left her highly selective private school after one semester to attend a state university and establish her independence. She felt that she could no longer accept dependence on her parents and their values as she considered herself to be part of a new generation of free thinkers. The Carsons had a great deal of trouble with this idea at first but soon decided that allowing Emily to be independent would cause a lot less hassle at home. However, now that the boys are considering expensive private schools, Emily's independence may not be the best financial decision for the family.

Mr. Carson is 55 and is concerned about protecting as much of his estate as possible for his upcoming retirement. When the Carsons got involved in financial aid planning, they learned that the parents' expected contribution for the two boys without Emily would be approximately $12,000. With Emily it would be approximately $11,750 for all three students, a difference of only $250 to which $500 should be added in additional tax savings generated by including Emily again as a tax deduction. The difference in total aid eligibility for the boys would be substantial. In each case the boys have no savings, so the only thing to be added to the parents' contribution is the boys' expected summer savings before their freshman year of $700. Even supposing that Emily was receiving a full $4,000 in aid as an independent student, the situation clearly is much better (see tables) for the Carson family if they file for aid with Emily as a dependent student.

The Carson Family (without Emily)*

Student	School Cost	Family Contribution	Aid Eligibility
Jordan	$7,500	$6,691	$ 809
Montague	8,500	6,691	1,809
(Emily)	4,000	0	4,000
Total aid eligibility			$6,618

* Family of five, two in college.

The Carson Family (with Emily)*

Student	School Cost	Family Contribution	Aid Eligibility
Jordan	$7,500	$4,620	$2,880
Montague	8,500	4,620	3,880
Emily	4,000	4,820	0
Total aid eligibility			$6,760

* Family of six, three in college.

If you add the $150 additional aid eligibility to the $500 in tax savings, there is a $650 advantage to the family—even more if Emily was not fully aided as an independent student. For example, assume that Emily only received $2,000 in assistance as an independent student. Then the case would be even clearer for having her file as a dependent student (see tables below).

The Carson Family (without Emily)*

Student	School Cost	Family Contribution	Aid Eligibility
Jordan	$7,500	$6,691	$ 809
Montague	8,500	6,691	1,809
(Emily)	4,000	0	2,000
Total aid eligibility			$4,618

* Family of five, two in college.

The Carson Family (with Emily)*

Student	School Cost	Family Contribution	Aid Eligibility
Jordan	$7,500	$4,620	$2,880
Montague	8,500	4,620	3,880
Emily	4,000	4,820	0
Total aid eligibility			$6,760

* Family of six, three in college.

The difference in aid eligibility would now be $2,142. This would be particularly important if this were all gift or grant dollars.

When you do your financial aid planning, be sure to consider carefully the impact of dependence versus independence.

Chapter 22

Social Security and Veterans' Benefits

A surprising number of students have benefited from social security and veterans' educational benefits. These can be a major source of assistance to a family that has lost the wage-earning power of one of its members. The amounts of these benefits can be substantial. In one case the benefits from both programs were so great that they more than covered the cost of a private school education. The mother in that case said that if her husband was still living, they could never have afforded that kind of education for their daughter.

Find Out if You Qualify

As a rule financial aid officers do not get involved in determining social security or veterans' benefits except that they may have to certify that a student is in school. However, they need to know how much the benefits are. In the past the financial aid forms have had questions about how much the monthly benefit will be for given periods of time. It is important that you supply this information correctly for your student since it will affect your financial aid. You are expected to know the monthly amount and how many months that the student is eligible for this benefit. If you are not sure, check with your social security or veterans' office in November or December before you fill out the form.

If you are not sure whether your student would qualify for these benefits, check with your social security office, particularly if the wage earner in the family has passed away or is unable to work due to some disability. Another area worth checking on is if your student is handicapped in any way. Is there a state agency that will provide rehabilitation funds that might help with college education expenses? Some people are very shrewd at following every channel and getting every dollar that they are entitled to. Others ignore what is being offered because they do not know or are too proud to explore the possibilities.

The Financial Aid Office Needs to Know

Why is it important for the financial aid officer to know what benefits your student will receive from social security? (For this discussion we will use the term *social security*, but in most cases the same kinds of things would apply to veterans' childrens' educational benefits.) In the past social security has been treated like a direct grant for education and, therefore, would reduce your other aid. If your student did not inform the financial aid office or the school until later, they would have to reduce the award when they did find out. It is far easier for you and the financial aid officer if you can get one accurate award rather than having to make changes. Most changes in social security, unless the family income has been reduced, end up reducing the award.

Financial Aid Treatment of Social Security Benefits

The treatment of social security benefits like many other areas has long been a topic of discussion in the financial aid community. The current practice is that in low-income families a portion of the social security income is assumed to be needed to help maintain the home for the student and the family. As the family income increases, more and more of the social security benefits are expected to be available for educational expenses. In most middle-income families, all of the social security benefits are assumed to be available for educational expenses. Families must be aware of this.

Cash Flow Problems

Some students maintain that they do not have enough money for school even with the parents' contribution, student contribution, social security, and aid. The student may then try to argue that the social security money is being used for a car payment or some other necessity. This is not a legitimate or acceptable argument. The student is then faced with trying to get help from home for the car payments or selling the car. If the student drops out of school, the social security payment will stop, and if the student stays in school, that money is needed for educational expenses.

Note that the social security benefits received *beginning July 1, after graduation from high school* are assumed to be available for educational expenses for the freshman year. Thus the money received over the summer should be waiting in the bank in September to help with the school bills. Students who spend this money over the summer and only come with their summer savings may be in for a rude surprise. They probably won't have enough money. If, for example, Jane Mabry was receiving $200 a month in social security benefits, she would be expected to have $1,300 available by the end of September to help with her fall bills.

July social security	$ 200
August social security	200
September social security	200
Summer savings (freshman)	700
Total available for fall	$1,300

Of course, if Jane reported savings, then she would be expected to contribute 35 percent of those dollars as well. Further, Jane must remember that throughout the year she is expected to contribute $2,400 (12 months times her $200 monthly check) toward the cost of her education from social security.

Find Out How Much Aid Officers Expect

It is not uncommon for a family receiving these social security benefits to use part of the benefits for living costs over the summer. However, unless this is taken into account by the financial aid budget (based on a low family income), to do so could cause the student to be short of money in the fall. If you are not sure about how much of your social security is being counted as available for school cost, check your aid award to see if they have listed the amount on the award form. If not, you may have to check with the aid office at the school. If you are considering several different schools, determine if all the financial aid officers are treating your social security contribution in the same way.

COMPUTATION OF FAMILY CONTRIBUTION WITH BENEFITS

In the case of students with social security benefits, the family contribution is computed in a slightly different way. As before, the parents' contribution is computed from income and assets, but the student's section is different. The student is expected to have summer earnings and to make a contribution from savings if there are any reported. In addition, the student is expected to contribute from the

FIGURE 22-1

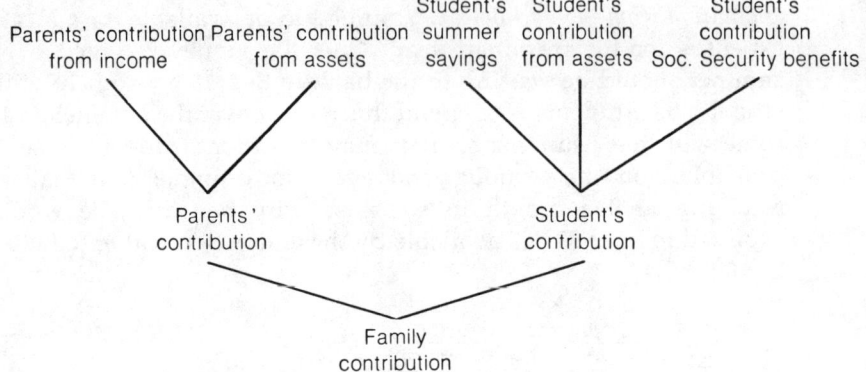

social security benefits in most cases at a 100 percent level (see Figure 22-1).

Student Assets Plus Benefits

It is evident that students who are receiving social security benefits may not qualify for large amounts of other aid unless the family is extremely needy or they do not have much in savings. However, look at a typical case where when the father died he not only left the social security but also an insurance policy of $5,000 for each of his children's education.

Harold Baker will receive $200 a month in social security benefits to help with his schooling. He has $6,000 in the bank for his education, the $5,000 from his father's insurance policy and $1,000 that he has earned on his own. Additionally, Harold knows that he is expected to earn and save $700 to bring to school with him in the fall. If we assume that there is no contribution available from his mother then Harold's situation would be as follows:

Expected contribution of Harold Baker:

Summer savings (freshman)	$ 700
35 percent of savings	2,100
Social security	2,400
Total contribution for Harold	$5,200

Thus, Harold would not have any eligibility at schools costing less than $5,200, but he would have aid eligibility at schools costing more than that. Of course, his situation might be different in his sophomore year, especially if there is a 10 percent increase in social security payments (to $220 a month) and Harold's expected summer earnings are now $900. Further, we know that this savings will be reduced by $2,100 to $3,900. Thus his situation would be as follows:

Expected contribution of Harold Baker:

Summer savings	$ 900
35 percent of $3,900	1,365
Social security	2,640
Total contribution for Harold	$4,905

The savings contribution would, of course, decrease each year; but you could, based on past history, expect the social security contribution as well as the summer earnings to go up. If Harold is choosing between schools, he should consider what his situation might look like over the next four years and try to project where he will best be able to afford to go to school. Harold may have to consult aid officers to understand what each schools' aid policies are toward students in his situation.

Assets of Rich Families

In many cases where there is a family contribution and the student is receiving social security benefits, the family contribution is generated not from the income of the remaining parent but from the assets that were left. Ingrid Stoddard's father did not leave her any insurance money, and she has no savings. Her mother, however, does have a family contribution because she was left assets. Unfortunately, these assets do not produce much income, but Mrs. Stoddard does not wish to sell them as they are rapidly appreciating in value. The home and the land around it which Dr. Stoddard had planned to develop were paid off by a mortgage insurance policy. Mrs. Stoddard estimates their value conservatively at $200,000, based on the appraisal that was done for Dr. Stoddard's estate. Further, she has about $50,000 in stocks and other securities that were left to her.

Unfortunately, none of this provides much income, and she is barely squeaking by in her living expenses. But her advisers believe that if she can hold onto her property for a few years, she may be able to get over $500,000 for it if a proposed new mall is developed. Since her income contributes nothing, the only contribution she is expected to make to Ingrid's education is from her assets, and that totals $5,408. Mrs. Stoddard is 48 and will have two children in school next year. Thus, Ingrid faces the following situation:

Expected contribution of Ingrid Stoddard:

Summer savings	$ 700
35 percent of savings	0
Social security	2,400
Total student contribution (Ingrid)	$3,100
Expected parent contribution (Mrs. Stoddard)	
From income	0
From assets	$5,408

Obviously, if Ingrid picks a school below $3,100, then she will be able to pay her own expenses. Above that level her mother will have to either use part of her assets, particularly the securities, remortgage the land and house, or encourage Ingrid to take a Guaranteed Student Loan. If Ingrid borrowed up to $2,500, that would cover her at schools costing up to $5,600. Beyond that level, Mrs. Stoddard would have to use some assets to pay the bills.

The situation is not as uncommon as you may think. Many families in this situation think they are practically destitute. They have no real income and are using the child's social security to help pay the grocery bills so they can hang on to the assets. The Stoddards need to reassess the long-range plans for education and financial resources with their advisers both in financial aid terms and also in terms of how Mrs. Stoddard is going to live and pay the taxes and maintenance. Clearly there is a substantial amount of money and it can all work out nicely, but she will need to plan more carefully than she has in the past.

The most logical place for Mrs. Stoddard to turn initially is to her security holdings to beef up her income. Further, she may want to talk with her advisers about her present need for money to live on and what will be needed to pay for the education of her children. It would be possible through financial aid planning to do an estimate of exactly how many dollars she will need to pay out for both children in addition to the children's projected earnings and social security benefits. With this information the advisors can then begin to get a real handle on the Stoddard's cash flow needs. Perhaps Mrs. Stoddard can work out a reverse mortgage with fixed payments. The bank would increase the mortgage and make payments to her at the level necessary for her to live and make educational payments until the property is sold or until she has found work.

Another opportunity would be for Mrs. Stoddard to consider going back to school herself. It would lower the family contribution and help her to develop a skill that would increase her income.

Chapter 22: Social Security and Veterans' Benefits

Plan Ahead

Enough of the Stoddards! This chapter is supposed to be helping with social security and veterans' benefits. Here, like everyplace else, the most important thing is planning. Plan to find out what your benefits are, if any, in advance of the time you complete the form. That way you can give the financial aid officer complete information the first time around.

Also plan how you will live without the student's social security benefits as part of the family income—they will have to be used for school cost. Project the situation a few years in advance to be sure that the family contribution, the student's contribution, and the social security benefits together with expected financial aid will be able to cover the cost. If you find yourself in a situation like the Stoddards, start now to figure how some of the capital can be made available to help with educational cost.

Chapter 23

Pell Grant (BEOG)

This is the core of all federal programs. It is an entitlement grant, meaning that it belongs to the student and is awarded directly by the government and not the aid officer at the school. Until recently only families with incomes below about $15,000 qualified for this grant. The Middle Income Assistance Act, passed in the fall of 1978, made the BEOG available to families with incomes of up to about $40,000. Each year inflationary adjustments are making the grant more and more available to higher income families. This is a grant worth taking seriously—the benefits now range up to $1,750 a year.

In the past you could apply for this grant by using the same form that you were using for most of your schools. The form asks if you would like to release your information to the Pell Grant Program or not. Be sure to check yes. This program costs nothing to apply to, and many families have been surprised by the amount of grant assistance they get. The Pell Grant form in general has utilized even less information than state or institutional programs in the awarding of aid.

The Pell Grant formula is different. It is not uncommon for two families that have approximately the same aid eligibility at a school based on the uniform methodology to have widely varying amounts in the Pell Grant. This is, in large part, due to the difference in treatment of assets and income in the parents' contribution section. Such variation bothers some students and their families. But it does not bother aid officers who understand that the formulas act on different situations with a variety of results.

There has been discussion in the financial aid profession for a number of years about the possibility of the BEOG formula becoming the means to distribute all aid. If you have money, nothing could work more to your advantage. The following comments and illustrations are based on the *Federal Register* of August 1, 1980. They will undoubtedly be changed before the academic year 1981–82.

The formula is considerably simpler in some aspects than the uniform methodology. For example, in looking at parents' income there is credit given for U.S. income taxes paid, a family maintenance allowance, and an employment allowance for a household in which both parents work or for a one-parent family. In contrast, the uniform methodology also gives allowances for state taxes and social security taxes. They both make allowances for large medical expenses. The key difference in the treatment of income is that in the uniform methodology there is a graduated scale of usage of parents' income (combined with assets). In the Pell formula it is a straight across-the-board 10.5 percent of income. The effect of these differences in the formulas is to make the uniform methodology better for low-income families and the Pell formula better for high-income families.

The Pell also produces an index called an eligibility index which is used to ration the federal money around the country. You will find out more about your eligibility index and how many Pell grant dollars it may be worth to you when you get your Pell Student Eligibility Report back in the mail after you have filed for financial aid.

Most schools have used the uniform methodology to distribute their institutional resources. If you have a high income and find a school that is using the Pell Grant formula, you may get more aid than you would under the uniform methodology. Usually the schools that will consider using the Pell index are large state institutions. This is because it would simplify their process somewhat and allow them to handle the entire student record with one formula.

Private and higher-priced schools are not likely to use the Pell method for calculating a family contribution because it would greatly reduce family contributions for those in the upper-income brackets. The use of the Pell method would quickly qualify people in high-income positions for more aid. Schools would then be faced with a shortage of financial aid funds and have to underaward aid to many students to ration their limited resources. This, of course, would change if the Pell formula were to be changed.

If you plan to educate one or more of your children in private schools, count on something like the uniform methodology existing for some time to come. In that case most of the things that we have talked about in this book are probably relevant to your financial aid planning. As far as I have been able to determine, all of the ideas mentioned would work as well or even better for the federal formula (Pell).

There are four tables in this chapter.

1. Estimated Parents' Contribution (see Table 23–1). This assumes that only one parent is employed and that there would only be one child

TABLE 23–1
Estimated Parents' Contribution*

Income	Uniform Methodology 1981–82	BEOG, 1981–82 (Pell)
$10,000	$ 0	$ 85
20,000	850	939
30,000	2,390	1,706
40,000	4,732	2,384
50,000	6,983	2,981

* Assumptions: Parents' assets under $25,000; age of parents, 46; four in family; one in college; one parent employed; state tax rate, 9 percent; and no medical expenses.

in school. Remember that income represents line 31 on the income tax return. The contrast here is between Pell contributions and the uniform methodology contribution. In this case the uniform methodology contribution is usually the same or larger.

2. Estimated Parents' Contribution with Two Parents Working. Table 23–2 is exactly like Table 23–1 except for the fact that now there are two parents employed, with the second parent earning $5,000. You can see the benefit that is derived from the employment protection allowance. You will note that in this case (as in Table 23–1) the uniform methodology generates a lower family contribution than does the Pell method at the $20,000 income level. Above that point the uniform

TABLE 23–2
Estimated Parents' Contribution with Two
Parents Working*

Income	Uniform Methodology 1981–82	BEOG, 1981–82 (Pell)
$10,000	$ 0	$ 0
20,000	322	781
30,000	1,626	1,549
40,000	3,481	2,226
50,000	5,732	2,823

* Assumptions: Parents' assets under $25,000; age of parents, 46; four in family; one in college; two parents employed, second parent earns $5,000; state tax rate, 9 percent; and no medical expenses.

methodology quickly moves ahead demanding a larger and larger parents' contribution.

You may wish to compare Table 23-1 and Table 23-2 and note the difference when part of the income is attributed to a second parent. For example, in the $50,000 income situation the effect of attributing part of the income to the second parents' work reduced the parents' contribution by $1,250. This may be a suggestion for those who own their own business and are not paying wages to their spouse.

3. *Projected Parents' Contribution from Income and Assets under the Pell Grant.* Table 23-3 will help you see the effect of the constant

TABLE 23-3
Projected Parents' Contribution from Income and Assets under the Pell Grant*

Assets	Income			
	$20,000	$30,000	$40,000	$50,000
$ 10,000	$ 781	$1,549	$2,226	$2,823
20,000	781	1,549	2,226	2,823
30,000	1,031	1,799	2,476	3,073
40,000	1,531	2,299	2,976	3,573
50,000	2,031	2,799	3,476	4,073
60,000	2,531	3,299	3,976	4,573
70,000	3,031	3,799	4,476	5,073
80,000	3,531	4,299	4,976	5,573
90,000	4,031	4,799	5,476	6,073
100,000	4,531	5,299	5,976	6,573

* Assumptions: two parents working, second parent earns $5,000; parents are any age; four in family; one in college.

percentage rate coming out of assets. If you reported a business or farm worth of at least $25,000, then there could be a significant reduction in some of these contribution levels by as much as $2,625. Once again as in the uniform methodology, a business or farm appears to be very important. Do not overlook the opportunity to report your business as a business (no matter how small it is) as long as it qualifies according to the definition on the form that you are completing. Many people have made this mistake and lost out—they did not get the additional asset protection that is allowed for a business or farm. In all these cases no matter what income or asset level you pick your student would qualify for aid at a school costing $7,000 even with only one in school. The same is not true under uniform methodology.

4. *Projected Parents' Contribution from Income and Assets under Uniform Methodology.* In making your choice of schools it may be important to take into consideration which formula will be used to determine your aid eligibility, Pell or uniform methodology.

TABLE 23-4
Projected Parents' Contribution from Income and Assets under the Uniform Methodology*

	Income				
Assets	$20,000	$30,000	$40,000	$50,000	$60,000
$ 10,000..........	$ 322	$1,626	$3,481	$5,732	$ 7,706
20,000..........	322	1,626	3,481	5,732	7,706
30,000..........	338	1,644	3,514	5,766	7,740
40,000..........	602	1,969	4,078	6,330	8,304
50,000..........	866	2,329	4,642	6,894	8,868
60,000..........	1,130	2,737	5,206	7,458	9,432
70,000..........	1,395	3,207	5,770	8,022	9,996
80,000..........	1,695	3,731	6,334	8,586	10,560
90,000..........	2,028	4,296	6,898	9,150	11,124
100,000..........	2,398	4,860	7,462	9,714	11,688

* Assumptions: Two parents employed, second employed parent earns $5,000; age of parents, 46; four in family; and one in college.

The comparison between the two is interesting. In Table 23-4 low-income people do better under uniform methodology and higher-income people do better under Pell. Fortunately, you do not have to worry much about how these calculations are made.

It is far more important for you to spend your time doing the best financial aid planning that you can in the hopes of maximizing your return. Be sure when you complete the forms to check every question carefully and have your back-up information ready and available. The financial aid officers at the school(s) to which you apply will decide what your maximum aid eligibility is. Your time is better spent providing the information needed to help with the largest possible aid award.

Section VII
MORE EXAMPLES

Chapter 24
Case Studies

Chapter 24

Case Studies

As this book has been evolving a number of examples have come to mind—important cases that might be of interest. Each situation is entirely different, but perhaps among these cases you will find hope that there may be assistance for you and your students. Cases here are similar to real situations I have seen. Further, note that many of the families have reasonably large incomes or assets. I use these cases because it is my belief that many people in these situations do not take advantage of the aid available to them. However, families with lower incomes and assets almost certainly qualify for some assistance at many schools and should definitely apply. To prove that point, the first example is a family with an income just above $20,000.

$20,000 Income

The Jacobs have an income of about $20,000 from his job as an accountant in a small manufacturing firm. Mrs. Jacobs has worked off and on, but since her diagnosis of cancer she has chosen not to work. She spends more time with her family, using her strength to do things around the home. There are two children, an older daughter who graduated from college sometime ago and a son, Ralph, who is about to enter school. They own a home that is worth about $40,000 and have about $15,000 in savings and investments.

Many times when we work with a family like the Jacobs many more details spill out that are not included in the formula—in this case, the family car is eight years old and almost rusted through and the house needs a new roof. Unfortunately, these things are not directly taken into account by the formula when your application is being considered. The only way some of these personal items can be effectively considered is to write a letter to the financial aid officer at the school(s) that your student is considering. Don't expect miracles. Many times the financial aid officer does not have a lot of discretion in what will be considered in calculating your student's aid eligibility. Financial aid forms do not ask you what kind of car you drive or give you special benefits because of your frugal nature. Theoretically, if the Jacobs wanted a new car, they would have been better off to buy it before applying for financial aid. This would have lowered their assets and thus reduced the family contribution by a small amount (unless they decided to finance it). Ralph Jacobs has had reasonably good summer jobs and has managed to save almost $1,000 by January of his senior year in high school. Mr. Jacobs is 50 years old at the time his son applies for aid.

Given the original situation:

The Jacobs' Family*

Taxable and nontaxable income............		$20,000
Assets:		
Home equity...........................	$40,000	
Cash and investments	15,000	
Net assets...............................		55,000

* Family size, 3; number in college, 1; age of oldest parent, 50.

The family contribution would be calculated as follows:
  A. Family contribution for Ralph Jacobs:

Parents' contribution...........................	$1,902
Student's summer savings (freshman)............	700
35 percent of $1,000 savings	350
Total family contribution	$2,952

Importance of Assets

If the Jacobs spent $5,000 cash for a different car and a new roof, then the situation would be as follows:
  B. Family contribution for Ralph Jacobs:

Parents' contribution......................	$1,736
Student's summer savings	700
35 percent of $1,000 savings	350
Total family contribution............	$2,786

You can see from this example that the last $5,000 in assets only changed the family contribution by $166, or less than 6 percent.

Number in Family

But if the Jacobs were a family of four with one in college, that would change the family contribution in the following way:

C. Family contribution for Ralph Jacobs (four in the family):

Parents' contribution	$1,431
Student's summer savings	700
35 percent of $1,000 savings	350
Total family contribution	$2,481

It is possible to go on making changes for a long time and thus affect the family contribution. You have already learned how much savings can affect a student's contribution; the number in college if increased could greatly reduce the expected family contribution. If part of the income was earned by the mother working, that would have a favorable impact on the family contribution because of the previously discussed allowance for two parents working. All of these things should be considered when you do your financial aid planning. Hopefully you will plan *before* you fill out your financial aid form and lock in your taxes for the year being considered.

$32,000 Income

The Hunts have a modest income in the $32,000-plus range and assets of $120,000, mainly in appreciating real estate which they wisely bought when they were first married. There are six in the family including the two parents. The eldest daughter, Jill, is the first to be going to college. The parents are 46 years old. In this case it will help to look at the family contribution with one in college and then see what happens as the second child enters school. With only Jill going to school, the family situation looks something like this.

The Hunt Family*

Taxable and nontaxable income		$ 32,000
Assets:		
Real estate	$120,000	
Net assets		120,000

*Family size, 6; number in college, 1; age of oldest parent, 46.

D. Family contribution for Jill Hunt:

Parents' contribution	$6,152
Student's summer earnings (freshman)	700
35 percent of $700 savings	245
Total family contribution	$7,097

Assuming that nothing else changed in the sophomore year for Jill except that Scott would be entering college (two in college), the situation might be as follows:

E. Family contribution for Jill Hunt (two in college):

Parents' contribution	$3,361
Student's summer savings	900
35 percent of $455 ($700 − $245)	159
Total family contribution	$4,420

It is easy to see what a major difference the second child in school will make for the Hunts. The Hunts will face a dilemma that is not uncommon in today's family; that is, where is the cash going to come from? In the original situation with just Jill in school, the parent contribution was $6,152. This works out to 12 payments of $512.67—quite a chunk out of the Hunts' already strained monthly budget. It is not so easy to raise four children on the Hunts' annual income. They are naturally hesitant about dipping into their capital, particularly that caused by appreciation in their house value. (This could be a possible solution if Jill was the last one in college and they could see the end of the tunnel of bills in sight.) As it is, their initial reaction was that if they have to come up with $6,200 a year for each child for each year of school, they could expect to pay out a total of $100,000. And this says nothing about the expenses for graduate school and so forth.

When the Hunts saw how financial aid works, they were somewhat relieved. They could see that they were not going to have to pay out $6,200 for each child for each year. In the second year when Scott starts they might be expected to contribute a total of $6,800—not too much of an increase over the original $6,200, especially considering that they do not have to feed Scott at home for nine months. As Mrs. Hunt says when Scott goes away to school they will have a much easier time buying groceries as everyone else eats normal amounts of food.

Cash Flow

The Hunts remained concerned about how they will come up with the cash necessary to make it through the first year of school. Because the school year is only nine months, they need almost $700 a month. This is where the GSL or Parents' Loan can come in handy. It was decided that Jill would take a GSL in the amount of $2,500 and that she would use all of her savings the first year. Thus, the family contribution would be made up as follows:

Family contribution for Jill Hunt:

Parents' contribution.....................	$3,197
Jill's summer earnings....................	700
35 percent of $700 savings	245
Remainder of savings	455
GSL	2,500
Total family contribution	$7,097

This would reduce the parents' need to contribute to $3,200 ($267 a month over 12 months or $356 a month over 9 months). Still a difficult job, but much more reasonable to them. They felt they could even use some savings to reduce the money taken out of current income to $200 a month. In the second year not as much trouble was anticipated. If both Scott and Jill took loans, then the family would have $5,000 toward the needed $7,000 parents' contribution.

School Policies on Bill Payment

Many families have trouble working out their financial plans especially for big college bills. Different schools have different policies about bill payment. Some schools are very hard-nosed; they want the money for the semester or quarter before the term begins. Others will accept delayed payments. Some even have payment plans of their own, or have joined a service that will collect the monthly payment from you. As a rule of thumb, I often suggest to people that they divide their parents' contribution by 12 and start setting aside monthly amounts into an account on May 1 before school starts. This will not work perfectly every time, but it seems to help a lot of people.

If like the Hunts you are counting on receiving a GSL, then be sure that you apply on time. Again some schools will let you simply prove that a loan is on the way in order to permit you to register. Others want and need their money before you register. If you are not sure of your school's policy, call the business office or the financial aid office and find out before your student faces embarrassing moments trying to register. If for some reason you cannot have the money on the due date, write the business office a letter to suggest a payment date or explain the reason for your delinquency. There is no guarantee that they will honor your request for an extension, but at least you will have tried.

Three in College

The Hunts wanted to know what would happen to Jill when all three of their children were in school. It is always hard to project into the future because family situations can change so rapidly (as can the formula under which the financial aid situation works). Even so a weak projection is better than none.

F. Family contribution for Jill Hunt (three in college):

Parents' contribution	$2,430
Jill's summer savings (senior)	900
Jill's contribution from assets	0
Total family contribution	$3,330

It is almost incredible to think that for the same student, the family contribution could drop from $7,097 to less than 47 percent of that, or $3,330. The main variable that changed is the number in college. It is quite possible that Jill would not have received any aid during her first year in school. But she would get increasingly large sums of assistance as she moved through school and her siblings joined her.

Remember that the $120,000 could be represented by a business worth $225,000 or a farm of the same amount, assuming that the family rented its housing. Thus, if you own a business that is worth a considerable amount even after you subtract the debts against it, there may be a chance that you will get help if your situation parallels the Hunts.

Effect of $90,000 in Assets

Many families do not have anywhere near $120,000 in assets. It would be interesting to see Jill's situation under different asset situations. Consider Jill Hunt in her first year of college. This time the family income will be $32,000 as before but now there will only be $30,000 in assets. ($90,000 less)

G. Family contribution for Jill Hunt ($30,000 in assets):

Parents' contribution	$1,732
Jill's summer savings (freshman)	700
35 percent of $1,000 savings	350
Total family contribution	$2,782

In this situation almost the entire family contribution could come from a Guaranteed Student Loan or Parents' Loan if the family felt it was necessary. Certainly if $1,500 was borrowed, the parents would have a much easier time of making the remaining expected payments of $232. In case D where we assumed $120,000 in assets, the parental contribution was $6,152. In case G where we assumed $30,000 in assets, the parents' contribution was $1,732. The difference of $90,000 in assets ($120,000 − $30,000) caused a change in parents' contribution of $4,400 [$6,152(D) − $1,732(G)]. Thus the $90,000 in assets caused an increase in parental contribution in case D of $4,400 each year. Another way of looking at this is that out of the $90,000 in additional assets (cases D, E, and F) the parents were only expected to give about $4,400 toward the cost of their daughter's education, or just under 5 percent.

$55,000 Income

Mrs. Schmidt recently returned to school and received her MBA. She is now making about $30,000 a year as a bank officer. Mr. Schmidt continues to enjoy his job and avocation of coaching at which he makes just over $25,000 a year. The Schmidts are 46 years old and have three children. One child, Bob, is a freshman at Universal State. He did not apply for aid at the time he entered school. Now that their second child, Leslie, is considering a private school, the Schmidts are beginning to feel a cash crunch. Because their increase in income is so recent, they do not have much in the way of assets. Their house is worth about $100,000, but it has a high mortgage ($75,000) because they remortgaged to help cover the cost of Mrs. Schmidt's schooling. Unfortunately, no one told them that Mrs. Schmidt could have borrowed $5,000 a year through the GSL program and thus not caused them to remortgage the house. The Schmidts have about $1,000 in cash. After Leslie, their third child, Jim, will start school the following year. The Schmidts are sure that Jim will want to go away to school—far away. The family contribution for Leslie for her first year with just her and Robert in school is as follows:

The Schmidts*

Taxable and nontaxable income		$55,000
Assets:		
Home equity	$25,000	
Cash	1,000	
Net assets		26,000

*Family size, 5; number in college, 2; age of oldest parent, 46.

H. Family contribution for Leslie Schmidt:

Parents' contribution	$3,002
Leslie's summer savings (freshman)	700
Leslie's contribution from assets	0
Total family contribution	$3,702

The Schmidts were surprised and decided that they had better file for aid for Robert for whom the family contribution would be about $3902. His expenses were exceeding that level, and every little bit would help.

Three in College

When the Schmidts looked ahead to Leslie's sophomore year, Robert's junior year, and Jim's freshman year, they found that they would only be expected to contribute $2,191 per student or a total of $6,573 (assuming that all the schools fully awarded). The situation for Leslie in her second year would then be as follows:

I. Family contribution for Leslie Schmidt (sophomore, three in school):

Parents' contribution	$2,191
Leslie's summer savings	900
Leslie's contribution from assets	0
Total family contribution	$3,091

The contribution for Robert would be $3,091, and the contribution for Jim would be $200 less, or $2,891, because as a freshman he would only be expected to save $700. The Schmidts were pleased that they might be able to make all the payments, particularly with the help of Guaranteed Student Loans or Parents' Loans.

Investment Strategies

Mrs. Schmidt posed an interesting question. She was contemplating investing in some oil-drilling program which would give them a write-off the first year against taxes. They planned to invest $10,000 and to write off $7,500 of it the first year. They figured that in their tax bracket this was an immediate savings of $3,470. Now this shrewd woman wanted to know the effect on financial aid of a drop in taxable income to $47,500 with everything else remaining the same. When the figures were calculated, the total parents' contribution for Robert and Leslie for the next school year, dropped from $6,004 to $4,428, or a total reduction of over $1,500. Added to their first year's tax savings, the total savings would be over $5,000.

Tax savings	$3,470
Reduced expected parents' contribution	1,576
Total savings	$5,046

Thus, as Mrs. Schmidt had surmised, the $10,000 investment would only cost the Schmidts $5,000, which made the 50 percent probability of payoff much more attractive for them. It was necessary to point out to Mrs. Schmidt that schools have a right not to fully award, and she was making the assumption that her children would attend schools that fully awarded. Further, the investment would have to be reported on the financial aid forms at its current market value. The impact of this plan on Leslie's situation would be as follows:

J. Family contribution for Leslie Schmidt (investment strategy):

Parents' contribution	$2,214
Leslie's summer savings (freshman)	700
Leslie's contribution from assets	0
Total family contribution	$2,914

This is $700 less than the original situation for Leslie. Mrs. Schmidt had an interesting interpretation of financial aid planning that included mixing her investment strategy with her financial aid strategy. As the income brackets affected by financial aid continue to move up, this will become more and more common as a means of maximizing individual family situations.

$65,000 INCOME

Mr. Wilder makes $63,500 a year, and Mrs. Wilder earns approximately $1,500 in extra money working with the local school system. They have three children—Julia, a sophomore at college; Richard, who is about to enter college; and a younger daughter, Tina. In addition Mrs. Wilder's mother, Mrs. Richards, lives with them and is fully dependent on them. Mrs. Wilder is her only child, and Mr. Richards' long terminal illness took away most of what little they had accumulated. Thus, the Wilders will be filing for aid with a family of six and two in college. They have about $30,000 equity in their $100,000 home. As Mrs. Wilder explained when I questioned her about the high income and low amount of assets, they were more interested in things other than collecting assets. However, they have recently realized from Mrs. Wilder's mother's experience that they need to accumulate something for retirement. So at the age of 45 Mrs. Wilder is going back to school. Her husband, 55, thinks that this is amusing at best.

The Wilder Family*

Taxable income............		$65,000
Assets:		
Home equity............	$30,000	
Net assets.................		30,000

* Family size, 6; number in college, 2; age of oldest parent, 55.

The concern of the Wilders was how much they would be expected to contribute to college cost and how much they would have to provide for Richard. The Wilders were advised that not all schools meet the full aid eligibility and that many have different policies on financial aid. Further, it was suggested that they should apply for aid for Mrs. Wilder and Julia. Mr. Wilder thought that it was really great to have his wife on financial aid and jokingly said he would also have her apply for food stamps. However, when it was explained how the aid system worked, he could see where she might qualify since Mrs. Wilder had chosen to do her masters' work at an excellent private university near their suburban home. The situation then for Richard was as follows:

K.   Family contribution for Richard Wilder:

Parents' contribution	$3,165
Richard's summer savings (freshman)	700
No savings.....................................	0
Total family contribution	$3,865

This assumed Richard was a freshman and that there would be three in school. If Mrs. Wilder decided not to go to school, then there would only be two in school and the expected parents' contribution per student would increase.

The Wilders then dropped a bit of a surprise. Mrs. Wilder was notified that she was a beneficiary in her uncle's will of a $100,000 legacy. This, of course, was not yet her money. The estate still had to go through all the normal channels to be sure that everything was in order. The Wilders wanted to know what effect this would have on the expected family contribution with three in school, assuming that they put this money in the bank when they received it. Of course, the following year the income would have to be accounted for, but in the meantime the assets would have the following effect on Richard's aid:

L. Family contribution for Richard Wilder (after $100,000 inheritance):

Parents' contribution	$4,985
Richard's summer savings	700
No savings	0
Total family contribution	$5,685

The Wilders could not believe that with three in school, a net worth of $130,000, and an income of $65,000 that they would probably be eligible for aid at any of the schools that they were considering for Richard. However, when we sat down to budget for them they realized that they needed all that help and more if they were going to continue to do even a portion of the things that they had been doing in the past. Mrs. Wilder was pleased to find that she might also qualify for assistance under these circumstances.

But what would happen if the Wilders were only going to have one child in college? It is unlikely that they would receive any aid because their family contribution would be far too great for one student. The important thing in that case would be to plan ahead if there was a chance that more would be going to school. Some clients try to make plans for the next four or five years based on the information that is now available.

CONCLUSION

It is possible to go on, case after case, hoping that you, the reader, would find one similar to yours. The message should be clear. There is aid available, and people in higher and higher income brackets are receiving help. I know a family now with an income over $85,000 whose children will be getting assistance at a number of fine institutions. Not many years ago this would not have been possible.

To help appreciate the aid eligibility for all the cases in this chapter, Table 24-1 shows different school costs and how much aid students would be eligible for in each case. Read the case and note the family contribution as well as the potential for aid. Remember, not every school fully awards their aid applicants but many do. Much of the time it is done with federal and state dollars at no expense to the institution—in fact, you will be doing them a service using these dollars and helping them to ask for more.

TABLE 24–1
School Costs and Aid Eligibility

	School Cost					
	$4,000	$5,000	$6,000	$7,000	$8,000	$9,000
Ralph Jacobs:						
A. ($2,952)............	$1,048	$2,048	$3,048	$4,048	$5,048	$6,048
B. ($2,786)............	1,214	2,214	3,214	4,214	5,214	6,214
C. ($2,481)............	1,519	2,519	3,519	4,519	5,519	6,519
Jill Hunt:						
D. ($7,097)............	0	0	0	0	903	1,903
E. ($4,420)............	0	580	1,580	2,580	3,580	4,580
F. ($3,330)............	670	1,670	2,670	3,670	4,670	5,670
G. ($2,782)............	1,218	2,218	3,218	4,218	5,218	6,218
Leslie Schmidt:						
H. ($3,702)............	298	1,298	2,298	3,298	4,298	5,298
I. ($3,091)............	909	1,909	2,909	3,909	4,909	5,909
J. ($5,046)............	0	0	954	1,954	2,954	3,954
Richard Wilder:						
K. ($3,865)............	135	1,135	2,135	3,135	4,135	5,135
L. ($5,685)............	0	0	315	1,315	2,315	3,315

Note: School cost − Family contribution = Aid eligibility
i.e., (G) $7,000 − $2,782 = $4,218

Several things became clearer to me when this chart was made up:

1. Almost every student that has been discussed so far would qualify for substantial amounts of aid eligibility at most expensive private schools. In some cases there is as much as $6,000 need.

2. In many of the examples the students would qualify for help at many less expensive institutions with total costs ranging from $4,000 to $5,000.

3. Only in the case of Jill Hunt's situation D (where there is just one student in college) does the student become close to being a full-paying student at most schools.

4. There are probably many students who limit their choice of schools because their families do not believe that they would qualify for aid. But just the reverse is true. Since aid eligibility theoretically increases with the increase in school cost, the student could have his choice of schools. And surprisingly the siblings in college might also receive assistance from their schools if they also filed aid applications.

Section VIII
THE FUTURE

Chapter 25
The Future

Chapter 25

The Future

Financial Aid Will Change

We can expect continual changes in the financial aid processes each year as a result of the shifting priorities of those in power and the political importance of financial aid. Clearly, one of the factors that will influence what the politicians do will be their perception of the political force of the educational community—students, faculty, administrators, parents, and those who just believe in the importance of education.

It is hard to specify the exact kinds of changes that we may see and how they will affect individual families. Some of the possibilities that have been discussed are as follows.

Reduction in the Federal Aid Programs

The Pell may be reduced so that it is only useful for extremely needy families, thus excluding many of the middle-income and lower-middle-income economic groups from much needed assistance. This has been discussed at some length. But in reality it could cause some major difficulties for a number of institutions that depend on their students having this money in order to have necessary enrollment. It is unlikely that the same conservative Congress that wants to save money will want to endanger the independent and public educational systems in this country by cutting off a major portion of their flow of funds.

Newspapers have been full of discussions about changing the loan programs. We should not forget that the loan programs were instituted as National Defense Loans many years ago. In the 1950s, it was recognized that education was one of the best defenses that a nation had in this increasingly technical world. Perhaps we will see adjustments in the loan programs to make them less attractive to those who may be abusing the system and to orient students to those fields that are most important for the nation. For example, if we need more scientists, perhaps they should receive a lower interest rate than business students. Loans have been built into the educational financing systems as an integral part of financial aid packaging. While change may be in order, it is difficult to imagine that this entire program would be eliminated. Severe reduction in loan programs could cause grave damage to some of our educational institutions whose students depend on this as a source of financing their education. How would the gap be filled? Is this nation prepared to pay the price of reducing its standards of education and perhaps endanger a significant part of the independent educational sector?

The College Work Study Program will almost assuredly remain and grow. It has always been politically popular for students to work for their education. Even in a period of changing political beliefs you can expect that this program will continue in much the same form.

Changes in State Programs

Significant changes in state aid may occur as a result of shifts in federal aid for a number of reasons.

1. Some state aid is subsidized by federal aid to the states. Changes in this federal aid could force significant changes in state programs.
2. States have differing levels of commitment to education. Those with a high level of education will probably not only continue the aid they have been providing but may actually increase it in order to make up to their citizens any aid loss from federal sources.
3. The economic conditions of the states will be a factor. In Michigan during the sales slump for automobiles of 1979–81, it became necessary to reduce state aid to education and, in particular, financial aid to students and their families.

In my opinion states will want to make every effort that they can to maintain and even to promote the building of the finest educational systems possible. This may well be an investment in their future, both in educating their young and attracting new business.

One of the major shifts that states may contemplate is to award financial aid on some criteria other than what is currently being used. In a time of limited financial aid funds, states, like the federal government, may wish to develop their own new methods of evaluating financial need.

Institutional Aid Programs

Institutions may very well get caught in a two-way squeeze play—reduced federal and state financial aid available to students and fewer students to go around due to the lower birth rate. This may be one of the places that the careful financial aid planner can pick up money. It may well become more and more commonplace to negotiate with institutions about how much you want to pay and when. Institutions need students to survive; they also need paying students. You will want to discuss the amount of the discount that might be available to your child.

You Can Help Yourself

Plan ahead; plan to apply for financial aid. Start early. Find out how the aid process works, what is likely to be available from your state and from the federal government. When you narrow down your choice of schools, find out how they award aid. Get to know the ins and outs of the financial aid office. Let the admissions office know that you want aid and how much you expect. Often if you can give them a dollar amount, they will try to lobby with the financial aid office for you. It is difficult to make a deal if you do not tell them what you want.

What looks on the surface to be a bad time for higher-income families seeking aid may be just the beginning of an opportunity to bargain for the best deal. Congress and various states may feel that education is too important to make significant cuts in these areas. America's high educational level is one of the things that is helping our nation now—to do away with that might further weaken our situation.

Using History as a Guideline

If we look back historically, financial aid has been increasing to upper-income groups for a number of years. I believe that it will continue to do so for those who plan.

Section IX
APPENDIXES

Appendix A
Glossary

Appendix B
Resources

Appendix C
Sample Questions

Appendix A—Glossary

Academic Scholarships Grants or gift aid awarded in part or entirely on the basis of academic achievement by the student. Financial need or aid eligibility is not necessary to receive one of these awards, but if you receive one and have aid eligibility, it will have to be considered as part of your resources to meet that aid eligibility. Not all schools have academic scholarships.

Academic Year The period from September to June is generally defined as the academic year. Some schools end in April, and others do not start until October 1. But in general the two major semesters or three terms (quarters) are included in the academic year. This becomes important in financial aid because aid is generally awarded on an academic-year basis.

ACT The American College Testing Program, a nonprofit company that has been one of the major processors of financial aid applications. Recently their form has been called the Family Financial Statement. Your high school guidance office should have the Family Financial Statement or a successor form for your convenience.

Aid A shortened version of financial aid referring to the moneys provided to help with educational cost. These funds are usually administered by the financial aid office at the schools to which you will be applying.

Aid Eligibility A term used to indicate the financial need that a specific student has at a given institution. The same student can have a widely varying need or aid eligibility at schools with different total costs. The formula is:

$$\text{Total cost} - \text{Family contribution} = \text{Aid eligibility}$$

Thus, if a student's family contribution was $3,900 and the student was considering three different schools with costs of $4,000, $6,500, and $8,000, the student's aid eligibility in each case would be:

Total cost −	Family contribution =	Aid eligibility
$4,000 −	$3,900 =	$ 100
6,500 −	3,900 =	2,600
8,000 −	3,900 =	4,100

Aid Packaging The process by which a financial aid officer creates an award for you based on your eligibility for various funds. To determine your eligibility the formula is: total cost of the institution you are considering less the family contribution.

Total cost − Family contribution = Aid eligibility

See Chapters 15 and 17 for a detailed description of how aid packaging works including the kinds of awards available.

Assets For the purpose of financial aid only certain assets are usually considered. They include the home, cash, stocks, bonds, other securities, real estate, and business or farm. In all cases when looking at the value of assets, financial aid considers current market value less debts against the assets, or the net worth of assets. Assets of both the student and the parents are considered.

Award Money provided in the form of grant (gift), loan, or work to help a student complete an education. It is the portion of the aid eligibility that is actually made available.

Basic Educational Opportunity Grant (BEOG, or Pell Grant) This is a federal entitlement program and goes to students that are determined to have need by the basic grant formula. Like other financial aid, the amount that a student may qualify for can vary from school to school depending on the cost of the school. This grant will range from 0 to $1,750 for students attending school in 1980–81. In the past the basic grant formula has been different than that used to distribute most of the aid—the uniform methodology. A student who has aid eligibility under the basic grant formula might have a very different aid eligibility under the uniform methodology and vice versa. In 1980–81 the income range of the recipients of these kinds of funds was from 0 to $40,000 a year.

Basic Educational Opportunity Grant Student Eligibility Report (BEOGSER) This is a document that will be returned to you by the basic grant (Pell Grant) processor to inform you if they need additional information or information verified, or what your eligibility for the basic grant is. Your eligibility for the basic grant does not necessarily say anything about your eligibility for other forms of aid, as traditionally the basic grant formula has been different and served as a rationing device for the Office of Education. You do not need to worry about this document. It will automatically come in the student's mail if the financial aid application has been correctly filled out. Traditionally, it has been in three parts and it is important that you keep all three parts together until you have decided which school the student will attend. If colleges would like a copy before enrollment, send them a photostatic copy.

Business Farm Supplement A form that has traditionally been available from high school counselors, the financial aid office, or one of the processors,

Appendix A—Glossary

either ACT or the College Scholarship Service. Some schools and states require this if you indicate that you have business or farm assets or income. If you are required to file this, be sure you get enough forms to have one for each of your business operations.

Campus-Based Programs A term used to apply to federal programs including the SEOG (Supplementary Educational Opportunity Grant), the CWSP (College Work Study Program), and the NDSL (National Direct Student Loan) which are administered locally. This means that within the rules and regulations set down by the federal government, the institutional financial aid officer will be determining your award for these programs.

College Board An organization of colleges, universities, and school systems connected with the Scholastic Aptitude Test (SAT) test and the College Scholarship Service.

College Scholarship Service A subsidiary of the College Board (the SAT people) that has been one of the major processors of financial aid forms. Most recently their form has been called the Financial Aid Form; before that it was referred to as the Parents' Confidential Statement (PCS). Your high school guidance office should have the Financial Aid Form or its successor forms for your convenience. The College Scholarship Service (CSS) also produces annually a number of publications that are very helpful in understanding financial aid and its current policies.

College Work Study Program (CWSP) This is a federally funded program. These funds are 80 percent from the federal government and 20 percent from the college. Students' earnings under this program will be limited to what is stated on their fund award notice from the college. If they want to earn more, they should talk with the financial aid office about repackaging their aid to increase their earnings, perhaps reducing a loan (NDSL). It is their responsibility to work to earn these funds, and they will receive a paycheck. These funds cannot be deducted from the student's bill nor may they borrow against future earnings from the college to pay their bills. As a rule these dollars will help with personal expenses and the next tuition bill.

Confidentiality of Records The financial aid community has been concerned about the privacy of records for some time, and most financial aid offices make every effort to keep all records locked and only available to those who understand the private nature of the information that you have shared. Despite a great deal of concern about personal records, in my years I have never had a parent complain that their records were not held confidential.

Cost The term *cost* in financial aid is usually used to refer to the total cost of attending a school including the following charges: tuition, fees, room and board, books, personal expenses, and travel.

Dependent Student Most students file for aid as dependent students, meaning that their aid is based on the income and assets of the student and the parents. This is the normal status of a student.

Direct Student Loan (DSL) See **State Direct Student Loan.**

Educational Support An agreement usually in a divorce decree or separation agreement that a parent will make a contribution toward educational costs at the college level. In many cases the exact amount of such payment is fixed for the four years of college. See Chapter 18 on Divorce.

Employment Allowance   When both parents in a family are employed or if one parent in a single-parent family is employed, a special allowance is given to account for the additional expenses that are incurred by families that must pay for services (such as child care) to help maintain the family. The allowance in the 1981–82 year was 50 percent of the lower wage earner's wages up to $2,400. This allowance can have a significant impact on the aid eligibility of a family (see Chapter 6).

Employment Protection Allowance   See **Employment Allowance**.

Equity   The difference between the current market value and the amount that you owe on an item. For example, if you have $10,000 in stock and owe nothing on it, then you have $10,000 in equity. If the value of the stock drops to $9,000, then your equity is $9,000. If you then borrow $3,000 against the $9,000, your equity is $6,000.

Family Contribution   The family contribution is a sum of the parents' contribution from income and assets as well as the student's contribution from income, summer work, and assets.

Parents' contribution + Student's contribution = Family contribution

The parents' contribution and the student's contribution are covered in detail in Section III.

Family Financial Statement (FFS)   Similar to the Financial Aid Form (FAF), this is put out by the ACT (American College Testing) organization.

Family Size   The size of the family (or members of the household) that will be living at home is very important to determine financial aid. The larger the family size, the larger the allowance to maintain that family and thus the smaller the family contribution.

Federal Form   Federal Financial Aid Form is the application for the Basic Educational Opportunity Grant (Pell Grant). See **Basic Educational Opportunity Grant.**

Financial Aid   Assistance given on the basis of need to help with college costs. Need is usually determined by a formula, such as the uniform methodology, that is applied uniformly to the family by a number of schools or organizations.

Financial Aid Form (FAF)   This is the form which has been put out by the College Scholarship Service. The processor has in the past used the information you provide on this form to determine the family contribution using the uniform methodology, as it has been described. This form and its successor forms should be available through your high school counselor or college and university financial aid offices.

Financial Aid Officer   Usually an official of the school whose responsibility it is to verify aid applications, to package awards, and to deal with students and families who have financial aid problems. This is an increasingly professional field.

Financial Need   The total cost of the school you are considering less your family contribution equals financial need. See also **Aid Eligibility.**

Grants   Gift assistance based aid eligibility. These include:

   Pell Grant (BEOG)—Federal noncampus-based program awarded to students based on need as determined by the federal formula.

Appendix A—Glossary

    Supplementary Educational Opportunity Grant (SEOG)—Federal campus-based program awarded by the financial aid officer.

    State grants—Many states have programs of grant assistance for their residents to attend colleges and universities. Most of these programs require you to go to school in your own state.

    Institutional grants—Most institutions have some form of grant program either endowed through gifts of alumni and friends or created out of current budget dollars. These are also awarded by the aid officers.

    Other Grants—Local, regional, and national programs to help students with need (aid eligibility) to attend college. Many of these require a separate application process because they are awarded by their own committees and not by financial aid officers at the institution you are planning to attend. (A good source of more information would be your high school counselor.)

Guaranteed Student Loan (GSL) Loans made through banks but guaranteed by the federal government. The taxpayers pay the interest until the student is able to assume that responsibility by leaving school or graduating. There is a six-month grace period before the student must go into repayment. The payment of interest may be further deferred if the student elects to pursue graduate study. Every family ought to explore this option discussed in Chapter 16.

High School Counselor An extremely important resource. Usually will have the necessary aid applications and may be able to inform you about local scholarship opportunities. Some high school counselors have handouts or at least reference material on financial aid and may even arrange special financial aid nights.

Home The place (home) where the student lives is the one for which the financial aid form should be filled out. In cases of divorce or separation, apply for aid based on the situation in the home where the student lives.

Honor Scholarships Similar to academic scholarships. Given for excellence in one or many areas. Usually may be awarded whether or not there is need, but if there is need, this award must be considered as part of the total aid package.

Household The household for financial aid purposes is the one in which the student lives—the grouping of people with whom the student resides the majority of time when not in school. For an independent student this could be one—the student. For a student that lives only with his mother, this would be two. For a student that lives with parents, three siblings, two grandparents, and an uncle, this would be nine.

Income The income being considered is that reported on the tax form as adjusted gross income, which has been line 31. The lower this figure, the better your chance of having aid eligibility and thus getting aid.

Income Taxes For financial aid purposes the emphasis is on federal income tax information on Form 1040.

Independent Student This has been defined as a student who is entitled to file for and receive financial aid based on the student's income and assets without regard to the parents' situation. In order for a student to qualify for this status, in 1981–82 it was necessary for the student and parents to be able to answer no to all the following questions for both 1980 and 1981 (see Chapter 21):

Did or will the student live with the parents for more than six weeks?
Did or will the parents claim the student as an income tax exemption?
Did or will the student get more than $1,000 of support from the parents?

Institutional Aid Many schools have their own aid programs. These may include gift assistance or grants, work programs, and loans. School resources for these funds come out of gifts by alumni and friends and from the regular budget of the institution. The amounts are usually determined by the financial aid officer at that institution. Some institutions use their own formulas for awarding their own aid.

Institutional Aid Application Many schools have their own aid forms which should be completed in addition to the standard aid applications. School forms may be extremely simple or more detailed in an attempt to get more information to help determine the needs of students. Check with the financial aid office of the school to which you are applying to see if the school requires its own application.

Land Contract A real estate term used to describe a method of purchasing property. If you have sold property and the new owners are making payments to you for a period of time, it is suggested that you read the section on this topic in Chapter 8.

Line 31 The adjusted gross income figure on Form 1040 U.S. Individual Income Tax Return. This figure is central to all financial aid calculations as it is an auditable number.

Loans There are a number of loan programs available to students today, including the new taxpayer-subsidized Parents' Loan Program (PLP), and more are being considered by Congress. Some of the most common are:

NDSL—The National Direct Student Loan is awarded by the institution's financial aid officer to students of need. This form of assistance helps to meet their need eligibility.

GSL—Students apply through their local bank for the Guaranteed Student Loan. This loan may be used as part of the family contribution and, therefore, may be used in some cases in addition to the financial aid offered by the college.

SDSL—The State Direct Student Loan is similar to the GSL, but it is available for those students who have been refused loans by their bank, credit union, or savings and loan. In this case the state is the lender.

Institutional Loans—These vary from school to school, but many institutions have some funds available to loan to students who have special needs.

Minister's Housing Allowance Ministers are often provided housing by their church in partial compensation for the lower salaries that they receive. In some cases the pastor literally receives money to help pay the cost of rent or

Appendix A—Glossary

home purchase in addition to salary. To put everyone on an equal footing, ministers are required to report their housing allowance or in many cases a figure for the housing allowance is assumed. Pastors who do not receive either housing or a housing allowance would be well advised to point this out to the financial aid officer if the award that they receive seems to be too small because a housing allowance may have been assumed automatically.

National Direct Student Loan (NDSL) A campus-based federal program awarded by the financial aid officer to help fill the aid eligibility. There is not a separate application for these funds as there is for the GSL or SDSL. If an NDSL is included in your award and you accept it, you will usually sign for it about the time of registration. This loan fund is funded by the U.S. government, the college, and former students who are making payments. The interest rate has been very low, 3 percent after you graduate or leave school, although recently it has been raised to 4 percent.

National Merit Scholarship Corporation A private, nonprofit corporation that together with companies, individuals, foundations, and institutions makes scholarship (gift money) available on the basis of academic criteria and need. More information can be obtained from your high school counselor.

National Negro Achievement Scholarship A nationwide system of honor scholarships for outstanding black students, partially based on need.

Need This is the same thing as aid eligibility. In the past the difference between what a family could contribute according to the formula and the cost of the school was considered need. In more recent years some schools are referring to this as aid eligibility, particularly if they are not going to be able to meet the full need of the student. Another reason for the term *aid eligibility* is that the same student could have different aid eligibility under different formulas; for example, the BEOG (Pell) formula, the uniform methodology, and a state formula.

Net Worth For financial aid purposes, net worth is the total value of your assets being considered in the financial aid formula less any loans that you may have against those specific assets. See Chapter 8.

Overaward When a school awards more than the amount of aid eligibility or need for that student. This is done sometimes to lure a good student to the school. Sometimes this occurs by accident, and it frequently occurs in the case of special interest groups.

Parents' Contribution This is the amount that parents are expected to contribute toward the student's annual academic expenses. It is calculated by adding the parents' contribution from income to the parents' contribution from assets. It will change substantially if additional members of the family decide to go to college. The parents' contribution is generally based on the information provided on the aid application form. Because the formulas have been different, it may be different for BEOG than for uniform methodology. See Section III.

Parents' Contribution from Assets Under the formula only certain assets are considered. Only a small percentage of assets are considered available to use for financial aid purposes under the formulas that have been used through the 1980–81 processing year. Usually under 6 percent of asset value has been considered available to help defray the cost of education. See Chapter 8.

Parents' Contribution from Income This is generally calculated on the past tax year. Thus, if your student is applying for aid for the freshman year, it will be based on the tax year which started in the middle of that student's junior year in high school. See Chapter 6.

Parents' Loan Program The Parents' Loan Program (PLP) was first authorized by Congress in the fall of 1980. Under this program, parents of students should be able to borrow up to $3,000 a year per student at 9 percent (a maximum of $15,000). See Chapter 16.

Pell Grant The new name for the federally supported grant program formerly known as the Basic Grant or BEOG. See Chapter 23 or Basic Educational Opportunity Grant in the Glossary.

Personal Expenses An allowance in total cost to cover the day-to-day living cost of students during the academic year, including such items as money for cokes, toothpaste, and campus movies.

Processing Year The year for which aid forms are being completed. Thus, during the 1981–82 academic year students complete the aid form for the 1982–83 award year. This would be called the 1982–83 processing year.

Processor An organization which processes the aid application forms using the agreed-upon methodology and then forwards the information to the colleges and organizations requested by the students. The College Scholarship Service has been the processor for the FAF form, and ACT has been the processor for the FFS form. There are other approved processors, but these have been the two major nonprofit organizations working in this area.

Room and Board These charges for dormitory room and food usually do not vary too much between schools. Be sure that they are included in the total cost budget you consider.

State Direct Student Loan (SDSL) A form of guaranteed student loan available to students who are refused loans by their banks. Contact the financial aid office at the college or university you plan to attend. In the past you could borrow up to $2,500 a year but not more than $7,500 for four years of undergraduate education. These limits have now been raised. (See Chapter 16.)

State Tax Allowance Because tax policies are different in 50 different states, those responsible for developing the formula in the case of the uniform methodology have allowed for different figures for state tax. A constant figure for each state is multiplied against the total income as reported to determine the state tax allowance. For incomes of $10,000 or more they have been as follows:

State	Percent
Puerto Rico, Texas, Wyoming	4
Florida, Louisiana, Nevada, Tennessee, West Virginia	5
Alabama, Arkansas, Georgia, Indiana, New Mexico, Ohio, Oklahoma, Washington	6
Alaska, Arizona, Idaho, Kansas, Kentucky, Missouri, Mississippi, Nebraska, New Hampshire, North Carolina, North Dakota, South Carolina, South Dakota, Virginia	7

Appendix A—Glossary

State	Percent
Colorado, Connecticut, Washington, D.C., Guam, Illinois, Iowa, Montana, New Jersey, Oregon, Pennsylvania, Trust Territories, Utah, Virgin Islands	8
Delaware, Hawaii, Maine, Michigan, Rhode Island	9
California, Maryland, Minnesota, Vermont	10
Massachusetts, Wisconsin	11
New York	12

Source: Reprinted with permission from *CSS Need Analysis: Theory and Computation Procedures for the 1981–82 FAF.* Copyright © 1980 by College Entrance Examination Board, New York.

In the examples generally we have used 9 percent as a state tax rate, since that appears to represent approximately the middle according to the way the population is distributed. People who live in states with rates above 9 percent would have increased aid eligibility over the examples, and people who live in states with lower tax rates would receive less aid eligibility.

Student's Contribution from Assets Generally students are expected to contribute 35 percent of their asset value for each year for assets that are considered for financial aid purposes. If a student lists as an asset $1,000 in savings, then that student will be expected to contribute $350 from that $1,000 toward the next year's college cost (see Chapter 11). Students' assets may include a variety of items: savings, stocks, bonds, land, and so forth.

Student Eligibility Report (SER) A form sent to Pell (BEOG) applicants to inform them of their eligibility based on the financial information filed on the application.

Student Savings See **Student Contribution from Assets.**

Student's Contribution The student's contribution is a sum of the student contribution from assets and the expected summer savings.

Summer Earnings See **Summer Savings.**

Summer Savings Each student is expected to work and earn money toward educational expenses over the course of the summer. Schools have different expectations about how much a student can earn and save during the summer. The general rules have been as follows for the summer between:

High school senior and college freshman	$700
College freshman and college sophomore	900
College sophomore and college junior	900
College junior and college senior	900

Supplementary Educational Opportunity Grant Program (SEOG) A campus-based federal program aimed at particularly needy students. To qualify for this the family contribution should be less than half the total cost of attending the institution. These awards are determined by the financial aid officer.

Taxes Federal taxes and the basis for your calculation of your federal income taxes are extremely important to the financial aid process. You should start your taxes early if you will be applying for financial aid.

Tax-Free Dollars As used in this text it implies that aid dollars awarded will not in general be taxed. The only aid dollars that might be subject to income tax would be those earned working if the student had substantial other income.

Tax Year The tax year which is referred to in financial aid is the standard personal income tax year beginning January 1 and ending December 31. Some of you may have different tax years for a variety of reasons. If that is the case, be sure you know how to handle this for financial aid purposes.

Travel An allowance for the cost of getting to and from school. The standard if a student lives a great distance from the school is to allow an amount equivalent to two round-trip air coach fares.

Underaward An institution may choose not to meet the full need or aid eligibility of the student for a variety of reasons. This is known as an underaward. A common reason for underawarding students is to ration funds. This is done by federal, state, and local governments as well as by institutions that need to ration their institutional funds.

Uniform Methodology The government-approved formulas that have been used for determining the family contribution toward educational expenses. This formula is used nationally by the College Scholarship Service (FAF) and American College Testing (FFS). The BEOG formula is different. Some states and some schools use their own formulas to distribute their own funds.

Appendix B—Resources

Resources

There are many sources of information about financial aid that are available to you as you go through the application process. The forms that are required depend on what you are applying for and what schools are being considered. The people are professionals who in most cases have a myriad of other job responsibilities in addition to keeping up with the changing regulations in financial aid.

One of the concerns expressed by parents is the apparent difficulty of getting accurate and specific information on the topic. There are plenty of handout materials prepared each year: but where do you find them and what do you do if you have questions after reviewing them? Each person who considers financial aid will find a wide variety of people to talk to about the topic—but probably only a few will be really knowledgeable and able to help.

Getting the best information is a matter of "digging." Try the high school guidance office as well as the admissions office and financial aid office as you visit schools. Remember that financial aid is a rapidly changing field and there are few experts in the field available to help you. The number becomes even smaller if you are looking for ways to make the system work for you.

Probably the best sources of current financial aid information are financial aid officers who deal daily with changes in the law and administration of programs. Remember financial aid planning, like tax planning, requires knowledge of the subject, and usually decisive action must be taken long before the return is due.

Forms

There are a number of major forms that you should become familiar with. Due to new legislation at the end of 1980, there may be additional forms or replacement forms for some of those listed below for the 1981–82 application year. However, this list should give you a good start.

1. *Financial Aid Form (1980–81).* This financial aid application is distributed by the College Scholarship Service which is part of the College Board, the people who put out the SAT test, the achievement tests, and advance placement, as well as a multitude of other services to the educational community. The completed form is sent to the College Scholarship Service (the processor) and not to the colleges. The processor (College Scholarship Service) scans the form and then keypunches the information into a data system for a nationally agreed-upon analysis (the uniform methodology). The colleges and agencies get a photostatic copy of everything that you send in on the form as well as a copy of the analysis done by the processor (the College Scholarship Service). At the time of this writing there are discussions about revising this form for the 1981–82 application year (1982–83 award year).

2. *Family Financial Statement (1980–81).* This application asks the same questions as the Financial Aid Form. But in the past to answer questions on this form you marked little boxes or circles on an answer sheet (a mark sense document). This allows the form to be machine read for analysis. This application is put out by the American College Testing Service, the company that puts out the ACT exam, the PEP exam, and many other educational services. The ACT company also has acted as a processor in performing almost the same analysis as the College Scholarship Service.

3. *BEOG Application.* The Basic Educational Opportunity Grant has been renamed the Pell Grant in honor of the program's original sponsor, Senator Claiborne Pell. In recent years the Pell Grant (BEOG) application has been included in its entirety in the two forms mentioned above. The Pell or basic grant application is the federal application for the basic grant program plus other federal programs beginning in the 1982–83 academic year.

4. *Institutional Application.* Many institutions will have their own aid forms. These will vary from a few questions to detailed information about the family and its situation. Each school attempts to design its own aid forms if one is needed to meet the demands for institutional aid programs. Some colleges have even collectively created an additional aid form in order to provide the aid offices at those schools with more detailed information.

5. *State Applications.* Most states have some kind of financial aid program. Each state has its own method of handling aid applications. Many states have elected to use either or both the Financial Aid Form and the Family Financial Statement with minor modifications or additions. Some even have their own needs analysis system.

6. *U.S. Income Tax Form 1040.* Almost all financial aid is based directly or indirectly on the previous year's income as reported on the federal tax form. This form is very close to becoming a financial aid form, and what you put on your tax return will have a major effect on your financial aid.

7. *Local Scholarships.* Some local organizations as well as state and national groups and foundations have their own aid application forms. Many of these organizations use a supplement to or a variation of the Family Financial Statement or the Financial Aid Form.

To determine which form to use, check the current admissions or financial aid literature from the school to which you are applying. It will usually say which forms are accepted, but one may be preferred. Another place to get this information is from your high school guidance office. A number of high schools have handout charts explaining which schools prefer which forms.

People

There are many people and organizations involved in financial aid. Depending on the individual you ask, you will find different levels of knowledge regarding aid and the strategies or planning that you may want to devise.

1. *High School Counselor.* The first place to start in your quest for financial aid information is your high school counselor. Originally the aid system was designed so that the high school counseling or guidance office could serve as a source for the information and forms necessary for financial aid. The theory behind this idea was good. But as financial aid has become more and more complicated and the stakes are higher, the high school counseling offices are not always prepared to provide the best answers to questions that families might have.

2. *Admissions Officer.* Usually when you visit a college you make an appointment with an admissions officer. This officer should make every effort to be sure that all your needs are met during your visit. The admissions director, associate director, counselor, or whatever, will probably talk with the student first and then ask you to join them and ask any questions that you may have. Almost invariably one of the first questions from Mom and/or Dad has to do with finances and then

financial aid. This is a good time to bring up finances—admissions people are knowledgeable on a wide variety of topics related to the college selection process. They can probably tell you how to apply and the kinds of awards that they give at their schools. These awards will be much like those given at the last school you visited, or the next school, only they may have different names.

Admissions people usually have available the forms necessary to apply for financial aid in case you have not been able to get them from your high school. They may also have any special forms required by their institution. They should have a pretty good idea of the schedule for financial aid and some knowledge of the kinds of grants, work, and loans that a student may receive based on his or her need. However, very few admissions people are trained to help parents with their in-depth financial aid questions.

3. *Financial Aid Officer.* You probably should ask the admissions office to make an appointment for you with the financial aid officer when you call for your admissions appointment, particularly if you are going a long way to visit the school. If you do make an appointment with the financial aid officer, try to have your information ready to discuss. Generally, before the appointment try to fill out an aid form, possibly an old one. And bring along last year's income tax form. Financial aid officers vary widely in their method of handling visitors. But if you are lucky and they are not pressed for time, then the aid officer will review your files and perhaps even hand calculate your analysis, giving you a realistic idea of how much aid you may expect. Aid officers can do this rather quickly. They can also go into some detail with you about the kinds of things that would or could make a significant difference in your aid. Unfortunately, at many schools the aid officers are already overburdened and they do not feel that they can take the time to do an in-depth review of your individual situation. If this is the case, try to be understanding, but it may be a signal to you about the school.

4. *Tax Preparer.* Another person that is becoming a larger part of the aid system is the *accountant or tax preparer*. At one time it was uncommon for parents to have their aid forms filled out by tax preparers or accountants, but today it is becoming more frequent. A word of caution—these people may be good in their business, but most of them do not know anything about financial aid. Most have never even applied for financial aid, much less studied it and how it works. You may find that your accountant or tax preparer can help you achieve some of the suggestions made in this book. Further, a professional can help you decide between the potential rewards in financial aid as compared to tax strategies.

Possibly training programs should be set up to help accountants and tax preparers learn more about the strategies of financial aid. This will become increasingly important if we continue to move in the direction of having people with higher and higher incomes qualifying for aid. One family had an income over $80,000 and qualified for assistance. That kind of family is likely to have an accountant working with them on their tax structure and, in the future, their financial aid structure. An example of the kind of things to be aware of in contrasting tax strategy and financial aid strategy is that the worst thing you can do for financial aid is to give your children money. Many tax advisors will suggest you avoid income taxes by giving money to your children. But this is contradictory to financial aid strategy and could cost you plenty in terms of financial aid dollars. (See Chapter 19.)

One of the things that you should do with your accountant or tax preparer is to let him or her know that you will need your taxes done in January if at all possible. Historically, it has been to the student's advantage to apply for financial aid early. The forms are not supposed to be filed (in 1980–81) until after January 1, 1981. Therefore, if the taxes can be done by the end of January, the financial aid forms can be filed with accurate information early in the financial aid processing year. If you cannot get your taxes done, you may file from an estimate. But people who do this usually have hassle after hassle until they have completed their taxes and can file an amended financial aid form. If you must make a choice between filing later or estimating your taxes, file an estimate and then correct it.

Programs

Some high school guidance offices sponsor a college night or, even better, a financial aid night. These programs will give you more detail about financial aid and what is available. But rarely do such programs go into aid strategies or give more than a superficial look at the financial aid application process. The reason for this is that it is difficult to lead a whole group of people through a detailed review of financial aid because of the variety of questions that come up and the lack of skilled presenters.

The best of these programs are usually those billed as financial aid nights—they concentrate on financial aid alone. Much of the time in these presentations is usually spent discussing the types of programs that you would be eligible for if you qualify. That is not really a problem; most state and federal grants are prescribed to be a certain size for a given set of qualifiers. The trick is to be sure that you get your family accurately represented on the application form in order to maximize your chances of getting assistance. Look for any hints of things that you can do to make yourself more eligible. If possible, review the financial aid form before attending a financial aid night so that instead of trying to follow along, you can be listening and fine tuning your application.

If you attend a special financial aid program at the college you will probably find that these sessions are well organized and thought provoking. The speaker is usually trained in financial aid and can show you much of the intricacy involved.

Materials

High school counselors usually have the necessary forms and even more importantly often know which schools prefer which forms. The system that was used the last two years (1978–79 and 1979–80) has had the application forms to the guidance office sometime in November. Most schools send them home between Thanksgiving and Christmas. If you will be applying for financial aid next year, mark it on your calendar. Start asking about those forms in late November. At the same time the guidance office will probably have available a number of brochures on financial aid prepared by the federal government, your state government, and possibly any major local scholarship groups. Each year the College Scholarship Service puts out a wonderful little booklet entitled "Meeting College Costs." It is well worth reading and should be available through the counseling office.

Appendix C—Sample Questions

The following list of questions is organized by chapter heading. Space has been left after each grouping in case you wish to write in your own questions about that area. It is hoped that selected use of these and other questions can help you get the most current information when visiting with college representatives, high school counselors, and financial aid officers and when attending financial aid presentations. You will want to adjust the wording of the questions to the appropriate situation. Having read this book you can readily understand that the way different schools respond can indicate a substantial difference in the way aid eligibility is determined. Remember to always obtain the name, address, and phone number of people you speak with so that you can return to them should you need additional information.

SECTION I. INTRODUCTION

Chapter 2. Should You Consider Aid?

1. How much is the school going to cost per year?
2. What is the estimated total cost for a student including books, spending money, and everything?

SECTION II. THE PROCESS

Chapter 3. The Application Process

1. When is the admissions application due?
2. Does the school require an institutional aid application?
3. When is the institutional aid application due?
4. How soon can you get the financial aid forms?
5. What is the deadline for filing the financial aid forms?
6. What are the forms and deadlines for state scholarships?
7. Is there any information on local scholarships that your student might qualify for?
8. Does the school have any scholarship competitions which your student can enter?

Chapter 4. The Application

1. When will the high schools or colleges have the actual aid applications that your student needs?
2. Will they mail you a complete packet of forms that you need?
3. What is the name of the financial aid officer with whom you will be dealing and how do you get in touch with that person?
   a. Name?
   b. Address?
   c. Telephone number?
4. How long does the school take to process the aid application?
5. When should you hear if you file on time?
6. Does the student have to be admitted before you can find out how much financial aid you might be entitled to?
7. Is your state aid program usable at the schools you are considering?
8. What is required in verification procedures?
9. What method does the school use for determining aid eligibility?
   a. Uniform methodology?
   b. Federal formula (Pell Grant or BEOG)?
   c. Institutional formula?

SECTION III. THE FAMILY CONTRIBUTION

Chapter 5. The Organization of the Family Contribution

1. Does the school use the adjusted gross income (line 31) from the U.S. federal tax form to determine need?
2. Is home equity considered an asset or not?

Appendix C—Sample Questions

Chapter 6. Parents' Contribution from Income
1. How are incomes treated in divorce situations by this institution?
   a. Income of natural parent not living in the home?
   b. Income of stepparent living in the home with the student?
2. How are ministers treated in relation to housing allowance?
3. How does the employment allowance work?
   a. What is the maximum?
   b. How does it work for two parents working?
   c. How does it affect a single-parent household?

Chapter 8. Parents' Contribution from Assets
1. How is home equity used in the needs analysis the school is using?
2. Do businesses and farms receive special treatment?

Chapter 9. Calculation of Parents' Contribution from Assets
1. Is there an asset protection allowance and how does it work?
2. What is the maximum rate at which parents' assets are used in the formula?

Chapter 10. Student's Contribution from Income
1. What are the expected summer savings for a student? How much is a student likely to have to earn to save the amount required?
2. How does the student's income figure into the aid eligibility calculations?

Chapter 11. Student's Contribution from Assets
1. What is the rate at which students' assets are going to be used?

SECTION IV. GENERAL STRATEGIES

Chapter 12. How Many Will Be in School?
1. How do additional students in college affect the aid?
2. If a parent is attending college, how does this affect the aid eligibility?

Chapter 13. Using Your Income Taxes in the Aid Application
1. How does the formula consider IRA and Keogh plans?
2. Does the formula being used consider depreciation any differently than does federal income tax?

SECTION V. AVAILABLE MONEY

Chapter 14. The Philosophy of Aid Packaging
1. What is the total cost for your student?
   a. Tuition charges?
   b. Fees?
   c. Room?
   d. Board?
   e. Personal expenses?
   f. Books?
   g. Travel?
   h. Other?
   i. Orientation?
2. How does the school package aid?
3. Is there a minimum expected family or student contribution?
4. Does the school meet full need according to aid eligibility? If not, how do they decide between students?
   a. Ability to pay?
   b. Athletic ability?
   c. Scholastic ability?
   d Music ability?

Appendix C—Sample Questions

Chapter 15. Sources of Aid

1. Does the school package the Guaranteed Student Loan or is that an option left for the student?
2. How many hours a week will the student be expected to work if a job is assigned under College Work Study?
3. If students do not wish to work or are unable to, do they lose out on aid, or can they obtain other aid in its place?
4. What is the rate of pay for the College Work Study students? If it is variable, how do you get a higher-paying job?
5. What are the state programs and how do they work?
6. What is the size of the institutional aid budget?
   a. For need-based aid?
   b. For scholarship aid?
   c. How many students share this amount?
7. Are upperclass students awarded aid on the same basis as freshman?
8. How will the aid package be affected if the students receive an honorary scholarship from high school?
   a. If reduced, will it come out of work?
   b. If reduced, will it come out of loan?
   c. If reduced, will it come out of grant?

Chapter 16. Loans

1. How early can one apply for a GSL?
2. Are there any new restrictions on the GSL?
3. Does the Parents' Loan Program exist and how does it work?
4. Are there limits on the amount that can be borrowed through the Parents' Loan Program or the GSL?
5. What happens if a bank or other thrift institution will not loan to your family under the GSL or PLP program?

SECTION VI. SPECIFIC STRATEGIES

Chapter 18. Divorce

1. In the case of divorce, which household(s) will be used to determine aid eligibility?
2. What about a stepparent's income?

Chapter 21. Independent Students

1. What is the definition of an independent student?
2. Does your institution have any special treatment of independent students—such as a minimum required family contribution?
3. Why shouldn't I encourage my child to go independent?

Chapter 23. Pell Grant (BEOG)

1. What are the most recent changes in the Pell Grant?
2. Is the formula being used for the Pell Grant different than the formula that is being used to award other aid at the institution?

Index

A

Acknowledgment forms, 19, 21
Admissions applications, 15–16, 19, 26, 231
Admissions officer, 25, 231, 247–48
Age of parent, effect of, 70–71
Agreement, education support, 159–72, 237
Aid eligibility, 22, 72, 78–81, 89–90, 94, 107–8, 117–19, 137, 153–56, 225–26, 235, 243
Aid packaging, 153–56, 236
Aid sources, 117–33; *see also* Honor awards; Loans to students; *and* Scholarships
   federal, 119–23, 125–30, 238–39
   handicapped, 17, 202
   institutional, 121–24, 131–32, 155, 188, 191, 197, 231, 239–40
   other, 17, 121, 132–33, 239
   social security benefits, 76–77, 201–7
   state, 119–23, 130, 230–31, 239
   veterans' benefits, 76–77, 201–7
American College Testing Program (ACT), 235, 238; *see also* Processor
Application for aid, 25–31
   asset information, 9, 52–69, 78–83
   code number, 19–21
   forms, 9, 15–16, 20–21, 25–31, 236, 238, 240, 246–47
   nontaxable income, 36, 41–42, 76
   tax return information, 9, 18–19, 29, 41–43, 100–114, 163
   timing, 15–19, 26, 30
   verification, 29
   where to send, 28–29, 31
Asset protection allowance, 70–73, 93

Assets, 236
   bonds, 60–61
   borrowing against, 98–99
   business, 64–66, 101–7, 236–37
   capital gains, 107–10
   cash, 66–67
   farms, 64, 66, 110–12, 236–37
   home equity, 8, 52–56
   land contracts, 61–63, 240
   nonliquid, 150
   not included in aid determination, 57, 60, 68
   protection allowance, 70–73, 93
   real estate, 52, 64, 66, 103
   securities, 63–64
   stocks, 57–60, 107–10
   trusts, 63, 182–86
   valuation, 9, 52–69
Athletes, 120, 131
Auto loan, 216
Award notice, 18, 38, 203–4, 236
Award period, 17–18

B

Base income year, 17–18
Basic Educational Opportunity Grant (BEOG); *see* Pell Grant (BEOG), Basic Educational Opportunity Grant *and* Student Eligibility Report
Basic Grant; *see* Pell Grant (BEOG), Basic Educational Opportunity Grant
Bonds, 60–61
Borrowing against assets, 98–99
Business assets, 64–66, 101–7, 236–37
Business income, 101–7, 236–37; *see also* Farms

257

Index

C

Calendar, 15–16, 19
Capital gains and losses, 107–10
Cash assets, 66–67
Changes in system, 4, 8, 21–22, 29, 90, 148, 195–96, 229–31
Collectibles; *see* Assets, not included in aid determination
College choices, limit, 16, 28
College Scholarship Service, 237; *see also* Processor
College Work Study Program (CWSP), 129–30, 154–56, 230, 237
Confidentiality, 9–10, 237
Consumer credit, 58–60
Costs, college and university, 5–6, 11, 117, 153, 237
  effect of, 95–96, 118

D

Debts
  collateral; *see* Stocks
  credit cards; *see* Consumer credit
  home improvement loans; *see* Home equity
  margin; *see* Stocks
  mortgages; *see* Home equity; Land contracts; Real estate assets
Discretionary net worth, 70, 72, 93, 98
Divorce and separation, 40–41, 159–72, 237

E

Educational accounts, 181
Educational expenses; *see* Costs, college and university
Educational support (supplemental) agreements, 159–72, 237
Eligibility; *see* Aid eligibility
Eligibility index, 209
Employment allowance, 40, 45–46, 238
Estate planning, 4, 185–86

F

Family contribution, 22–24, 35–39, 135–37, 238; *see also* Parents' contribution *and* Student's contribution
Family Financial Statement (FFS), 26–27, 30–31, 235, 238, 246
Farms, 64–66, 110–12, 236–37
Federal aid
  application, 15
  sources, 119–23, 125–30, 238–39

Financial Aid Form (FAF), 26–27, 30–31, 237–38, 246
Financial aid officer (office), 25–26, 31, 38, 75, 117–24, 131, 134, 136, 147, 201, 203, 219, 231, 238, 248
Forms, 9, 15–16, 20–21, 25–31, 236, 238, 240, 246–47; *see also* High School Counselor *and* Pell Grant (BEOG), Basic Educational Opportunity Grant
Formula for aid, 22, 29–31, 33–83, 95, 126, 208–12, 242, 244

G

Gifts to students, 79–80, 173–81
Grants, 119–20, 125–27, 130–32, 202, 238–39; *see also* Aid sources, other; Handicapped, aid to; Institutional aid; Pell Grant (BEOG), Basic Educational Opportunity Grant; Scholarships; Social security benefits; State aid; Supplemental Educational Opportunity Grant (SEOG); *and* Veterans' benefits
Guaranteed Student Loan (GSL), 125. 127, 130, 134–52, 155, 195–96, 219, 221–22, 239
Guardians, 146, 152, 186

H

Handicapped, aid to, 17, 202
High school counselor, 17, 27, 30, 121, 130, 132, 237, 239, 245, 247
High school guidance office; *see* High school counselor
Home (household), student, 40–41, 47, 50, 159–61, 239
Home equity, 8, 52–56
Honor awards (scholarship, prizes, etc.), 119–23, 132–33, 140, 239
Household, student; *see* Home (household), student

I

Income averaging, 43
Income; *see* Nontaxable income; Student earnings; *and* Parents' contribution, income; Tax return information
Income determination, parents; *see* Parents' contribution, income
Income supplement, 72, 93
Independent student, 90–91, 187–200, 239–40
Individual Retirement Account (IRA), 113

Index

Institutional aid
application, 15–16, 27
sources, 121–24, 131–32, 155, 188, 191, 197, 231, 239–40
Institutional aid forms, 27, 240
Insurance, 57, 60, 68
Investments; *see* Assets

J–L

Joint Accounts with students, 79–80, 180–81
Keogh Plan, 113
Land contracts, 61–63, 240
Loans to students, 82, 119–20, 134–52, 230, 240; *see also* Guaranteed Student Loan; National Direct Student Loan; Parents' Loan Program; *and* State Direct Student Loan

M

Maintenance allowance, 40, 47, 88
Margin, 58–60; *see also* Stocks
Medical and dental expenses, 19, 40–42, 46–47
Minister's housing allowance, 7, 41–42, 240–41
Mortgages; *see* Land contracts; Real estate assets; *and* Home equity

N

National Direct Student Loan (NDSL), 128–30, 134–35, 141–42, 154–55, 240–41
National Merit Scholarship Program, 18, 121, 241
National Negro Achievement Scholarship, 241
Need, 17, 30, 238, 241; *see also* Aid eligibility
Net worth, determination of, 67–69, 70–73, 92–93, 241
Nonliquid assets, 150
Nontaxable income, 36, 40–43, 76

O–P

Oil ventures, 112
Parent; *see* Home (household), student; Single parent; Stepparent; *and* Divorce and separation
Parents in school, 91–94
Parents' contribution, 22–24, 73, 87–89, 241
assets, 35–37, 52–73, 93, 241
income, 35, 40–51, 89, 242

Parents' Loan Program (PLP), 125, 127, 130, 134, 149–52, 219, 221–22, 242
Payments (college bills), 219–20
Pell Grant (BEOG), Basic Educational Opportunity Grant, 15, 26–30, 37, 76–77, 125–27, 130, 154–55, 208–12, 229, 236, 242, 246; *see also* Student Eligibility Report
Pell Grant formula, 30–31, 76–77, 126, 208–12
Pell Student Eligiblity Report; *see* Student Eligibility Report
Planning, 6–9, 11–12, 19, 25, 41, 60, 82, 90–93, 99, 101, 111–13, 172, 178, 191–95, 206–7, 212
Postgraduate study, 96
Processing year, 17–18, 242
Processor, 22, 26, 30–31, 242; *see also* American College Testing Program (ACT) *and* College Scholarship Service

Q–R

Qualifying for aid; *see* Aid eligibility
Real estate assets 52, 64–66, 103; *see also* Home equity
Record keeping, 19–21, 55, 76, 143

S

Scholarships, 119–20, 131
academic, 235
local, 17, 31
National Merit, 18, 120, 241
National Negro Achievement, 241
special, 16, 132–33
Securities, 63–64; *see also* Stocks *and* Bonds
Separation and divorce; *see* Divorce and separation
Single parent, 46, 50–51, 71, 164; *see also* Divorce and separation
Social security benefits, 76–77, 201–7
State aid
application, 16, 27–28
sources, 119–23, 130, 230–31, 239
State Direct Student Loan (SDSL), 134, 147–49, 237
Stepparent, 40, 160–61
Stocks, 57–60, 107–10
Stopping out, 94
Student dropouts; *see* Stopping out
Student earnings, 21, 37, 74–77; *see also* Student's contribution
Student Eligibility Report (SER), 27–28, 127, 209, 236, 243
Student home; *see* Home (household), student

Students, number in college, 87–99
Student's contribution, 22–24, 37–39, 243; *see also* Social security benefits *and* Veterans' benefits
  assets, 78–83, 243
  income, 74–77
Student's savings; *see* Student's contribution, assets
Summer savings, 74, 243; *see also* Student earnings
Supplementary Educational Opportunity Grant (SEOG), 125, 127–28, 130, 153–56, 243

T

Tax allowance, 40–44; *see also* Taxes
Tax-free dollars, 6–7, 12, 22, 60, 73, 80, 91, 99, 179–80, 244
Tax return information, 9, 18–19, 29, 41–43, 100–114, 163

Taxable income; *see* Tax return information
Taxes
  income (federal), 7–9, 40–41, 100–114; *see also* Tax return information
  social security, 40, 43
  state and local, 40, 43–44, 242
Trusts, 63, 182–86
Types of aid; *see* College Work Study Program (CWSP) Grants; Scholarships; Loans to students; Parents' loan Program (PLP); *and* Aid sources

U–W

Uniform methodology, 29–30, 44–45, 68, 76–77, 208–12, 242, 244
Valuation of assets, 9, 52–69
Veterans' benefits, 76–77, 201–7
Work programs; *see* College Work Study Program (CWSP)